Strategic Recreation Management

Strategic Recreation Management is a comprehensive and up-to-date introduction to the fundamental principles, managerial techniques and practices in the public administration of recreational services. It covers every key facet of public management as it concerns recreational service, including organizational, operational, planning, developmental, and managerial procedures, as well as examining all the contextual factors that influence the delivery of recreation, such as political pressures, economics, social considerations, physical resources, and citizens' perception of the field and its performance.

Each chapter offers illustrative case studies from the real world of recreation management, with chapters sequenced to represent the typical day-to-day challenges and issues in recreation service. Authors Jay Shivers and Joseph Halper have many years' experience of working in the recreational sector, as educators and practitioners, and the result is a textbook that provides the perfect foundation for any degree-level course in recreation management, as well as being an indispensable reference for all professionals working in recreation service.

Jay Shivers is Professor Emeritus, University of Connecticut, USA. He has been engaged in the practice and study of the field of recreational service for over 60 years and is the author of 27 major textbooks and numerous articles in refereed journals.

Joseph Halper is an internationally recognized parks and recreation administrator knighted in Sweden for civic merit. He has served as the head of the largest urban park and recreation systems in the United States including New York City and Los Angeles County. His experience encompasses 35 years as an administrator and educator in this field.

Ratio sine exercitatione inutilis, exercitatio sine ratione caeca est.

Strategic Recreation Management

Jay Shivers and Joseph Halper

Routledge
Taylor & Francis Group

LONDON AND NEW YORK

First published 2012
by Routledge
2 Park Square, Milton Park, Abingdon, Oxon OX14 4RN

Simultaneously published in the USA and Canada
by Routledge
711 Third Avenue, New York, NY 10017

Routledge is an imprint of the Taylor & Francis Group, an informa business

British Library Cataloguing in Publication Data
A catalogue record for this book is available from the British Library

Library of Congress Cataloging in Publication Data
Strategic recreation management / edited by Jay Shivers and Joseph
Halper. – 1st ed.
  p. cm.
1. Recreation–Management. 2. Recreation–Planning. 3. Strategic
planning. I. Shivers, Jay Sanford, 1930– II. Halper, Joseph W.
GV181.5.S73 2012
790.069–dc23   2011024836

ISBN: 978-0-415-78363-7 (hbk)
ISBN: 978-0-415-78364-4 (pbk)
ISBN: 978-0-203-14822-8 (ebk)

Typeset in Times
by Taylor & Francis books

Dedication

I dedicate this text to the individuals who were most influential in forming my understanding of what constitutes effective administration. First, and absolutely important, the ethical base was established by Harlan Gold Metcalf at the State University of New York at Cortland. This was followed by my early field experience in association with Joseph Curtis, who provided me with an appreciation of the importance of interpersonal relations in community dynamics; an essential quality for leadership in this field. Lastly, a knowledge of the techniques involved in achieving organizational objectives was imparted to me by my friend and colleague Richard Bader.

I recognize my life's partner and wife of 50 years, Arline Rimmer Halper, for her encouragement and leavening influence in the selection of material for my contribution to the book. I acknowledge also the challenge of my three sons Jamie, Michael, and Keith, who in their own exciting and successful careers have both tested and modeled many of the concepts I have examined in this presentation of administrative practice and theory.

I am also indebted to the talented people I have been privileged to work with during my career in public administration and from whom I have taken much wisdom. They include my mentors, colleagues, and friends, Sam Aldrich, Casey Conrad, Robert Gamble, Seymour Greben, August Heckscher, John Lindsay, Ellen Linson, Herbert Rathner, James Ridenour, Berit Stanton, Frances Wallach, and my co-author Jay Shivers.

Joe Halper

I dedicate my portion of the text to Jed Mark Shivers, whose professional career has spanned 25 years to date, as a medical school administrator.

I stand in awe of his technical skill and competence, his diplomatic sagacity, his integrity and loyalty. He epitomizes the professional who has earned the respect and esteem of his peers by his work ethic, intelligence, and diligence. Moreover, he applies good common sense to his dealings with others and that is why he is universally liked and admired. This is my son of whom I am justifiably proud.

Jay S. Shivers
Storrs
September 1, 2011

Contents

Figures

Acknowledgements

We appreciate the information willingly provided by professionals in recreational service throughout the United States. We are certainly thankful for the variety of critiques received from readers of the manuscript prior to publication. These informative statements assisted us in making the text more accurate and readable. We owe particular recognition to Dr. Jan Louise Jones of Southern Connecticut State University for her assistance with web sites; to Mark Gordon, Web Master for the Prince William County Department of Parks and Recreation, for his contribution; Dr. Sungho Cho, of Bowling Green State University for his technical assistance in schematic production; Shane Reilly of Wells Fargo Advisors for timely technical support; and Jason Knight, Legislative Aide, Connecticut General Assembly for technical support.

The presses, publishing houses, and professional journals mentioned specifically in the endnotes graciously consented to allow reproduction of quotations from their pages and publications. For these permissions we express our gratitude.

Preface

This book is intended primarily as a text for use in institutions of higher education where professional courses for the preparation of recreational service personnel at the management level are offered. Although public recreational services are administered by jurisdictions other than local governments, and some recreational services are offered by private and commercial agencies, courses for the professional preparation of recreationists are typically related to the field of public management.

The terms *management* and *administration* will be used interchangeably throughout this text. Management is the process performed within an organization in order to achieve its purposes. It is in this manner that the administration of an agency is defined as a system of joint effort and coordination. The concept of management espoused here concerns the collection of functions and responsibilities that permeate the organization so that every person in the operation plays a significant role in the process.

Administration consists of organized effort on the part of two or more persons in an activity which the individual cannot accomplish alone. Thus, properly speaking, administration is essentially concerned with some goal and action pertinently instigated to achieve that goal. Public recreational service administration, under a superstructure of managing specialized personnel, materials, facilities, and finance, is concerned with the goal of providing services of a recreational nature to all the people in the community.

Public recreational service administration is immediately concerned with the study of how effective services of a recreational nature can be performed for the citizens of any community, at the least possible cost, and without duplicating other agency functions.

Strategic management deals with techniques and practices pertaining to business organizations, government organizations, and non-profit organizations. The text is designed to familiarize readers with the accepted standards, procedures, and techniques employed by corporate, entrepreneurial, and functional level managers. Readers will have an understanding of the role of management in any modern organization that includes human resources, finances, ethics and agency responsibility, communications within organizations, decision-making, and organizational motivation.

The text deals with every facet of management as it concerns recreational service – including organization, operation, planning, development, controlling, and technical procedures. It describes the basic elements of the field: liability factors in a legal framework of operation; community structure; socio-political practices; social implications and typical municipal settings of the recreational service agency. An investigation of all the social agencies which may have direct or indirect influence on the amount and type of recreational services offered within the community is included. The text treats the internal structure of the public recreational service department and the managerial functions that are based on daily operations of the system. Emphasis is placed on fundamental principles and practices of managing recreational service departments. Management practices, with the exception of those functions regulated by law or custom, may be found in all sectors of society. Therefore the text may be useful to administrators serving in private and quasi-public organizations.

The material is oriented to the consideration of management from the standpoint of departmental problems. Departmental management draws its form largely from uniform practices within the municipal government as a whole and, to a large extent, is governed by state and municipal laws. Problems of managing particular programs and facilities of individual units are not included except as they illustrate or relate to universal problems involved in the management of all types of recreational places.

The book offers the reader an understanding of the role of management and how to develop plans and execute strategy in the pursuit of organizational goals. There is a fundamental need to reduce organizational ineffectiveness. Citizens want to know just what they are supporting in public recreational service. The requirement for accountability, at a time when corporate, political, and personal ethics and morality are being examined and questioned to a greater degree than ever before, is obvious. Society is becoming more aware of the abuse of individuals in the public and private domains. Therefore, the manager must become intimately engaged in the coordination of organizational goals with employee needs and constituency demands.

The text is organized into four major parts: Part I, "Planning, strategy, and policy", deals with fundamental concepts of strategy, planning, policy-making and leadership; Part II, "Establishing recreational service", concerns legal establishment, department structure, organization, executive and commission relations; Part III, "Management functions and responsibilities", deals with human resources management, information technology, fiscal management, budgeting, and budget types, public relations; Part IV, "Primary influences on management practices", concerns liability, program practices, resource planning, physical plant maintenance, office management, record keeping, and, finally, evaluation of recreational service.

The advantage of this organization is logical progression. The sequence of chapters is in the order that might arise in the establishment, development, and operation of an agency or system providing recreational services to a public constituency. There have also been included forces that create or alleviate problems for the operation of the agency. The reader is introduced to each topic by definition and discussion. Each chapter, although it may stand alone and be perused independently of the others, is authoritative in itself and has been placed as a supplement and complement to preceding chapters. Thus, the reader is able to follow the complete development and day-to-day managerial practices of any recreational service system in the public sector, from its inception to operational problems and methods for their solution. Essentially, the book approaches the science and art of strategic management in recreational service logically and with the factual data that can reduce conflict and be of use to recreationists every day on the job.

New trends in the organization of recreational services, as presented here, are in conformance with the best thinking in municipal government. Lines of authority and responsibility are clearly set forth for large or small units. Legal and other provisions and suggestions are made for a rich cooperative program. The term *recreational service* has been deliberately used throughout the text. This use denotes our conviction and acceptance of the functional fact that agencies of whatever designation which supply or provide the public's demand for recreational programming and places are performing recreational services. Since functional names are usually preferred in designating departments of governmental services, it may well develop that *recreational services management* will comprehend all that is now connoted by other existing titles.

The work combines the pragmatic outlook of the agency executive and the academic orientation of the university professor. The synthesis of these viewpoints and analyses has resulted in a more complete and useful text that tells how to manage. It offers crystallized and acceptable methods for handling current operational problems and for resolving then successfully. The text should fulfill a vital need of practicing managers and provide definitive information for those who teach and learn in higher education.

Part I
Planning, strategy, and policy

1 Strategic management in recreational service

Strategic management focuses on the achievement of the organization's objectives. A strategic plan articulates how to gain those objectives. The organization's objective or purpose for which the field was created has to be explicit. It is formulated so that action follows. The objective of the field is to broadly educate people about the worthy use of leisure and provide the spaces, places, personnel, and opportunities for participation in safe, enjoyable, beneficial, and satisfying activities.

Mission statement

The mission of the public recreational service department or system is to enable the constituency, during their respective leisure, to participate in recreational experiences in areas that are safe, healthful, most conducive to satisfying personal and social needs through learning new recreational activities, honing acquired skills for a higher quality of life, or both. It is the purpose of the recreational delivery system to plan, organize, and conduct a comprehensive program of recreational activities designed to appeal to the skills, tastes, talents, and appreciations of the constituency, to offer equal opportunity for engagement; to provide the specialized indoor or outdoor areas and facilities necessary for the conduct of a varied recreational program; to maintain the physical plant for the health, safety, and welfare of all those who participate; and to provide the professional personnel required to teach, advise, or counsel actual and potential participants so that all who are served may feel fulfilled and lead more enhanced lives. In this manner the aspirations of the field are realized. The organization's mission statement should reflect the aspirations.

Strategy conceptualization

Strategy arises from the need for direction and focus in the manager's search for and establishment of new opportunities to provide the services for which the organization was instigated. The primary goal for recreational service agencies is to enable actual or potential participants to engage in experiences that are enjoyable, satisfying, and stimulating to the interests of the individual performer. The goal sets the condition for the development of objectives which leads to the achievement of the stated mission. Objectives determine the performance levels that the organization wants to attain.

Strategy is a collection of decision-making rules for guidance of organizational behavior. This means the ability to measure the current and expected performance of the organization. Rules for developing external relationships in the organization's environment are concerned with what activities will be developed, how the program will be operated, for whom the services will be provided, and how the agency will attract potential receivers of the service. These particular rules are termed *agency strategy*. Rules in the developing internal relationships and procedures within the organization are termed *administrative strategy*. Rules by which the organization operates on a day-to-day basis are viewed as *operating policies*.

The process of agency strategy formulation defines the general directions in which the organization's position will mature and develop. One consequence of that strategy must be to bring about projects by focusing on those areas identified by the strategy and to screen out those functions which are inconsistent with the strategy. Strategy formulation tends to be based on partial and variable information about alternatives. As research and experience discover specific options, a feedback element needs to be in place so that doubts about the course of the action to be taken can surface.

Feedback

Feedback tends to serve as a precautionary device to reduce the possibility of faulty decisions. Objectives represent the ends-in-view that the organization seeks to achieve, while strategy is the means by which the ends are obtained. A given strategy may not have the same value to the organization when objectives change. Moreover, as objectives and strategy are expanded throughout the organization, it is not unusual for hierarchical relationships to materialize.

Deliberate strategy formation

Although strategy produces no instant outcome for the agency it does have an absolute contribution to the department's overall performance. While management is a practical application, strategy is a topic of interest to management throughout the system and also to many of the line and staff personnel whose functions are vital to agency productivity. This concern is noted because those involved make significant contributions to strategy formulation and are also the primary practitioners seeing to its execution. The strategic plan has become the instrument for redirecting the organizational intent.[1] It produces improvement in the department's performance and does not rely upon adaptive and unsystematic response to contingencies. Explicit strategy formation is necessary when there is rapid disruption in the environment in which the organization functions. This could mean a change in the political climate, technological innovations, changes in demography, population movement, economic recession or retrenchment, and other impingements affecting the organization's services.

Under these circumstances, traditional organizational patterns and experiences are no longer capable of coping with either new opportunities or new dangers. Unless there exists a unifying strategy, the likelihood is that the various divisions of the system will develop independently, perhaps in a contradictory manner, and have disparate reactions. When these conditions are allowed to persist the organization is no longer able to focus on its mission and inconsistencies in service will result. A categorical new strategy is also required as the objectives of the department change radically in consequence of new demands imposed on it by social needs.

Strategy implements actions that tend to threaten the agency's traditions or the often-heard plaint, "This is how we do it here."[2] The typical response is to sabotage or fail to accommodate the innovation.[3] This is a well-known phenomenon. Machiavelli wrote the most succinct description of this reaction:

> It must be considered that there is nothing more difficult to carry out, or more doubtful of success, nor more dangerous to handle, then to initiate a new order of things, for the reformer has enemies in all those who profit by the old order and only lukewarm defenders in all who would profit by the new order.[4]

The perceived threat to the organization's historic outlook and political process elicits confrontation by the old guard instead of expanding energy to face the challenges instigated by the environment. Individuals and groups tend to resist any change that is viewed as a threat or discomfort caused by the discontinuity imposed by those who regard strategic decision-making as imperative to effective organizational function. Until there is widespread dissemination of information that teaches those personnel directly affected by strategy that the benefits far outweigh personal costs, the innovation will meet with procrastination or outright hostility. Strategy must be flexible so that external threats to the system can be minimized. This is done by utilizing whatever technologies are available for upgrading the efficiency of personnel, by employing the resources and capabilities of the system in ways that are timely, and by an internal educational program which informs all concerned about the need for systematic acquaintance with the desired outlook.[5] It is important to buy in the individuals in the organization who will be key to the implementation of the plan by their early involvement in its development.

Strategic plan formulation

The strategic plan is the basis for decision-making which guides the process of determining which alternatives to take. In fact, problem solution is a major factor for the establishment of a strategic position. Problem-solving is typically based on scientific method and may be described as the identification of the problem, collection of raw data pertinent to the problem, refinement of the data specific to the problem, selecting an approach that appears to be justified given the information available, testing the alternatives, and arriving at a solution.

Approaches to strategic solutions

In formulating a strategy for the conduct of the recreational service system, consideration must be given to optimizing the efficiency of the department's ability to allocate its resources in ways that carry out its primary mission. Strategy carries with it certain social objectives, which correspond to the needs and aspirations of the clientele to be served, as well as the employees of the organization. As a guiding rule for decision-making, strategy enables the department to become flexible in its response to and handling of internal and external turbulence that may constrain the ability to act. In this way, the department is responsive to the social goals for which it was created.[6]

Rationale for strategic management

Strategic management is concerned with producing results. Strategic management is a process of organizational action that includes psychological, sociological, and political variables. Therefore, strategic management focuses on what is to be done and the people who will carry out the functions designed to fulfill the organization's mission.

The focus is on the processes of management which are relevant to the public sector of society. Of course, any organization can utilize strategic management to maximize outcomes valuable to the organization.

Of necessity, all forms of human association require elements of management. Whenever there is the need to mobilize material, fiscal, natural, or human resources in order to accomplish some set purpose, management procedures are called into play. Management is certainly a cooperative undertaking, the net result of which is to gain a specific objective.[7] While the specific objectives of organizations may vary considerably depending upon the differing environments, ideology, and problems confronted, there are processes held in common. The precise form of management differs because of local conditions and the nature of the organization in question. Strategic management comprehends the formulation of strategies, designing the agency's or system's capacity to perform.

Organizational goals. Such goals are those anticipated conditions that the agency wants to realize. It is understood that policies must be formulated that will enable personnel to carry out their functions in the most effective and efficient manner possible. Effectiveness is the capacity to get things done. Efficiency is the ability to get this done without wasting time, effort, or expense. Simply put, effectiveness is doing the right thing. Efficiency is doing things right. Organizations are effective to the degree to which the mission is achieved. Efficiency is concerned with the minimal use of resources in terms of money, material, or personnel to produce what is necessary; that is, the most comprehensive and balanced recreational program possible.

Tactical goals. Since the organization is typically arranged by major divisions, carrying out specialized functions designed to achieve the agency's mission, tactical goals define the outcome of the tasks these divisions perform in order for the organization to reach its overall objective.

Effective goal setting is characterized by distinctive and measurable outcomes concerned with areas significant to agency operations; goals should be realistic and challenging, but capable of being attained. Additionally, there is a known period for the performance to be completed and such performance, when successful, is directly associated with accomplishment of the organization's mission.

Organization

Organization itself is the assignment of tasks necessary for the achievement of the goals that have been envisioned. It is concerned with the allocation of the resources to the various divisions enabling their personnel to operate in a manner calculated to achieve the objectives previously set for them.

Managerial leadership or the use of influence to stimulate employee motivation in achievement of organizational goals requires two-way communication.[8] Constant communication to and from peers and subordinates permits steady integration of personnel in the decision-making process and constitutes the most effective means for reaching organizational goals.[9] Many organizations are in accord with communication from the top down. It is important that the decision-making process allow for input from all levels of the organization.

Managerial control

Managerial control is exercised by monitoring employee activities that are measured by establishing standards of performance. In this way, the organizational personnel focus is enhanced through a systematic feedback process to make necessary corrections in a timely manner. Evaluations and assessment of performance deal with the entire organization as well as concentrating on the work of each individual. It is the outcome of individual effort that contributes to the overall achievement of the system. All such evaluation becomes part of the communication processes and each employee understands his/her position within the agency structure and how they are performing.

Dimensions of management

All efforts to establish a set of generally applicable principles to all situations have thus far failed. Therefore, any claim that management is a science is likely to be received with skepticism. Nevertheless, students of management must continue to attempt to apply scientific principles to this area. In an increasingly complex society, the only logical managerial approach to problems is the scientific method. Although scientific methods and certain technical devices may be utilized within public management processes, management is not as yet a science. A body of knowledge concerning the field has been accumulated from research into the way outcomes are generated, why interactions between people are significant, and purely mechanical aspects of regulating material goods (storage, distribution, allocation, purchase) for efficiency, economy, and speed. But management is not yet susceptible to science in the true sense of the word.

The art of management confirms that, while a tremendous portion of the work may be learned, transmitted, recorded, and filed, crucial decisions are often based neither on scientifically acquired research nor on obvious fact. Certainly, the function of the manager can be systematically analyzed and classified. There are particular professional features and a scientific aspect to management. However, too much decision-making critical to public management at the policy level is still romanticized or made by "feel." This condition has to be overcome. Only through the acquisition of knowledge and continual professionalization will the manager and management itself become reliable features of the culture in which they are embedded. Today, the individual manager's experience, knowledge, and sensitivity to situations and prevailing conditions remain the critical factors from which value judgments and systems are derived and defined.[10]

Scientific management. Scientific management principles may be successfully used in organizations, but more recently human resources have come to be recognized as being quite different from the machines or materials that compose part of the resources on which the system works. Science tends to view management as essentially devoted to technical features or division of labor and specialization. However, concentration on mechanical features to the exclusion of the human factors involved has come to be seen as a fundamental error. Technology can be applied wherever repetitive movements are required or where facts alone constitute the basis of making decisions. When, as is the usual case, the human element is a component of the work situation, another important facet must be understood. People are not susceptible to manipulation as are inert items; they are much too unpredictable, even on the basis of probability tests and surveys. Human beings cannot be subject to precise calculations, because they are susceptible to whimsy, fancies, subjective influences, and varying beliefs. From scientific practices has come the recognition that management is not a science when it deals with people.[11]

The technological advances made in computer processing, data analysis, and automation are not compelling reasons for assuming that management is, can be, or should be a science. Basic understanding brings the realization that, in the social contexts of which economic and technical units comprise but one segment, the human resource is of infinite importance. Interpersonal relationships involving stimulation, morale, cooperation, creativity, flexibility, and receptivity to change, can satisfactorily be resolved only through an acute understanding of probable human perception and an ability to respond appropriately in terms of such understanding.

Scientific principles and practices greatly aid public management in organizational analysis and efficient production, but the field itself heavily relies upon human relationships because these are integral throughout its processes. Cooperative or collective endeavor is the touchstone of management. Public management comprises every area and enterprise under the aegis of public policy and should not be thought of as mere policy execution. Managerial adroitness permeates the enactment of legislation, the adjudication of legislation, and the shaping of value judgments that become policy statements. It includes organization, policy execution, and supervision of personnel, finances, and the practices fundamental to the effective operations of agencies charged with carrying out the specific functions of government.

Nature of public management

Management is formed of three components: (1) determination of policy, because policy is essential to direct the activities of the institution, system, or agency; (2) policies must be translated into substantive operations to achieve the prescribed ends; and (3) the operations must be put into action. Therefore, managerial achievement comes from sound interpersonal relationships: between the manager and those who set the policy; between the manager and his/her chief subordinates in stimulating, leading, and supervising the personnel who will execute the policy of the agency; and among the operating personnel, because production (whether of goods or services) depends on cooperative relations.

Although there is a blurring of distinct spheres of interest between policy-making and management, owing to the strong influence exerted on policy-makers by the manager and realities of the workplace, a discrete function may be clearly observed. Management is always subordinate to policy. Despite the reliance of executives, political leaders, and legislators on managers who supply them with relevant facts on which to base decisions (thereby permitting the manager to subtly influence policy decisions), policy-making is not a responsibility of management. Execution of policy by ethical means to reach desired ends is the essence of management.

The chief purpose of public management is to administer the public's business in the most competent manner possible. Management is a highly complex process which has evolved gradually with the maturation of society and is a direct outgrowth of the division of labor, requiring special learning and skills. The manager requires an ever-expanding body of knowledge, both formal and informal, to equip him/herself for competency.

Cultural impacts on public management. Public management in any society is a reflection of that society's complexity. As the social order becomes more complicated, the range and variety of all public services increase. Furthermore, as environmental and human relationships are modified, stress is focused on the need to redirect public programs to fit such changes. Among the significant factors that influence adaptations and public management are demographic changes; technological improvements; environmental pollution; educational innovations; social movements and ideologies; the political system; the interrelationships of public, quasi-public, and private sectors on each other; social problems and disintegration; and economic resources and their utilization.

Demography. Demographic changes are typically reflected in the kinds, numbers, and degrees of services rendered by public agencies. When population increases or decreases, an analogous movement in the fiscal position of the public service occurs. Therefore, increases in population require a corresponding increase in governmental budgets. In municipalities all money is expended on police and fire protection, health services, garbage collection, education, public works, low- and middle-income public housing, public recreational services, and other needs.

As population increases, usually covert problems become all too apparent in urban centers: congestion, crime, racism, ecological destruction, overload of traffic, violence, and other conditions created by an enigmatic and complex social structure requires assistance from higher and higher governmental levels. In an era when international terrorism intrudes into the lives of millions of innocent people, citizens look to their government to deflect or eradicate the cause. Such exigencies require the vast expenditure of money, materials, and people away from the normal allocation in the preservation of the social fabric.

At a stressful time public management assumes the burden and undertakes those actions necessary for the maintenance of social control and an expected high quality of life. Actions that can deal with a rapidly changing social scene in the most expeditious way possible are essential. Any social system in transition is characterized by its complexity and requires a public service that can adjust to and arrange its procedures in conformity with swiftly moving events.

Technology. The 21st century will witness a more rapid advance in all forms of automation including fiber-optics for the transmission of information. This constitutes a major force for change in society. Many of these innovations have had a significant impact on public management. All of them together open vistas for a better style of living than has heretofore been imagined. Technological advances make possible massive leisure, mobility, affluence, and an entire complex of permutations with enormous influence on the way people live.

People are witnesses to history as it is being made through instant mass communication, primarily television; with even greater impact from blogging, tweeting, Skyping, e-mail, and smart phones. Although newspapers, magazines, and some radio broadcasts still provide detailed information necessary for the thorough understanding of news events, television carries the initial impact to millions of people around the world; along with other electronic devices. With instant communication and rapid transportation, greater knowledge about other peoples, their beliefs or ideology, is transmitted in a way that has been previously unknown. For some it is exposure to a way of life that promotes envy or even hatred. For others it is a process of widespread interchange of ideas, ideals, values, and respect for other opinions.

Politics and economic pressure

The merit system was adopted as an employment practice in the public sector. It requires appointment in the civil service to be made on the basis of educational and experiential qualifications by examination. This system is prevalent in most public jurisdictions and provides a degree of protection to public sector employees from arbitrary political ideology and economic philosophy which play an extremely important role in decision-making in the public sector. Increasingly, the politician's influence on public management is felt in terms of political appointment to high office as well as employment of personnel in managerial, technical, and subordinate positions. If the political official believes in a "spoils system" or a patronage approach to public management, his/her election to office may mean the demise of, or a considerable hindrance to, the merit system of employment. In many instances, political rewards for assisting individuals to gain some high office actually means the placement of party figures in public office, typically spelling the decline of public service. Of course, political appointees or personal friends may have the talent and skill necessary to perform competently, but this is not usual.

Governmental agencies saddled with political appointees develop bureaucratic tendencies, are less efficient than organizations in which each employee must prove his/her technical worth, and are less likely to have a favorable cost–benefit relationship between the financial needs of the agency and the expectations of public service. Political influence and orientation of elected officials invariably has repercussions on the management of any public agency within the level of government in question. Policy decisions concerning personnel practices, pressure brought to bear on the agency for specific services or favors for particular groups, favorable consideration for some practices as opposed to others, all these are intimately connected, sometimes subtly and other times more overtly. Pressures have a decided impact on the management and execution of prescribed functions of a single agency or the government at large.

Philosophical orientation. The economic philosophy of the chief executive, or political superior, also influences agency responsibility and function. A philosophically conservative elected official may view the function of government as purely maintaining the status quo. A fiscal conservative may oppose social services, require a lowering or maintenance of current tax lines, or attempt to discontinue the social welfare functions of government, or simply downsize. Economic philosophy is mirrored in the services that government offers. Actually, nothing is more significant to public management and the operation of public services than the economic ideology that elected public officials hold. Whatever the economic philosophy, it is translated into functions and services or diverted to sustain the particular public posture the office holder believes the constituency desires. Within this framework public policy is made, and public managers either abide by decisions rendered or take their leave of public service. Indeed, managers may attempt to influence policy decisions, but once policy is decided they must execute it.

Management skills. Conceptual skills, positive human relations, and technical performance are the hallmarks of adroit managerial competence. All of these characteristics produce outstanding organizations. Conceptualization has to do with the ability to generate ideas that serve as the foundation for meeting the needs of people – both within the agency and externally for the constituency. Firmly established in this configuration is the ability to understand employees and give them the stimulation necessary to motivate high-quality performance. This requires insight into human behavior, an understanding of ego needs in terms of recognition or a reward structure that indicates the esteem in which the employee is held. Such involvement tends to displace friction, misunderstanding, and lack of endeavor with highly motivated and agency-identified personnel.

Technical performance on the part of the manager really means the ability to gain adherence to organizational goals by cooperative activity. People are the vital resource by which the agency is able to provide the disinterested service demanded by its constituency. The manager must be able to advance organizational goals by creating an environment that is conducive to success. This suggests favoring performance over planning and a desire for action. The emphasis is on what the organization does best. There is a continuation of building on strengths as well as the development of entrepreneurship among staff members so that improved productivity will occur. Of necessity, controls are imposed that both regulate and expand behavior. While there are clearly defined limits, there is simultaneously broad autonomy and great freedom within those limits. In this way the manager provides the leadership and perspective to enhance the system's performance.

2 Planning for strategic management

Planning precedes all management; particularly if there is to be a paradigm shift from bureaucratic inertia to innovative use of personnel, money, technology, and problem-solving.[1] Strategic planning enables organizational goals to be set and facilitates a general view of organizational life, both internally and externally. It is the difference between crisis and strategic management.[2]

The internal environment consists of all of the human resources of the organization, attitudes toward work performance, and relationships that develop in meeting objectives. Of course, the tools for operational effectiveness must be available. Strategic planning is where an organization wants to be at some future point and how it is going to get there. It is the process by which an organization makes decisions that affect its long-term performance. The strategic planning process requires continual attention to changes in the organization and its external environment.[3]

External forces that impinge upon the public organization may be viewed as political, competitive, economic, or social influences. Insofar as politics plays a role in agency operation, it may be seen as an attempt to use the department as a dumping ground for political party hacks by the placement of non-professional cronies or relatives in positions; these are common practices in a patronage system. An example of this is a discourse that took place between a county political party leader who raised the question of the meaning of the term *qualified* in an attempt to resolve the conflict over a pending appointment to a position. The difference of opinion between the county patronage chief and the professional department head came down to the semantics of what the word *qualified* means. The patronage chief's definition was that the candidate had his district leader's support for the position and the department head quoted the position qualifications adopted by the county civil service commission.[4] It is not an uncommon practice to use the public sector organization to bolster political fortunes by catering to a small supporting segment of the population at the expense of the majority. Significant moneyed interests, whose contributions enable them to gain unwarranted access to, or have influence with elected officials are an external force with which administrators in the public sector will have to reckon. Under such circumstances, lobbyists and special pleaders can and do exert pressure on public sector administrators that may be contrary to the public good. Such pressure may be directed towards obtaining concessions concerning a particular ideology, philosophy, opinion, or sectarian view that is questionable or, perhaps, inimical to the rights, status, and needs of the constituent population.

Questionable or unethical (illegal) activities have immediate impact on organizations, to such an extent that managers can be hard-pressed to maintain their organization's equilibrium. The outcome of attempts to retain the capacity to perform in the public interest by professional managers frustrating politically instigated negative activity can be a politically initiated backlash that hurts the organization as well as the career of the professional manager.[5] Care should be taken by senior administrators to secure insulation to prevent capricious acts detrimental to the administrator or the organization. This can be accomplished by contractual undertakings prior to accepting employment or by developing a supportive constituency through consistently performing well in the public interest, or both.

Chief executives, either elected or appointed, generally believe that any person with a general management background can be successful in specialty agencies. They aver that credentials and specific experience in a particular field is unnecessary or insignificant, and that management skill is everything. Although it seems unlikely that police, fire, and health executives would be chosen without the appropriate education and experience, it is not rare for an individual without the qualifying credentials, apart from management ones, to be appointed to an executive position in the field of recreational service. This premise on the part of city managers is rejected as erroneous and harmful to the execution of the departmental mission. Department executives require specialized education and particular experience so that they can better understand the problems, conflicts, and demands recreationists[6] face from stakeholders, and the other environmental pressures generated in today's social milieu. An analogous case in point is the nomination of a non-credentialed corporate executive to be the Chancellor of the New York City public school system.[7] She was asked to resign five months later.[8]

Public and private agencies may attempt to arrogate to themselves responsibilities or tasks that are functions of the recreational service department. An example would be the police department's establishment of Police Athletic League programs in recognition of the value of such programs both for the department's public image and in terms of the potential for developing relationships with marginal youth populations that have adversarial attitudes to police contacts. Religious-based non-profit organizations that see the potential of attracting youth to their causes or constituencies can also be a concern.

Agencies that see themselves in competition with the department for funds or jurisdiction may attempt to undermine the department in an attempt to gain control of the resources involved. Economics always has a direct influence on the type of service and the extent to which any organization can offer opportunities to its constituency.[9] Tax resources, income derived, and budgeting considerations are based on current economic conditions and can cripple or enhance the achievement of the agency's goal.[10] Social influences reflect the mood, understanding, and willingness of citizens to participate in the offerings of the agency and to support its functions. These are some of the forces that are arrayed for or against the public agency. As a strategy it is recommended that these organizations be considered as a legitimate part of the recreational service delivery system and they can be valuable allies and partners.[11] Fortunately, recreational service might often have committed organized support due to the public's positive perception of the nature of the service. Recently, the governor of California, in response to a serious budget deficit, ordered the closing of state parks among other public program funding cuts. The public outcry opposing this was many times more vociferous than that regarding any of the other proposed service cuts and the decision was subsequently reversed.[12]

Strategic planning

Strategic planning is a rational approach to defining the organization's future direction for a period of three to five years. It requires the identification of organizational objectives and evaluation of the agency's ability to satisfy them.[13] It determines the organization's capabilities, the development of services designed to satisfy patron or client needs, and provides an opportunity to remove obsolete or unproductive activities. It increasingly involves concern for investigation and analysis of social and political trends, assessment of their impact on the organization, and selection of those components resulting in programs that maximize recreational opportunities. From this orientation it can be seen that planning is a logical means for assessing and determining an organization's place in the social order. Having taken account of the environmental situation, technological advances, social and cultural constraints, political realities, and economic conditions, the planning process becomes an integral part of the managerial system.

To administer a recreational service agency effectively, the service manager needs to develop strategic planning skills. The following is an inventory of the most crucial of the skills that this form of planning requires:

1. Scanning the environment within and external to the organization including an evaluation of the strains, weaknesses, opportunities, and threats facing the organization. This is commonly known as a SWOT review.[14]
2. Developing a mission statement expressing the vision and values of the organization. The document defines the purpose of the organization.

3. Establishing goals and objectives with the tasks and timeline necessary for their accomplishment. The employment of a planning/tracking system such as the Program Evaluation Review Technique, known as PERT can be helpful in the implementation and tracking of the strategic plan.[15] Inexpensive user-friendly software is available to support this system.
4. Strategic leadership and planning formulation can be applied to any organization in the sectors of society. The Blue Ocean Strategy (BOS) enables the development of effective strategy enactment and facilitates communication.[16]

The most effective way to introduce strategic planning in an organization is to develop the plan as a group process; involving the stakeholders and those who will be tasked to enact it.

This will empower the personnel involved in the implementation and secure the needed buy-in of the stakeholders, assuring a higher degree of success. Effective management of multiple projects can be achieved by the senior management by focusing only on the elements that have fallen out of the timeline or cost projections associated with a project. The manager is thereby provided with the support essential for achieving the organizational objectives or goal successfully.

Budgeting as a strategic planning tool

The budget document is a fiscal expression of the single year's portion of any strategic planning as well as the operational plan for the period. There are several types of budgeting processes that are commonly used by public agencies. The type employed is dependent on the information needed by the organization to express its funding requirements. The following is a description of the type of budgeting techniques and their purposes. More detailed explanations will be provided in the chapters on financial management and budgeting.

*   Historic Based Budget is the most common and least labor-intensive process. It reflects the current programs and costs adjusted for inflation. It can also be arranged to include new activities with projected estimated costs.
*   Line Item Budget is an accounting of all the items required to perform the projected programs with cost extensions. This type of budget gives management the maximum control of financial expenditures, but does not link the expenditures to expected outcomes for them.
*   Program Budget expresses the outcomes projected to be achieved by the expenditures for specific programs. It generally provides authority for the manager of the program to expend a set amount of funds for a particular program to achieve an agreed-upon outcome without restriction of specific items or services to be purchased.

- Zero Based Budget makes no assumptions based on previous costs or operating experience. The calculations for each item are based upon information that is developed specifically for the year, identifying each projected item or cost in a program. This allows a fresh look at the cost–benefit of programs as each projected cost for personnel, supplies, or equipment is accounted for by program. This is the most labor-intensive budget process. However, it offers the most transparent plan for evaluating and decision-making purposes.

Combinations of the various budgeting processes are used to achieve the planning result desired or the method of presentation adopted by the governmental entity.

Planning initiation

Where does planning begin? A number of considerations determine the initiation of any planning procedure, especially one that may change the personal relationships and organizational perspectives of employees. Top-down planning efforts begin with the policy-making body and the chief executive of the agency. Advantages of this are that the executive who is most knowledgeable about the organization as a whole, and policy-makers informed about the details, mission, and purposes of the agency, drive the development of the plan. The top-down approach works best when success is dependent upon the ability to make high-level organizational changes in response to environmental threats and pressures. Legitimate authority is established by ordinance or delegated by the responsible elected officer and resides with the agency executive in this model.

Bottom-up planning, on the other hand, begins at the lowest level of the organization where the service or activity is performed. It is initiated by those who are closest to the operations or recipients of the service. The bottom-up planning process appears to be most advantageous when the primary criterion of agency success is its responsiveness to patron needs and demands. This planning model is effective for empowering staff and gaining the desired commitment to achieve goals developed in this manner. Management in all cases should empower staff to perform their assigned tasks by delegating authority commensurate with responsibility.[17]

Planning components

The introduction of strategic management requires a number of intermediate procedures so that a logical foundation for change can be prepared. Problem identification, analysis, projection, and implementation are the methodological components deliberately formulated to transform the agency's capacity and responsiveness. The threats, opportunities, applied pressures, patron demand, economic, or political necessity require an agile response. In some instances the organization aggressively pushes innovative programs to satisfy its target population. In a more usual behavioral mold bureaucratic indifference to public demands is offset by responsiveness to the vociferous outcry from high-profile pressure groups. The elements contributing to the manner in which the agency responds stems from tradition, size, and latent organizational inertia, the connection of personal skills to environmental needs and, specifically, the capacity of management.

It is logical to discover a correlation between the strength of organizational response to public demand and the personal abilities found within the agency. This is determined by the drive and perception of managers to make decisions and the speed with which flexibility of structure enables the organization to respond.[18]

Problem identification. Problem determination develops as problems arise within the community or agency. Once a problem is raised or identified, the sequential process of solution begins. The salient features of the problem are described. Identifying the opponents and proponents as well as the relative influence and effect on the stakeholders involved. Objectives are set up and programs are formulated for resolving the problem.

Analysis. Following determination of a problem, cost-effectiveness must be examined. Justification and verification of the investigation by appropriate research techniques, so as to permit other people to appreciate what was performed in the analysis, should be carried out. All cost-effectiveness studies should use methods that fit the need. Therefore, operations research, economic analysis, mathematical concepts, and other pertinent investigatory techniques may be drawn upon to create a proper presentation.

In this way, a formalized system for assuring valid and reliable information necessary for making intelligent decisions becomes reality. Program plans are translated as monetary needs for the annual appropriation and accounting process. Conversion to electronic data-processing and cost–benefit analysis is not an attempt to eliminate the intangible aspects of human judgment from the decision-making process. Rather, it is a means for perpetuating better public services so that strategic decisions may be made in allocating scarce resources, substituting intelligent solutions for decisions based on emotion or external pressures.[19]

Projection. A managerial system that can offer optimum benefits to the department and community should be selected. Excellent software programs are available for this purpose. The assumption is that with all pertinent data collected and possible scenarios cast, the most logical alternative will be chosen to meet demand. This process, when routinized, particularly with the help of computer simulation, should produce decisions able to realize the primary objectives and goals of the organization. It is important that access to the information generated by the system is made readily available to all members of the organization to achieve a coordinated result in practice.

Examination of the organization's capacity for response requires close observation of behavioral characteristics. These include prevailing values, management focus and reaction to change, managerial skills, knowledge, and entrepreneurial attitudes. The latter are of particular importance at a time of shrinking funding resources available to the public sector through the tax base.

Structural relationships within the organization, including authority, responsibility, information generation, and performance outcome, must be assessed.

Implementation. When the strategic management system has been selected, it must be installed in the organization for operational effect. Absolutely vital to the success of the process is the professional staff's acceptance of the new system and its conformity to the requirements that the system will impose on decision-makers and problem-solvers. Equally significant, though of lower priority, are the cost factors and the amount or kind of inconvenience that installation of the new system may have on current operations. To stimulate employees so that they will accept the system and perform tasks effectively to achieve success, a basic educational program should be inaugurated. The maintenance of employee morale is an important factor in determining the success of the strategic management system. The executive must do everything he/she can to remove the potential resistance to the planning system which can occur when a new management system is introduced.

Staff members at every level must be notified when initial consideration is given to a new management system. Implicit in the educational program is the involvement of the affected employees to participate in the design of the new system. Identification with the new system does much to enhance commitment by the users. Personal involvement with a new plan invariably produces satisfaction in having participated in its development. Organizational problems are always encountered whenever a new system is introduced in an organization. However, if the new system can be shown to produce benefits that employees value, and if particularly affected employees are sought out for their opinions or suggestions in the development of the new system, ready acceptance of the process can be anticipated and accomplished.[20]

Types of plans

Tactical plans. These are intermediate steps designed to assist in the execution of strategic plans and to accomplish a particular segment of the organization's strategy. Tactical plans have to do with scheduling events, deployment of personnel, or allocation of resources. It is important to designate authority commensurate with responsibility. Essentially, divisional managers, one step removed from the executive level, formulate tactical plans. Thus, the manager of the plant and maintenance division, central office division, or recreational program division will have input concerning tactical plans; whereby the strategic mission of the agency is fulfilled.

Operational planning. This focuses on determining the day-to-day activities that are required to achieve the long-term goals of the organization. Such plans necessarily outline the tactical activities that must occur to support and implement the strategic plan. Operational plans are more specific than tactical ones and address short-term issues. Operations are based on daily needs of each section or sub-unit of the division. They will be developed in terms of participant numbers; issuance of supplies, materials, or equipment to carry out activities; public information releases to inform potential users of times, places, and activities; custodial or janitorial work to be performed, and other such priorities. Operational plans can be characterized as standing or single use plans. In the former, the plan is relatively long-lived and routine. In the latter, the plan is put into effect for a limited time or for a particular case. Operational plans are developed at the agency's middle management and lower levels and referred to those units contributing to the tactical effectiveness and efficiency of the organization, which, in turn, further the strategic goals of the agency. In the final analysis, managers need to plan because planning leads to higher performance and aids in coping with the complex situations which confront them.

Contingency plans. This kind of planning is necessary in environments that change rapidly or in unpredictable ways. Such planning necessitates the development of two or more plans based upon different operating conditions. Scenarios are developed which examine or explore possible projected environmental changes if certain alternatives are taken. With these plans in reserve, the organization is in a better position to react to situations where possible threats or opportunities are unforeseen. Even if an exact scenario has not been developed, the approximation of possibility to actuality enables the agency to effectively respond to needs and demands placed upon it. Contingency planning offers a tactical advantage to the agency for rapid and accurate problem resolution.

Finally, planning is a linking mechanism that sets the relationship of goals, plans, and controls. It establishes procedures for ensuring that the organization is moving in the right direction and making progress in the achievement of its goals. It enables managers to coordinate a broad range of organizational activities while it defines the responsibilities of individuals and task groups and assists in the coordination of their activities to achieve organizational objectives. The planning function forces managers to think ahead and consider resource need as well as potential opportunities and dangers that might arise in the future.

Establishment of the managerial system

Once the new process has been clarified, the most logical procedure is its institutionalization and use in the organization. Is it most effective to install the system on a sequential basis or *in toto*? The former method permits proper acquaintance with the new system, allows time for the adjustments necessary when the employees are attempting to learn about new performance requirements, and enables user learning to occur faster.

Another basis for examining a sequential introduction is that the system's various components can be tried out, improved, or changed when and where necessary prior to the establishment of the system across the whole organization. Despite the purity of design and model, establishment and operation may indicate some needed corrections or modifications. Even in the sequential establishment, some disruptions may occur as the old system is phased out. Establishment of a pilot program affecting a limited element of the organization is a good way to introduce a new system safely and simplifies making changes as issues arise.

The executive should reserve the permissions process as one monitoring aspect of the system. A significant feature of operating the system is that it must be able to cope with the daily load of problems or input. Thus, the significance of strategic management begins to become clear when a total system is developed and the sub-units or components are seen in the context of a total system. Because components of the system can be readily identified, observed, and measured, a more rational approach to providing quality solutions occurs.

3 From strategic planning to organizational design

Organizational effectiveness and efficiency does not develop in a vacuum. When the agency determines that the time is propitious for the installation of strategic functions, it becomes necessary to formulate activity patterns so that strategic management and the enhancement of managerial capabilities to initiate strategic functions can occur. To implement innovation in the provision of recreational services the agency is required to maintain its current posture while repositioning itself to pursue the kind of organizational change necessary for maximum effectiveness and optimal efficiency.

The need to accommodate an organization's design to meet current and future challenges is ongoing in a dynamic agency. The administrator responsible for the process can expect a degree of resistance from those affected by the changes, regardless of how minor they may be. This can be attributed to the general fear of the unknown and the vested interests of some stakeholders in the status quo.[1] The following discussion concerns organizational designs currently being employed to effect various modifications that are prevalent in this sphere of operations.

Transitional needs

There are number of dimensional differences that can assist the transition from a present arrangement to a new organizational structure, which promotes innovation and the ability of the organization to meet the challenges of changing conditions. This suggests that agency success will rely on rapid and frequent redeployment of resources and strategic repositioning. Whether the agency expects to champion innovation as a fulcrum for growth or in response to increased turbulence in the environment is an important factor in the organizational design to be considered. Moreover, it adds an important facet to innovation.[2] This additional dimension makes awareness of substantial strategy modifications significant by eliminating some activities while adding new ones. If the agency is going to encourage wide-scale strategic innovation, its redeployed resources may demand initial and continuing divestment. Divestment tends to be a most difficult and poorly executed process of organizational change. Some agencies, whose routinized operations are amazingly dysfunctional, still shrink at the idea of cutting down or cutting out these largely ineffective activities. Inertia may often deter suggestions for improvement and impede the changes that are necessary. When divestment practices are implemented the major portion of lower performance activity can be substantially reduced and the resources in personnel, finance, and material formerly committed to those activities can be rechanneled for greater organizational effectiveness.

Traditional organizational structure

Historically, organizational structure has been vertical and mechanistic with specialized tasks, strict hierarchy of authority, vertical communication and reporting systems, few or no teams, task forces, or integrators, with a centralized decision-making function.[3] There are agency personnel who are wedded to the chain-of-command, orthodox hierarchical structure because it has always clearly defined their respective functions, responsibilities, and authority.[4] The hierarchy protects those individuals who are only comfortable within a programmed niche or whose personalities require the imposition of authority or dependency upon an authority figure. Many authority figures restrict the choices that subordinates can make and this is consonant with the type of domineering behavior projected.[5] Some individuals in an agency feel cast adrift when they cannot lean on an established or customary policy or structure for authorization. They are unable to deal with the questioning and free-swinging response that accompanies structural change producing a more open or democratic system. In short, they adhere to a hierarchical structure because they have had little or no exposure to anything else; or because they need to feel that their position is insulated from intrusive demands that more skilled or knowledgeable individuals possess.

Organizational structure has usually been arranged in pyramidal form, with a base consisting of all non-managerial personnel who either carry out the functions for which the agency was established or who are in support roles and whose tasks are to assist line personnel to carry out their functions more effectively and efficiently.[6] The next level up is often comprised of supervisory personnel or specialists whose major function is to oversee base and support personnel. Supervisory responsibility includes making sure that work performance is carried out in a timely manner in accordance with preset policy. In this regard, the supervisor has real authority and is in a position to apply sanctions or to reward work well done.

The third level contains middle management personnel who are assigned responsibility for sub-units, bureaus, or divisions of the department and the personnel employed therein. The peak of the pyramid is reserved for upper management or the chief executive officer of the system. This vertical structure has top-down development, with the executive employed first and then the succeeding levels implemented as the department expands.

Under such a system all decisions, or any other influence affecting departmental performance, response to constituent demand, or the development of appropriate programs, spaces, plans, and equipment distribution reside at the executive level. There is little call for more effective communication in the form of questioning policy or carrying out orders. Figure 3.1 depicts the ramified public recreational service department hierarchical structure for direct service to the constituency. This bureaucratic structure ensures that policy transmitted is put into effect as received. Obedience to orders and carrying out the functions of a particular position is all that matters.

The key aspects of this type of management consist in establishing a clear chain of command in a span of control where personnel can be effectively supervised. The span of control imperative is heavily dependent on effective communication. This has been greatly enhanced by such developments as mobile phones, computers, e-mail, instant messaging, texting, and Skype that provides rapid communication and even visual capability when desirable. Adherence to orders and carrying out the function of a particular position, as testified in detailed job descriptions, is the goal of the organizational design. This design is most appropriate in a military-type organization, where compliance to orders is of paramount consideration, but creates some major issues in a recreational service agency that is constituency oriented.

Whether a specific policy developed by upper management in any top-down management style organization actually meets the needs of the people it is supposed to serve or whether it is unresponsive, untimely, and ineffective is rarely brought to question – particularly in large organizations where the executive officer is distant from the point of service delivery. It is only when there is constant complaint, obvious deficits, and political jeopardy that remedial measures may be taken. When under political or economic pressure to change the organizational structure radically some of the positive attributes of the department can be lost. Therefore, agencies must continually think about modification of structure in incremental ways to forestall serious errors as the department scrambles to maintain itself in the face of rapid change.

The centralized aspect of the bureaucratic structure precisely defines and fixes the agency and its subdivisions by their respective functions. Organizing by function in this type of design has its advantages and supervision of the function can be performed with a high degree of expertise when the chain of command of a unit is under the immediate direction of personnel with technical expertise in the function. However, the range from hierarchical (mechanistic) to a horizontal or flat organization includes both decentralized and centralized structures.

This in no way implies that the executive should perform all the duties within the department; however, it does mean that delegation of appropriate duties, authority, and responsibility to staff members who are subordinates is a necessity. Each person within the department thereby knows his/her

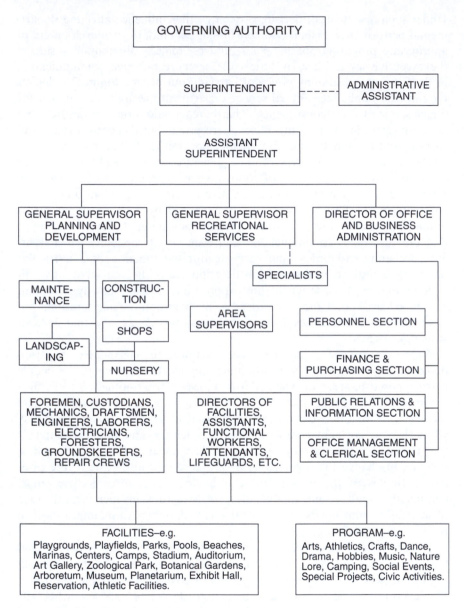

Figure 3.1 The ramified recreational service department.

function, to whom and for whom he/she is responsible, and the chain of command for the alleviation of problems that cannot be solved on his/her level.

Centralized executive control with delegated authority and responsibility essentially calls for the establishment of a definite line organization with direct triangular communication branching from the chief executive at the apex down through administrative, supervisory, and operational levels. This structure, it is thought, allows for a sound foundation of control and co-ordinated activity.

It may very well be that certain functions can be more efficient and effective operations if there is a high degree of repetitiveness, standard responses, and well-known activities. For example, centralized personnel management may contribute to the more efficient processing of new employees insofar as recruitment, induction, examination, and placement are concerned. It is also likely that a centralized industrial shop may be more effective in the necessary maintenance of automotive equipment, or material repairs in terms of volume purchases, that is, buying in bulk, storage, and inventory control, as well as purchasing supplies, materials, or equipment for the entire department (economies of scale). Other centralized functions may involve the development of community-wide activities performed simultaneously and in identical modes, public relations dealing with the overall image of the system, legal decisions affecting the entire system, policies concerning private use of public facilities, and other slow-moving developments to which incremental modifications can be made. These centralized duties may be continuously sustained even when the department is moving toward an innovational or decentralized system.

All organizational structures require that the individual charged with the operation of a unit of the department be given the requisite authority to execute that responsibility. An important principle of effective management is that authority must be coterminous with responsibility. The failure or the achievement of that unit then rests with the individual in whom authority and responsibility reposes.

A new pattern for organizational structure

In an organization such as a recreational service agency that is constituency focused, the imperative is for the organization to have the ability to accommodate the local cultural values of the population it is serving. Individual neighborhoods or communities in the same political jurisdiction may require different approaches. The overriding concern in this situation is the empowerment of the personnel closest to the point of service on making decisions.[7] This type of organization is best formed on a geographical configuration based on community considerations as opposed to a functional design favored in a hierarchical organization. A structure that supports innovation and that will support customization of service delivery tends to be horizontal and flat.[8] It features shared tasks, lessened subservience to strict hierarchical demands and is, in fact, characterized by few rules and little conformity to superior/subordinate relationships. One of the outstanding features is that authority is gained by expertise rather than position at the point of service delivery.[9]

In this structure the need for teams, task forces, and integrators is vital. There is a pattern of informal decentralized decision-making throughout the system.[10] Generally, the horizontal structure comes about where there is widespread recognition of the need to customize programming to meet citizen demand. Additionally, the utilization of electronic equipment in every office and facility creates a diffusion of knowledge about almost all operations and enhanced two-way communications ability so that solutions can be generated and handled on the spot as the condition or situation warrants. Information technology (IT) and its dissemination throughout the organization drive the horizontal structure. Typically, decentralization of authority comes about as a result of dynamic or rapid change within the socio-political environment. It might occur in consequence of in- or out-migration, because of industrial demand or the lack of it. In some instances capping property tax, increasing income tax, or the abolition of income tax might seriously affect the ability of the system to react as quickly as it should in order to meet the demands of its constituent population. Radical political development resulting in a higher demand for quick action might necessitate the need for individual offices or facilities of a far-flung system to take the responsibility for making decisions at the local level instead of waiting for the centralized bureaucracy to move. Where an answer is needed immediately, where conditions differ to such an extent at neighborhood, district, or regional centers that localized policy, decisions, and authority to function must be embodied in the system, then decentralization and empowerment of staff at the lowest level practical becomes a vital part of management. Whenever solutions must be generated quickly so that the system is enabled to make the most satisfactory rapid response to articulated desires, decentralization is seen as a key to success.

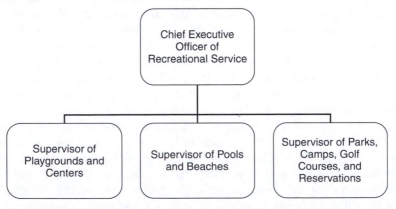

Figure 3.2 The flat or horizontal organization.

The team and its functions

Decentralization operates best through team effort and local management expertise in developing close-knit associations of peers working in horizontal or vertical structures depending on need.[11] Teams are created by the organization as a formal part of structure or informally to act for short periods to deal with situations of limited duration. They comprise work-groups formed by the manager and his/her subordinates or selected from across the spectrum of the organization for the expertise brought to the situation. When coordination is an imperative, teams come together across hierarchical lines in order to facilitate activity in gaining access to the knowledge, skill, and experience that specialists have.[12]

The team

A team is composed of two or more people who interact and coordinate their work to accomplish a specific goal. Team members may be selected for their expertise and/or interests from any sub-unit of the department whether of a line or staff designation. Thus team members who have a common vision and goal will be involved in regular interaction, see themselves as collaborating in a shared mission with collective responsibility for goal achievement, and provide consultative efforts to peer members of the team. These individuals may represent recreationists, plant and maintenance personnel, public relations personnel, or others, depending upon need. Team size may range from 2 to a maximum of 12, with the optimum being 7.

Measures of successful outcomes by effective teams will be based on productivity, that is, the amount of work performed in accomplishing a task or resolving a problem. Personal satisfaction inherent in the tasks to be performed is extremely important in creating a climate for success. If members have a sense of ego-identification with the team, its mission and efforts, it is likely that they will have a greater desire to see that the team achieves the objectives that have been set. Deriving personal satisfaction from accomplishment is a proven assessment for determining effectiveness.

Team leadership

Teams typically change leaders depending upon the situation confronted. Leadership roles are rotated or shared as the team responds to some problem or demand that requires specific skill, knowledge, or experience. It is not unusual for team members to serve in a leader role at one time and act as a follower at another. Team members have individual and mutual accountability. This means that individuals bring their particular capability to the team and work to the extent that they can, being accountable for that aspect of the task which requires their input. Teams may also be identified as ad hoc committees that are created to deal with tasks which do not regularly occur. Sometimes, special-purpose teams are created outside the organization to undertake a project of special significance to the system. These special-purpose teams are called into being only until the issue that required them to be formed is resolved; then they are dissolved. For example, a problem-solving team consists of employees within the vertical structure meeting to discuss ways of improving quality, efficiency, and work in and within their domain. Figure 3.3 displays both vertical and horizontal teams.

It is possible that the team may come to an independent conclusion for a given situation that differs in some degree to that of the organization. It is probable, however, that in working out the permutations involved, the team's outcome will be congruent with that of the organization. Inevitably, mutual accountability pervades team effort. In all discussions within the team decisions are made as to work performance and each member shares the work.[13]

Horizontally structured teams established from a number of sub-units or divisions of the department may also be organized for the same reason.

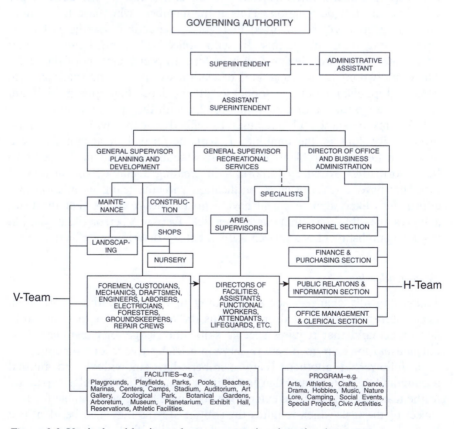

Figure 3.3 Vertical and horizontal teams recreational service department.

In the former instance, the work situation of a division may be substandard and therefore the team is initiated. In the latter instance, low morale, department-wide inefficiency, and poor working conditions may require input from across the board so that improvement may be brought about.

In certain situations, where there is great geographical distance among department members because of the size of the metropolitan area, county, or region being served by the recreational service system, virtual teams may have to be implemented. The virtual team uses computer technology and software so that distant members can collaborate on projects and reach common goals. While computers are useful in many departmental functions, a virtual team effort is typically initiated because of the wide dispersion of members, making travel time to a central meeting place an inefficient and uneconomical use of personnel.

Teams as transitional forces

Formation of teams may be used as a transitional tool to introduce re-alignment within the organization. This device is often applied to gradually shift authority in a hierarchical organization. It has been a helpful technique to deal with the need for acceptance by the major losers of authority, who are those in the middle and low management positions. Finally, there may be legal problems that arise with regard to meeting the terms of contracts in effect, seniority rules, due process procedures, along with other obstacles that are ingrained in the transition of organizations to new organizational designs.

Benefits of teams

There are benefits that outweigh disadvantages that might accrue as a result of team development. Primarily, the rise in the level of worker effort is recognized. Team member satisfaction motivates greater worker productivity. An invaluable asset is the empowerment of employees to bring their own knowledge and skill to task performance.[14] In the final analysis, organizational flexibility grows out of team implementation. This contribution does much to increase the rapid response necessary to solve confrontational problems and aid the department in maintaining itself in whatever social, political, or economic environment it is embedded.

The traditional ethos by which recreational service systems operate has come into conflict with the demands of a more sophisticated, consumer-driven society. The need to change historical or generic patterns of operation has come under pressure from both patrons (potential participants) and recreational professionals themselves. The shift from a recreational service system characterized by public service monopoly, hierarchy, and top-down attitudes to one having diverse providers, networks, and empowerment of service recipients is most strikingly seen in contemporary American society.[15]

Public recreational service as a system

If recreational service is seen as a system by which opportunities are delivered to the public rather than as a special agency actually providing recreational experiences per se, the organizational patterns will be quite different from extant agency types. Figure 3.4 depicts the networked system that such a structure would demand.

A coordinating, instead of a performing, department will constitute the best possible recreational service. Under such circumstances the entire resource potential of the community, in terms of sectors of interest, personnel, natural, financial, and artificial means, will be mobilized for the most effective service that can be made available. As a service delivery system its most significant feature may be one of coordinating diverse community resources rather than of having a permanent performing staff to instruct or supervise recreational activities. Examples of this proposed role are the relationships currently enjoyed by community recreational departments with youth sport organizations exemplified by Little League Baseball and the American Youth Soccer Organization (AYSO), where the public agency

Figure 3.4 The recreational service delivery system.

provides facilities and support such as leadership training or public information as needed. The recognition of the recreational value to the participants of the conduct and management of the recreational activities they are engaged in are critical to this form of service delivery. Some combined form of specialized department with permanent staff acting in a coordinating capacity with regard to community resources for recreational purposes may be most effective.

Typically, the structure of the agency is settled long before a manager is employed. If the manager has a strong sense of organizational value he/she may attempt to alter what is found. Insofar as the manager has a choice, a determination of the most important factors must be made and organized along the lines that offer the best possibilities for implementation. Responsibility for creating a structure that will prove the most effective in carrying out the mission of the agency is a continuing one. The manager must be prepared to move patiently, as well as definitively, and to introduce modifications in a manner that will allow for the gradual building up of support from stakeholders both internal to the organization as well as in the public domain.

Structure and change

Even though the term *structure* connotes formalized lines of authority, some representational form is necessary if a system is to produce the kinds of results that professionals want and recipients need. The most striking consequence of modification of the recreational service department from a monopolistic and hierarchical entity into a more decentralized flat or horizontal agency will be in terms of patron focus. Most significantly, the system will become more efficient in delivering recreational services. Thus, patrons will be able to choose freely among recreational providers, which will reduce the need for centralized planning, improve on frequently slow response time, and overall quality. Public recreational service authorities will serve to inform people of the options available to them. To strengthen freedom of choice and expand supply, publicly funded, private or quasi-public recreational service providers can be outsourced to offer service.

What will happen to the traditional hierarchical line and staff organization? It may go the way of all obsolete functions. Will this destroy career opportunities in the field? No! In fact, the implementation of flatter organization types may well cause the field to grow in ways that cannot be envisioned at the present time. For example, basic financial incentives and options for recreationists to begin their own businesses could revolutionize the delivery of recreational services to people everywhere. It is possible that publicly supported private contractors would be able to expand the varieties of recreational activities far beyond that which is currently supplied in the public domain. Organizations that offer particular recreational experiences could be compensated on the basis of direct provision to consumer groups.

In other words they would be paid for what they actually deliver. Public financing of private recreational providers does not mean that all commercial providers or businesses that have a recreational connotation would be placed on contract. For example, the typical places individuals frequent for recreational experiences, such as restaurants, bowling centers, taverns, cinemas, opera houses, golf courses, tennis clubs, swimming pools, marinas, hotels, spas, and the like would not be eligible to receive public tax support. These enterprises, with some recreational aspect, have always been established as profit-making businesses which charge those who want the service or experience a fee. Instead, the public recreational service system would, in effect, become the clearing house and coordinating institution of the community. Its major function would be to catalog the entire range of recreational resources within the community and, by contract, enable private specialists and/or companies employing recreational personnel to deliver those services of which they were capable. In this way economies of scale would be significant; only a core of recreational professionals and activity specialists would be required to be employed by the public agency because the agency would no longer be directly involved in the transmission of recreational experiences to clients, except in highly specialized situations. For those citizens who could not afford any but free recreational service and for whom the public agency is the organization of last resort, the public department would still be available.

Recreational professionals employed by the public system would have general oversight of contracting parties in order to be assured that appropriate and effective recreational services were made available to people using them. With this combination of decentralization, patron-driven influence, as well as the incorporation of positive economic incentives, the field of recreational service could be reordered. It can be expected that, in the future, recreational service recipients will be less tolerant of deficits in the supply of recreational experiences, options, information, and their own lack of influence. Public recreational service cannot stand still in a changing world, particularly with the competition for limited public tax resources available to support it.

4 Strategic decisions for policy-making

Policy is the result of decision-making. It is a statement, usually formalized in writing, which results in substantive action within any agency. It is the end product of a process of information-gathering and proposed solutions to anticipated or previous problems. Policy formulation concerns managerial decisions taken in consequence of the operations of the recreational service system. The decision-making process is intimately bound together with the primary mission of the system and methods for achieving objectives so that the mission can be accomplished, and inevitably focuses on the use of critical resources or situations which appear advantageous to agency success.

The need for policy

The amount of information that comes to the manager complicates his/her responsibility for decision-making. However, it is only by accumulating information about the issues that a rational judgment can be made so that policies will be best designed to satisfy constituent needs. The sheer volume of inputs needed to reach a decision that will enable sound policy to be formulated can be demoralizing. Unless knowledge of the environment is encyclopedic, spillover damage from policy can exacerbate the very problems the policy was supposed to resolve. Nevertheless, there are procedures that can be utilized to obtain the kinds of information necessary to reach a logical decision concerning policy design.

The essential procedures of logical problem-solving concern actions those managers undertake when they attempt to do their best in decision-making that can be done under the circumstances. Often, managers are confronted with problems for which there is incomplete knowledge, unresolved uncertainties, restricted ability to process data, and all other typical constraints, which can hinder rational thinking about the usually ill-defined problems that necessitate policy decisions. The manager needs to approach problem-solving by asking a considerable number of difficult questions. These questions inform significant goals or values that seem to be hanging in the balance and which require certain conditions to be met for a solution to be satisfactory. This means that the solution will probably be one of the best available. Among the questions that need answering are those that involve threats to or opportunities for the organization; requirements that need to be met in order to avoid dangers, achieve objectives, limit costs, and seek out alternatives that might probably solve the dilemma. Of course, additional questions will have to be posed so that facts may be ascertained, previous information can be retrieved, and new information can be obtained.[1]

Policy-making is an ongoing activity in which managers engage; it tends to have great importance for agency organization, control, and direction. Moreover, policy usually affects operations over an extended period, and inevitably focuses the use of critical resources on situations which appear advantageous to agency success.

If policies are defined as general guides for employee behavior in the achievement of objectives as well as lines of action necessary to control or promote certain activities, then it is necessary to recognize that several policies may be required in order to fulfill an objective. Each policy may need support and linkage to other policies if the specific mandate is to be carried out.

Policy determination

The development of the major elements of policy for any recreational service system will undoubtedly involve the following: (1) some designated component of the agency, the environment of which the agency is a part, or one or more operations carried on by the agency will be affected; (2) a desirable sequence of events will be implemented so that specific behaviors will occur; (3) a particular alternative will be chosen from among several possible courses of action so that a desired result is obtained; and (4) the intent of the decision-maker or makers will be clearly perceived through the publication of some statement which notifies all who are affected. Some policies offer tangible benefits to those who make up the constituency of the system. Other policies prevent, control, or direct behaviors that have been deemed hazardous, destructive, or deleterious.

Most people are apt to think that policy is decided upon through a series of steps (or a group of linked moves), such as: (a) initial appraisal of, or investigation into the problem; (b) identification of goals or objectives; (c) soliciting possible policies to achieve the goals; and (d) selection or decision. Looking at policy in this way is useful for some purposes, but it gives the impression that policy-making arises from a single person. This is obviously not true. This view fails to elicit or infer the specifically political facets of policy-making, its usual disarray, and the resultant emphatically diverse ways in which policies develop.

The impinging forces of the political environment, containing as it does various ideological viewpoints, special interests, particular aspirations, the political possibilities of constituent demands, or the economic realities of fiscal resources, all lead to certain compromises. Sometimes policy creates consequences which have little or nothing to do with the problem it was supposed to solve. On occasion policies are instituted to take advantage of opportunities rather than resolve problems. In some instances, conditions occur and ipso facto become policy because of importunate planning or the lack of foresight and no planning.

Policy-making is a complicated process whose parameters are frequently unobserved or only dimly seen. The mix of interacting forces necessitated by differentiated demands and requirements produces results that are described as policies. How this happens and how reasonable procedures can be introduced into this sometimes chaotic process is subject to analysis and, perhaps, comprehension. Still other policies are generated to encourage personal performance so that waste of valuable resources is either limited or restricted and the delivery of primary services is made more effective.

Problem confrontations and solutions

Problem generation besets the field. Strategic managers tend to anticipate problems before they arise and initiate procedures crafted to produce solutions. Worst-case scenarios should be developed as an exercise for logical resolution using an if–then system to propose alternative courses of action. By putting in sequence the likely series of events that might occur under certain circumstances or conditions the manager may be able to stockpile the best solution available for the projected case. The dictum, "whatever can go wrong, will go wrong" should be the guide by which the manager prepares to implement the tactics developed to counteract issues that cause stress. By foreseeing possible future problems and finding probable actions to be taken, the manager will have placed him/herself in a position of strategic importance.

Managerial procedures for the determination of solutions to departmental problems provide the system with the necessary flexibility or adjustment mechanisms through which valid responses can be found for environmental changes.[2] Management is the system's self-regulating instrument, and it presupposes that departmental problems are assigned to administration for resolution. The ultimate aim of all managerial procedures is to find satisfactory solutions, which then become program experiences for public consumption through participation. For effective solutions to problems confronting a recreational service system, some process that involves all factors of the department's performance, the devising of a general procedure for handling operational matters, system-wide simulation or model construction, and the assembling of information directly related to the department's ability to perform must occur. The final step is the utilization or application of specific data that can produce optimum levels of effectiveness.

Recreational service departments may be looked on as systems with meaningful direction whereby the cooperative efforts of many people are required if the aims of the system are to be realized. The aims of every public recreational service department are a varied and comprehensive series of individual, dual, group, and mass recreational activities and experiences that lead directly to human satisfaction, enjoyment, and enhancement of the quality of life.

The policy-making milieu

The environment of the recreational service system incorporates the social, cultural, and economic impacts that prompt the policy decisions which managers make and also affect the impact of their decisions upon the policy target. Resources that affect and influence policy are both human and instrumentalities. Human resources are those which are translated into constituent demands, desires, or claims for specific services; or personnel skills, knowledge, and ability to perform required duties and responsibilities in carrying out the mission of the department. Instrumentalities are financial support, program development, materials, supplies, and equipment that indicate whether the department has the means to carry out its mandate.

Policy-makers assimilate information derived from the available resources and develop policies based upon them. The results of policies usually become program services, which either satisfy the recreational needs of those who participate or are rejected by participants and non-participants alike. In the latter instance new policy must be developed to counteract whatever dissatisfaction arises from an inadequate program or other services. Included within the process of policy-making are also the conflicting values, behavioral variations, jurisdictional infringements, insufficient resources, or non-compliance with procedures that cause friction and other injurious confrontation.

For the purposes of this text, it has been found useful to differentiate between legislative policy and administrative policy. Legislative policies have typically been articulated by boards, commissions, or other designated executive bodies, that is, the city council or board of supervisors, and are usually broadly stated. Managerial policies, on the other hand, are typically specific in nature and almost always limited to a particular subject, problem, or issue. Thus, a legislative policy that "the department will attempt to support area suppliers whenever possible" may become interpreted at the management level into a procedure that "when two suppliers of materials or goods bid for contracts and one is not from the community, the local supplier, not necessarily the lowest bidder, will be selected."

It should be emphasized that the manager of the department will probably influence legislative policy-making because of the expertise that the manager brings to the position. The professional invariably has more pertinent information about the operational needs of the agency than anyone else at the policy-making level. It behooves him/her to supply information to policy-makers so that they have the ability to make rational decisions. Where the manager answers to a legislative body, it is possible that said body would delegate the translation of legislative principles into a policy statement. Furthermore, the manager may also initiate policy in terms of general principles.

Policies at the managerial or legislative level are determined from among the alternatives offered in terms of resources available or other controlling conditions. At the managerial level, however, they become the principles which guide the decision-making process throughout the organization. For example, at the legislative level, the manager may decide that, for promotion to supervisory rank, professional education and breadth of experience will count for more than seniority in the department. In coming to this decision, the manager will have considered the variables of personal merit, education, ability, and seniority. At the managerial level, when several individuals are being examined for supervisory candidacy, the criteria employed in selection will be based upon professional education first and then length of service with the department.

Policies are injected into operational workings of an organization in several ways. From a legislative orientation they are the objects of the decision-making process. From a managerial orientation they become the basis for problem-solving when implemented. The presumption here is that policies are developed upon rational models, although this is not always true.

Policy variations

To appreciate the operation of any organization, especially a large one, the pattern of personal relationships within the agency needs to be understood. Such patterns tend to be displayed in the habitual policies that are adopted by the agency in its operation. Assessment of a department usually discloses the various kinds of policy in effect and the methods by which such policies are instituted.

Conventional policy

Conventional policy is determined by custom, precedent, and usage. In its extreme form, such policy is restricted, inflexible, and demands conformity. It is reduced to a formula which is its own end and is not conducive to logical intervention. There are agencies which do things in certain ways, not because there is any rational basis for the action but simply because things have always been done this way and nobody challenges the object or method. Conventional policy may once have had some rational basis for its inception, but times change and so do conditions. Unless the organization is able to move with the times, it stands in the unforgiving position of risking becoming stagnant. Conventional policy produces static and finally stagnant conditions. Such policy is too rigid to be able to cope with rapidly changing situations.

Essentially, the policy of convention relies more upon historical precedent that it does upon rational decision-making. This policy variety discourages questioning and requires adherence to long practice without explanation. Historical practice is habitual and appears as a natural order of things. Those who support such policy do so without any thought of change. In fact, it is considered irrelevant to offer rational suggestions for the modification of conventional policy. Each agency apparently establishes fundamental rules that are generally accepted even though those who accept them would be severely pressed to offer any reason for them. In a contemporary organization it may start with a legislative decision that establishes a precedent which then endures long after the cause for the decision has been forgotten and the condition that demanded it no longer exists. When such policy is only part of the organizational culture and affects performance in trifling ways it has little consequence on agency efficiency. However, when it leads to static rigidity in an environment requiring the ability to adapt to rapid change, then serious problems can be expected.

"But we've always done it that way around here" may be the agonized cry of the traditionalist. This is not a rational answer to situations which require change. Organizational policies that were once based on sound reasoning and proved effective when they were initially introduced sometimes continue long after the reasons for their development have passed from the scene. Their only value is that of tradition.

Dictum

The policy of dictum – like any autocratic pronouncement – is the willful issuance of guiding statements by one person. Such policy is exemplified by the arrogation of power by an individual and the capricious development of policy for the daily operation of the organization. Policy of this type is fast fading from the scene because it implies an entrepreneurial or charismatic personality that is not widely known in an era of technocratic managers. Policy by fiat, when observed in agencies, has the effect of requiring subordinates to maintain constant contact with the boss so that clarification of what is really wanted is understood. Since the boss is under no obligation to maintain the same policy from moment to moment, subordinates generally have problems in determining how they are supposed to behave at any given time; they have little discretion to act without first consulting the promoter.

Usually, policy by dictum is undesirable because it produces frustration among subordinates. There are instances when such policy procedure may be effective. That occurs when the situation is uncertain and rapidly moving events demand something close to instantaneous modification. Not hampered by precedent or logical processes in the development of policy, the arbitrary manager utilizes his/her knowledge of the agency's resources and personal "instincts" to guide the organization.

Policy by dictum provides tremendous leverage and discretion to the individual who is the source of such policy, but dampens the enthusiasm of co-workers who are thwarted in their desire to perform and who remain in limbo as they try to anticipate what is expected of them. Such a policy is diametrically opposed to group or team decision-making. The only time that arbitrary policy is worthwhile is when subordinates gain satisfaction through a high level of interpersonal relationships as well as the expectation of great rewards from slavish devotion to the boss. Contemporary conditions are not conducive to such policy or relationships. Where this is in effect, the organization may be placed in jeopardy.

Logic

Policy created from needs and based upon accurate and pertinent information, as in the case of systematic management and problem-solving mechanisms previously discussed, permits enlightened managers and frees organizational employees from the willful acts of a head. The concept of policy as defined by a legislative body, rather than one person, is well known in the literature. However, much policy is, and should be made by individuals. In any modern organization, rational policy is usually expressed in terms of principles, which guide behavior and set the operational tone of the agency. Generally policy of this type is supplemented by procedures, standards of performance, and monitoring techniques. Usually, these procedures are understood to be managerial policies designed to explain how legislative principles will be executed.

The rational model provides guidelines for handling recurrent situations or activities, or for avoiding behavior, which is undesirable. Policy should propose intended behavior concomitant with agency goals. Policy based upon logical input produces consistent and coordinated action. Individuals within the department are able to guide their own actions and anticipate the actions of others because the policy is stable and not subject to whim. With rational policy, each member employed by the system has a common set of guidelines to follow. Logical policy development contains both the reasons why behavioral guides are necessary and the particular restrictions which control behavior. These two components, the rationale and the specifications, incorporate the fundamental factors of the soundly designed policy. For example:

Rationale: The department resolves that its professional staff will be recognized on the basis of merit and ability. It is determined that this is the most equitable method of compensation.

Specification: Systematic evaluation of departmental personnel performance will be conducted on a routine basis and regular review of individual compensation will be conducted in terms of position requirements and performance.

Rationale: The safety of agency patrons is an essential responsibility of the department and all personnel associated with it. Scrupulous care must be taken to avoid placing patrons in jeopardy through error, lack of information, or negligence. To this end a safety education program will be devised, employees will inspect physical properties for damage or hazards, and patrons will be warned against dangerous practices or prevented from engaging in behavior which might lead them to injury.

Specification: Warning signs will be posted at all appropriate places, to prevent behavior inimical to the health or safety of patrons.

Whether in the form of a legislative statement, as in the first policy above, or in that of a definitive rule limiting action, as in the second managerial statement, these policies offer the reasons justifying the actions. When conditions change, if ever, so that the rationale becomes invalid, the policy could be changed. It is unlikely that a safety program will ever not be needed. The vagaries of human nature being what they are, people will wittingly or unwittingly place themselves in danger in recreational situations because they do not believe that any danger exists in the "safe" environment of a ballpark, playground, or other recreational area. When, however, justification for a policy can no longer be found, the policy should be changed or abolished. The real danger is that policies take on the trappings of tradition, become fixed, and are no longer derived from rational needs. When the reasons for policy are clearly understood, the danger of policy by precedent and rigid adherence without question can be radically reduced.

Clarification of the rationale for policy statements is useful in another connection. When personnel in a system understand the logic that justifies a constraint, they are more likely to accept it as a reasonable guide to their own behavior. While there are certain personality types, oriented to authoritarian attitudes, which tend to accept constraints with little or no question, others, who are more democratically oriented, require the reasoning behind the rules before acceptance is given. Managers who explain their policies instead of attempting to enforce prescribed rules of conduct through edict are usually confirmed by a more willing acceptance on the part of subordinates.

Rational policy-making requires both explanation and specificity. However, if the policy is to be considered worthwhile, and capable of implementation, other elements will need to be included within the parameters of the policy. Policy should be the outcome of the values of the decision-makers. Once policy is determined it must be capable of acceptance by those who are affected by it. Despite a logical basis and excellent design, policy can be circumvented or subverted by disaffected subordinates. This stipulation suggests that co-workers should be participating in the decision-making process, which formulates policy whenever feasible. Policy should be elastic to accommodate itself to different circumstances. Permitting exceptions need not invalidate the policy. There are conditions or situations where exceptions can be made, but all exceptions require justification.

Policies provide stable rules that are in effect until they are modified; for this reason, decisions arrived at at various times will be consistent. Legislative policies are meant to govern the entire system, not only distinct parts of it. Since the same policy is constant throughout the organization, decisions that are made are probably going to be more consistent at any given time than in circumstances where policies are arbitrarily arrived at or non-existent. Policies based upon logic and factual input permit flexibility. Because they are designed rationally, with the reasons for their existence explicitly stated, they can be evaluated and changed as conditions mandate change. This is in direct contrast to those policies which are dynastic in type or created by managerial caprice and are, therefore, much more difficult to assess or modify.

Scope of policy

Whatever inputs there are to recreational service departments, it is probably safe to say that most departments are motivated by the beliefs of the decision-makers that the primary function of the department is to supply recreational opportunities to all community residents. The perception of the manager is that recreational services should be offered in such a manner that every person, regardless of ethnicity, disability, youth, age, or socio-economic status would receive whatever is required for personal satisfaction. The specific objectives, then, are the promotion of recreational experiences which can meet individual needs, take place in areas that are easily accessible and have the kind of recreational activities demanded, have sufficient personnel to take care of instructional and supervisory functions, and have availability of a diversified range of areas on which recreational activities may be experienced. All of these conditions are normally offered because there is an adequate supply of money to produce the delivery of services.

However, the manager is also aware of the fact that fiscal support for the comprehensive delivery of recreational services is less than what is required in all respects. Still, the mission of the agency remains to be fulfilled. There are diverse lines of action, which may be attempted. There can be an appeal to the governing authorities of the community for more funds to meet the needs; grant proposals to state and federal authorities may be written to obtain funds for such purposes; there may be a public relations campaign promoted which seeks direct support from the people of the community; it may be determined that only selected populations will receive well-publicized delivery of programs; maintenance items or other capital budget features may be delayed or neglected so that money can be diverted to program opportunities; or some combination of all of the above. Whatever option is selected, it will be transmitted to the rank and file of the agency through written materials as well as verbal communication by line supervisors who will have the real responsibility for executing the policy. However, the process does not stop with policy implementation. Every policy probably generates some reaction. The more people who are touched by the policy and the greater the significance to them, the surer there will be repercussions. Subtle or overt changes may have to be made as the full impact of policy begins to be felt by those concerned.

Any number of questions can be raised about policy as it affects the public and the operation of the agency. "Is the policy worthwhile?" "Does the policy do what it was intended to do?" "Was there a miscalculation with concomitant adverse effects?" All of these questions must be examined, but before any definitive answers can be obtained, there is the necessity for investigating policy, economics, service delivery, and impact.

Economics

Almost all policies that are enacted by the recreational service department will involve costs in one way or another. Except for purely symbolic statements designed to mollify particular social groupings or uplift their morale, the expenditure of public money is to be one expected outcome of policy implementation in the public sector. In times of economic retrenchment the question of budgetary allocations to recreational service departments becomes an explosive issue. There are many city services competing for the same tax dollar. To most citizens recreational services represent a frill, hardly to be compared to the more significant functions of health, police, fire, sanitation, and the much-maligned educational system. To discuss public recreational services under such circumstances is a risk. Few managers want their budget allocations cut. Public recreational service departments may be able to justify financial requests, but whether the governing body will honor such requests is another issue.

During times of financial stress, public recreational service agencies are nearly always cut back in terms of manpower through attrition, furlough, or discharge. Moreover, maintenance support is curtailed. Materials to operate activities are kept to a bare minimum. Any change in operations that is likely to cost money will be rejected. When citizens are hard pressed financially, then the tax burden is among the most critical and sensitive issues which can be raised. Each substantive policy becomes a money-spending decision. Governing authorities focus their attention on budgetary problems, and costs are generally seen as a fundamental component insofar as the production of services is concerned. While spending alone will not satisfy the demands for service, it does permit the purchase of those items that will produce the service. By judicious manipulation of line items and the creation of policy that requires high-profile action for the most vociferous groups, the recreationist manager can obtain financial support for the continuation of public recreational service. Until the economy begins to strengthen and the community once again begins to appreciate the value of public recreational service, the manager may have to formulate policy that curtails comprehensiveness in favor of exclusivity.

Service delivery

Policies may be judged in terms of the level of output obtained. Incorporated in this area are such questions as *per capita* expenditure; what program is actually purchased by such spending; and what combination of capital outlay, personnel expenditure, and activities are generated? Although the level of spending may indicate the degree of service attained, allocation of funds does not necessarily provide the quantity or quality of service that is required. There is little question that money is extremely important to the provision of recreational service delivery, but there is no guarantee that sufficient budgetary allocation will produce a corresponding level of service. The real performance levels in public recreational programs are undoubtedly influenced by factors beyond the control of the department. The needs of the recipients, extra-departmental pressures, severity of deficiencies to be overcome, and other impinging stresses, are environmental conditions over which the recreational service department may have little or no influence.

Impact

Recreational policy effects are disposed differentially within the community. Certain policies will affect every person living in the community, while others have greater significance for particular populations. For example, a safety policy enacted to prevent accidents and injuries from occurring may only affect those who utilize or participate in certain activities or areas. Nevertheless, the policy has been implemented with the idea of it affecting all citizens equally. On the other hand, some policies are enacted which influence only certain socio-economic classes or particular neighborhoods within the community. Policy may be enacted which discriminates against ethnic or economic groups. Some groups may receive more services in terms of facilities, leadership or activities. That there is variability in service cannot be denied. To the extent that persons who reside in one neighborhood as opposed to another, because of racial, religious, ethnic, social, or economic differences, may enjoy more or less service of a particular type reflects their need or the manager's perception of the need.

Policy does not necessarily attain the objectives set out for it. Although the department may offer the delivery of services, such services may not have their intended outcomes. The thrust of service may be effective or not. Impacts of delivery are the outcomes that services have upon the intended recipient population as well as on other aspects of the environment. Certain impacts will be deliberate or planned; others will be accidental, coincidental, or unanticipated effects. Non-intentional impacts occur because of the nature of urban life and the paucity of information about the potential influences that policy implementation can have.

One example of unanticipated results may provide clarification of the concept of impact. The summer vacation may produce tension and an increased hostility among unemployed youth in the inner city. The department, in order to diminish unoccupied free time, establishes a series of popular music concerts, which brings an influx of youth into the city center. The decision to alleviate pressure may encourage the very outbreaks that the department hoped to prevent. The expected outcome, instead of providing a few hours of respite from alienation, was not realized and in fact became a main contributor to riotous conditions. This situation can occur when managers are not sensitive to problems that traumatize some elements of the potential patrons of the service. Whenever there is insufficient information about conditions and the consequences that might accrue as a product of specific policy, the actuality of unintentional negative effects is always present. An external aspiration of adroit managers is to formulate policies whose chief outcomes are planned and whose unanticipated ripple effects are either innocuous or minuscule.

Decision-making and policy

Logic should be the basis on which decisions are made. Emotionalism should be omitted from any process in which rational outcomes are expected. In analyzing the logical procedure it must be recognized that no agency has sufficient resources available to reach decisions that completely reduce unforeseen consequences to a bare minimum. The most logical procedure would include: (1) identification of the problem; (2) listing of all resources available; (3) setting out the objectives of the agency in order to fulfill the mission; (4) determination of priority of objectives; (5) determination of the costs of each line of attack and the sequence of events that might flow as a consequence of adoption; (6) choice of the objectives that appear most amenable to fulfillment in association with the greatest benefits and accommodations; (7) formulation of the policy which incorporates the actions necessary to accomplish the task.

Managers who follow this procedure require information about all the potential opportunities and all possible outcomes developed from each opportunity. This need for information, unless retrieved or generated through electronic data-processing (EDP), constitutes a huge responsibility. Furthermore, although cities have begun to use computers and EDP on a vastly expanded and routine basis, only the most progressive recreational service departments are either equipped with terminals or have the skilled personnel assigned to program and operate computers.

It is vital to collect intelligence. Unless the manager is prepared to gather information in some other way than the ideal mentioned above, his/her time will be almost completely absorbed in analyzing such data. Moreover, when the information is collected and analyzed, the manager cannot be biased for or against any alternative. Decisions have to be made on the basis of systematically collected information – thus, several hindrances to developing policies based upon a logical decision-making process immediately come to mind: (1) too much time will be spent in the collection and examination of information – then there is not enough time to pursue all the projected consequences of each possible alternative; (2) the price of gathering and analyzing pertinent information may be prohibitive; (3) sometimes discrepant objectives may be amalgamated and simultaneously followed within the system; (4) there may be organizational practices that thwart intelligent and cooperative actions; and (5) the political climate will place restrictions on what is practicable.

Constraints on logical decision-making

Almost all the problems which public recreational service departments face have been developing for scores of years. There are no easy solutions to these problems nor will they disappear quickly. Despite this fact, managers are constantly urged to develop policy that will lead to the instantaneous solution of these problems. Politicians work within reduced time frames and are therefore compelled to press their appointed officials for action on problematic conditions that abound throughout the community.

Time limits. Managers are harried beyond their means to produce policies that will be effective. But the formulation of policy takes time. The collection and analysis of information on which to base substantive policy requires a great deal time. Time is the commodity in shortest supply and it is one of the major reasons why policies cannot be developed in logical fashion. The pressure of having to make decisions without the necessary study of pertinent information or the accumulation of information about the consequences of various alternatives abrogates conformity to logical procedure. In short, there is insufficient time to work out all of the ramifications involved.

Cost limits. Another decisive factor that prevents logical decision-making is the financial resources required for collecting information. Of all of the kinds of information needed none is more important than accumulating data which show the needs of people. Specialized information, which indicates methods for obtaining objectives, also requires considerable effort, cost, and time to obtain. Even after the information is gathered, there still remains the necessity for analysis and application. Managers have only a limited amount of time to devote to decision-making. They can reflect upon few items simultaneously and can assimilate a restricted amount of data dealing with any one problem. Because capacities for collecting information are curtailed by existing resources, when does the manager end the search for information and stop examining what has been obtained? Ideally, the reply is never. Reality, however, demands that at some agreed point in the process of policy formulation there will have to be some decision. When this occurs, a value judgment will have been made and some policy will emerge.

Too often, managers cease their investigations when they perceive a method of work that involves the least radical change in their ongoing operation. They do not seek out all the likely alternatives until they discover the most appropriate one. Rather, they act pragmatically and investigate until they establish a technique that works, something that will offer a modicum of relief from recognized difficulties without jeopardizing the bureaucratic status quo or causing instability among the various pressure groups that are the agency's constituents. Thus, the search for information continues until the manager feels that he/she must act. The costs are far too great and the pressures for policy commitment are too profound to continue a search until the single best mixture of objectives, data, and policy design has been found.

Discrepancy limitations. Recreational service departments operate under disparate policy statements. Some of these, unless the manager has been extremely careful, may be diametrically opposed. Such an obvious concept cannot be unexpected when it is recognized that a public recreational service department serves numerous interests and diverse constituencies. The department must, therefore, respond to many demands of which there are bound to be conflicts. How the department resolves the variety of inconsistencies that can occur does not contribute to the logical development of policy. It is not unusual to find departments advocating two policies that are completely antagonistic. One example is racial integration. Many urban departments are faced with de facto segregation across neighborhoods. The promotion of decentralized management with concomitant dispersion of facilities does little to enhance racial integration, which is an avowed interest of the department. It is clear that the department's policies may sometimes fail to support its goals and may actually hinder or frustrate compliance.

Discrepancies are not only observed in terms of incompatibility. Policies may also be in conflict insofar as cost–benefits are concerned. There is inadequate information concerning departmental objectives and ineffective measuring devices to appraise their relative worth. Managers have little idea of whether additional dollars allocated to certain recreational activities will produce greater benefits for the same population as would money devoted to maintenance operations of facilities. Even the primary objective of recreational service provision cannot be clearly measured in terms of which policy will more nearly meet the recreational needs of the public to be served. There is no substantial evidence that any one policy for supplying recreational services will be more effective than would any other policy.

Organizational limits. If logical decisions require the ability to organize practices that are commensurate with a selection of objectives that are designed to satisfy the basic mission of the agency, then the organizational procedures of urban departments are not capable of optimal functioning. Rather, there are innumerable ways by which an organizational structure frustrates the agency's mission. In fact, it is not unusual for several departments, with overlapping responsibilities, to have identical objectives and pursue different policies concerning the same or diverse goals, without any attempt at coordination.

One glaring example may be that responsibility for public recreational services is divided between three or more departments. When the school system, recreational agency, park department, and housing authority all have impact on the provision of public recreational service, there is bound to be duplication, gaps in service, competition for the same clientele, inefficiency, ineffectiveness, and waste of time, money, and effort. All of these agencies may have recreational service as their stated objective, but the policies developed in pursuit of that idea may be responsible for the frustration of coherent and coordinated activities.

Political limits. There are many services that the recreational agency can provide, but does not because of political interference by elected officials. The political climate may not permit the introduction of new activities, the construction of new facilities, or the employment of qualified workers because of infringement by politicians on the hiring practices of the department – for example, through patronage. Political feasibility also has reference to the social environment in which the department is situated. A variety of special interest groups may attempt to exert, or actually exert political influence over the governing authorities to compel the recreational service department to satisfy their particular needs, regardless of any logical input of factual information. Attitudes toward taxation, social philosophy, perceived need, or emotional issues tend to cloud factual representations. Elected officials, for the most part, are simply unwilling to mortgage their political futures by doing what is logical when, in effect, they can display themselves as listening to the demands of people and pass themselves off as popular heroes. Seldom have the interests of various pressure groups – who require symbolic or actual gestures to appease their needs and to obtain their votes – been subordinated to logically developed policies. Under such conditions political feasibility really means that parks, playgrounds, centers, or other necessary facilities will not be sited and constructed where logic dictates, but where special interests want them placed. In the final analysis, the judgment of what can be done about a specific question is decided not by what is logical, but by what potential voters will buy and what "wheeler-dealers" will accept.

Standard operating procedures. These actions are employed by managers to avoid the strict requirements of the logical model. Standard operating procedures designate which of the various criteria that might be pertinent are really to be examined in reaching a particular decision. Routinized practices simplify inputs, thereby making decisions less difficult. Managers use certain methods in formulating policy. One is the inclination to believe whatever information is presented by subordinates, rather than to discover new sources of information by themselves. For example, in dealing with union representatives, the manager may permit subordinates who first approach him/her to be the supplier of their opinions, rather than the facts, and base his/her subsequent decisions on their biases. Able managers will seek other sources, try to determine the facts, and make decisions over policy with as much knowledge of the situation as it is possible to obtain.

Adjustments and concessions

The inability of decision-makers to adhere to the exacting directions of logical procedure does not mean that their choices are disordered, random, or determined without recourse to rationality. According to the strict pre-scription of logical behavior there is little that can be done by recreationists except to compromise. While concessions have to be made in relation to the impediments that develop from practical policies, special pleading, and other constraints, there are techniques for contending with complexities that sanction judgments to be made without the complete analysis required by the logical pattern. Among social resource conserving practices are con-fidence in the equilibrium between routine activities and unmet needs to draw attention to the necessity for policy change; avoidance of confronta-tions; the utilization of standard operating procedures to simplify perplexing conditions; and the inclination to make adaptations to demands, instead of implementing decision-making procedures that pursue definitive objectives or policy. Not one of these techniques conforms to the stringency of logic, but they are all applied by managers seeking bases for reaching decisions in the push–pull environment of time, money, and informational constraints. Underlying each of these factors is the managers' dislike of deviating sub-stantially from usual activities. Managers prefer order and stability. Any attempt to hasten decision-making procedures is done to assist durability in an environment with increasing disposition toward inconsistency. Of course, it is also valid to state that some managers are entirely self-interested and do unprincipled things in their quest for status and power. As Barzini writes:

> There is, at all times and in all countries, a behind-the-scenes brutal truth which shocks the uninitiated in the discovery of it; great decisions are never entirely noble; great leaders in all fields are by no means as witty, handsome, magnanimous, and farsighted as their official bio-graphies make them out.[3]

Complaints, for example, are looked upon by managers as warnings of dissatisfaction with current services. Increasing complaints, falling atten-dance, increased vandalism, or other signals may lead to the design of new policies on manpower assignment, budget allocations, activity proposals, or advisory group establishment. Complaints can become the chief yardstick by which managers determine when unsatisfied needs are so pressing that modification of policy, or new policy is necessary. Managers who depend upon complaints to signal the need for change do not develop policy logically but simply wait for demands to become strong enough before action is taken. Some managers delay decisions continually, seeking to assess who has the balance of power. If there is equilibrium, decisions will be put off until there is a clear-cut dominance exhibited by one side or the other.

Choosing implementation strategies

There are a number of important aspects to remember about decisions. Initially, the decision by itself does not change anything. A manager can decide to begin an innovative program, employ a new supervisor, build a new swimming pool, or change the agency's personnel performance evaluation system, but the decision alone will not put itself into effect. Once a decision is made, there is no possibility of knowing whether it is good or bad. It is only when the consequences of the decision emerge that results can be evaluated.

The outcomes of decisions are long-lived. Something more has to be done. This additional something is implementation skill. Without implementation, decision-making is futile. While it is true that inordinate amounts of time and effort are spent in the decision-making process, often little or no thought is given to implementing decisions and handling their ramifications. In this sense, good managers are good analytic decision-makers; even more important, they are highly skilled in managing the outcomes of their decisions. The important action may not be the original decision, but what happens subsequently, and what actions are taken to ensure success. In truth, the most significant skill that a manager may have is handling the consequences of decisions. Where organizational barriers interfere with action, the essential ability is the capacity to get things implemented.

Democratization of the decision-making process

The keys to effective implementation are sensitivity to those who will be affected by the decision and appropriate planning and consideration of the resources necessary to carry out the decision. Therefore, managers must observe the impact of the decision objectively and make corrective adjustments where necessary. The evaluation of past decisions, along with other information, should power future decision-making as part of an ongoing decision-making feedback loop. Primarily, then, goal identification is extremely important if achievement is to occur. The manager must determine patterns of dependence and interdependence; that is, the individuals who are significant or influential in accomplishing the predetermined goal. Viewpoints of these significant others need to be considered. Important questions concern those who are more influential in the decision and their bases of power. The manager must be aware of his/her power base in order to exert more control over the situation. The manager's strategies and tactics for exercising influence in the prevailing environment need to be the most appropriate ones if they are to be effective. Finally, the manager must decide on a course of action to achieve his/her goal.

Group decision-making

Implementation does not have to be difficult if it is founded upon leadership and interpersonal relations. By interpersonal relations is meant the entire spectrum of behavior between persons acting reciprocally in situations of informing, cooperating, changing attitudes, problem-solving, and persuasion. This involvement with interpersonal relations in various organizations comes at a seminal time in social history.

Individuals have long been thought of as instruments of organization. Rather, the organization must be conceived as an instrument for the betterment of society. To serve the needs of people best, the quality of interpersonal relations within the organization must be improved. To this end, each member must develop self-awareness, sensitivity to others, and skill in communication. This change calls for empathy and personal commitment if implementation of objectives is to succeed.

Managers who lack confidence in their subordinates invariably feel that any discussion by lower levels of personnel in the organization will lead to conflict. Conflict in the situation is not a negative. Discussion generated may lead to more appropriate alternatives than the one previously determined by the manager. As information technology is widely dispersed at all levels of the organization, most, if not all, professionals should have enough information to make quality decisions. Therefore, delegation of decision-making is possible and probable.

Implementation may be achieved by developing a shared vision among those who are called upon to do the work of the agency. By setting goals cooperatively and sharing the methods for gaining the goal, all personnel contributing to such efforts may ego-identify so closely with the ends in view that a common perspective regarding what to do and how to do it pervades the system and enables all those concerned to coordinate their behavior. In short, people will be able to perform cooperatively without having to depend upon orders from higher authority. Sometimes, this technique is both time-consuming and expensive, particularly during crisis situations. There are times when the manager must act immediately to exploit a positive condition that may not prevail for any length of time. There simply is no time for prolonged discussion or for input from all factions. Only command and action can be considered at this juncture.

Policy implementation and practices

All policy should be based on well-known standards of practice, which are widely accepted within the field of recreational service. To the extent that a manager can apply such standards of practice to the facts generated by systematic research concerning local conditions within which the department functions, policy will be developed and actions taken to implement it in ways that may nearly correspond to a logical model. Anticipatory policy-making is of greater benefit to the department and the population being served than defensive or "after-the-in fact" policy. In the former instance, policy is derived from knowledge and facts regarding the operation of the department. In the latter instance, policy is developed because of some incident or problem, which prompted the policy statement. Almost always, defensive policies result from poor planning, damage to things, or injuries and even death of people. Implementation of policy under these conditions invariably indicates lack of recognition of tension; lack of awareness of hazardous areas, facilities, or environments; inadequate supervision of personnel or patrons; incompetence or negligence, or any one, some, or all of these negative attributes. Policies that ensue because something went wrong are akin to locking the barn door after the horse has been stolen. The policy will not alter the facts, although there is the assumption that future deleterious conduct, dangerous practices, or unsafe conditions will be avoided. Anticipatory policies, on the other hand, indicate positive qualities and concern on the part of the knowledgeable manager. While few practitioners can claim to be seers, capable managers try to foresee difficulties and act to prevent them.

Implementation of policy requires that certain pieces of routine information be placed at the manager's disposal automatically. They should assist in keeping him/her alert to the daily operations of the system. Other techniques can be employed to signal the existence of potential problems to the manager before they escalate into full-blown crises. When leadership is present it is probable that those who are influenced will act in ways beneficial to the organization, thereby handling problems at lower levels before they exert a degree of interference that might disconcert the agency and/or the manager.

Every skilled manager realizes that, in order to meet anticipated exigencies, certain policies regarding personnel, safety, facilities, record keeping, public relations, and activity have to be developed. It is not good to have to muddle through thorny issues regarding clientele, riots, and priorities concerning patron use of facilities, concessions, or chain-of-command procedures. It is better to have instituted clear policy statements as goals so that all concerned have the benefit of written guides when nettlesome situations arise or sensitive issues present themselves for response.

Successful implementation

Implementation should be successful when the manager and his immediate counselors explicitly discuss objectives in detail and specify the essential requirements for a beneficial selection of actions in accordance with significant goals or values involved in the run-up to policy-setting. This executive group must consider a number of workable alternative policies. There can be no accomplishment when one alternative is considered to the exclusion of other possibilities. Absolutely reliable information is required for critically analyzing the pros and cons of all available alternatives. Information has to be complete so that an informed decision can be made. Closed-minded bias cannot be permitted to form the basis for policy decisions or their implementation. The costs and risks associated with all the possible alternatives need to be examined thoroughly. The manager must be able to work out specific details for action, surveillance, and emergency plans. Alertness to possible problems in implementation and contingencies, with a program for monitoring these, may mitigate difficulties and secure the desired result.

Group decision-making is becoming more common as organizations focus on delivering improved service to patrons while pushing decision-making to lower levels of the workforce. This means that the manager has to bring his/her subordinates along by disseminating information about the goals and expectations of the agency. It is necessary that all professional personnel become involved in the solutions to problems that the agency faces. Since it is the subordinates who will carry out or implement policies that have been decided upon, it becomes necessary that those who execute policy believe in its efficacy and have a stake in its accomplishment. Thus, the first question the manager must ask is whether a solo decision made will be acceptable to and complied with by subordinates. Widely sharing information and the ideal that supports it should help to achieve goal congruence.

Probably the most important aspect of policy implementation concerns the need to integrate those who will carry out any new policy into the earliest stages of discussions dealing with policy formulation. People who participate in the decision-making process, particularly when it has a direct impact on them, are more likely to follow through on proposal implementation to the extent that their opinions have been solicited, their worth appreciated, and their contributions valued. Since they are ego-involved in the process and identify with the policy that has been developed, it is very likely that they will want to see the policy implemented and will do everything in their power to fulfill that ambition.

5 Leadership

The basis for strategic management

Despite collegiality and democratic orientation, organizations are hierarchical. That is the reality of society and human perception. Everybody expects the arrangement of an organization to include entry-level positions and a broad-based workforce that is responsible to higher levels of supervision until the executive is reached. However, leadership may exist at every level of an organization and it is this leavening catalyst that enables decisions to be well dispersed throughout the system.[1] The distribution of the decision-making function permeates the agency and enables personal resources to be brought to bear at points of conflict or stress. Leadership must be the key element in strategic management.[2]

Leadership

Leadership is non-coercive influence with others. This phenomenon of human behavior has nothing to do with positions or conferred status. It is both the ability to have insight into the needs of others and the process of satisfying these needs with material or psychic payoffs.[3] By ability is meant proficiency in reading people. This is concerned with empathy and acute perception. Empathy enables the possessor to recognize and understand verbal, gestural, and postural meanings that people use all the time. It is related to unarticulated wants or demands that the perceptive individual correctly interprets. Tone of voice, gesticulation, facial expression, or other signals convey how people feel about a given subject or object, and provide intellectual material that can be used to stimulate behavior coinciding with the objectives of the leader. Of course, the unspoken vocabulary operates. One characteristic of groups that affects leadership is the system by which communication is available.

> Communication is the form of interpersonal exchange through which, figuratively speaking, persons can come into contact with each other's minds. The mechanism of communication includes the encoding, through symbols, of information; the behavior transmission and the perception of these symbols; and their decoding. Following the

exchange of a message, if the exchange has been sincere and reasonably accurate, transmitter and sender have more nearly the same information about one or more referents of the message than before. Such equalization of information is not the goal of communication; it is only a relationship between the participants, usually not recognized by them, through which the motive satisfaction to which communication was instrumental can be attained.[4]

Related to and critical for communication is the welding of individuals into a cohesive union.[5] The capacity of individuals to share their resources (skills, knowledge, experience), submerge personal ambitions in group goals, and coordinate their efforts for the common good cements the process of interpersonal relationships. Adopting a common goal and working together in voluntary association occurs as each person recognizes and identifies with the values to be gained from such cooperative activity. Leadership is the catalyst that produces cooperation and coordinated effort. Communication is the indispensable method by which a compelling vision is received. All leadership is founded on an idea that someone successfully transmits to one or more others.[6]

Human communication is reciprocal and rests upon the language of speech and symbol for meaning, intensity, and clarity. Human communication depends upon information which comes back to the sender so that modifications can be made to sustain equilibrium (negative feedback) in order that continued interpersonal relationships can be enjoyed. Conversely, positive feedback requires change and interrupts equilibrium. Neither positive nor negative feedback is damaging, but serves a particular function, which is conditioned by the given situation.

Individual change, group alteration, or organizational rearrangement springs from the acquisition of new ideas, points of view, reactions, and behaviors with regard to other persons, objects, or circumstances. Such change is based upon the individual's intelligence and interest, and in surmounting barriers to learning. The most effective learning in interpersonal situations needs a stable relationship and willingness to change on the part of those engaged.[7] Communication involves a relationship between and with individuals. A person who transmits must communicate with someone else if leadership is to occur. The attention of the message recipient is required or no communication can take place. Therefore, recognition by the receiver of the sender is vital. Recognition confers status, acceptability, and focus.

For the leader to successfully communicate ideas to those wished as followers, a determination of their thoughts on particular matters must be made. Whether or not the would-be leader's ideas coincide with theirs is unimportant. The leader, when he/she knows the ideas people hold, can adjust views to resemble those to be influenced.

When the necessary attention has been gained so as to impart personal views, the audience may slowly be educated to the leader's own point of view. If it is radically different from the potential followers' orientation, there is less likelihood of the ability to communicate and therefore leadership status probably will not be accorded.[8]

Position power

The real problem in nearly all organizations is position power. This is the legitimate prerogative that attaches to particular positions within any agency. Position in an organization carries real authority and can be used coercively. Every person who is employed in a supervisory role has the ability to demand certain accommodating behaviors from subordinates. The ability to reward and punish or coerce performance is headship.[9] Headship passes for leadership in many hierarchies because those involved do not understand the difference between influence involuntarily gained and that which is acquired voluntarily. The "I-am-the-boss" syndrome pervades many organizational corridors and is accepted as the outcome of natural events due to hierarchical structure. Headship is not leadership. It is influence that accrues because of the position held rather than any real attempt at enabling individuals who voluntarily follow ideas.

The differences between leadership and headship are apparent. However, because most organizations are arranged hierarchically, positions tend to be filled by people who may not hold with democratic philosophy or may subscribe to autocratic tendencies. In such circumstances the functioning of the leadership process is distorted. Appointed to a position of power over others, the incumbent may be concerned only with his/her particular ideas or ways of doing things and therefore pressures subordinates to conform to the operating system or incur penalties. When people are threatened with concerns for their economic security or career success they may succumb to the threats. Only those who are confident of their own skills, knowledge, and experience will have the intestinal fortitude to separate themselves from the organization and find work elsewhere. Therefore, it is much more likely to find subordinates in the former category remaining in the agency. These are probably not the most highly productive, creative, imaginative, or enthusiastic employees. It is much more likely that their performance of their duties is somewhat reluctant – indicative of merely doing what is required for the remuneration involved.

Task performance may be successful in headship situations, but the morale of those within the agency will be depressed and performance will require greater degrees of intimidation in order to produce the results desired by the head. It does not take long before disintegrating morale and a disinclination to do anything but lock-step activities cause decreasing output. Headship works for a brief while insofar as task orientation is concerned. However, deteriorating interpersonal relationships, dissatisfaction, conformity, and fear combine to bring about reduced productivity and eventual disaster. If the headship condition continues in place, high employee turnover of competent subordinates who leave must occur, leaving in place disaffected, demoralized, and uncaring workers.

Real leadership[10]

Real leadership can occur in virtually every arena of organized activity. Whether in the public, private, or quasi-public domains of society, leaders, in the truest sense of the word, can be found everywhere. These are the people who challenge how things are done, whose ideas are so attractive and compelling that they inspire others to commit themselves voluntarily to behave in ways that coincide with the leader's objectives.[11] Leaders offer the means whereby others are enabled to perform to the best of their ability and, in the process, tend to cooperate and coordinate their actions with others in the same group.[12] The leader serves as a role model whose outlook, values, and presence[13] stir emulation by others to the extent that they identify with and share the vision (idea) held by the leader. Dwight Eisenhower's concept of leadership is: "A leader's job is to get others to go along with him in the promotion of something. To do this he needs their good will."[14]

Opportunists. All leaders are opportunists. They seize the moment or occasion to initiate new ideas, solve problems that others find intractable, offer assistance to those who require it, and tend to shake up the system or question accepted attitudes and methods in their quest for the successful achievement of ends in view.[15] Ethical leaders have a humanitarian outlook. They are concerned with bettering the situation of their followers.[16] Whether this means a higher quality of life, greater personal satisfaction, a sense of purpose, or more material benefits, the leader's attraction comes in consequence of consistency, credibility, and reward. This is no pie-in-the-sky guru mumbling about some revelation from on high, but a down-to-earth realist who perceives the situation accurately and acts in ways designed to enlist others in the cause.

Leaders are not interested in controlling others. Control signifies the failure of confidence in the ability of others to perform in an appropriate fashion. The more control the greater the mistrust on the part of those who look to leaders for support and consideration. Leaders must be highly enthusiastic about the things or ideas which motivate them to perform.[17] Energy and enthusiasm are the dynamics enrolled in the belief system that propels the leader's action. By articulating his/her convictions in a persuasive way and becoming involved (maintaining contact) with the followers, differing points of view, needs, wants, and desires will probably be more forthcoming, thereby creating conditions for greater engagement, ego-identification with the leader's goals, or in an increased sense of personal satisfaction in achieving those goals.

Collaboration. There is no leadership without followers. Among other things leaders serve as beacons to those who follow. They guide the behavior of others in a relationship that marshals the personal resources of constituents for the accomplishment of some shared vision. The quest for excellence requires collaboration.[18] Collaboration is really cooperative endeavor in the pursuit of a desired outcome. The recognition that success stems from assisting others to perform effectively grows out of the inescapable perception that the efforts, skills, and knowledge of more than one person are required to be applied to the solution of problems or the attainment of a certain objective. Shared values and compatible goals enhance trust. In circumstances where reliance on others is essential, those involved will expect assistance from others because of self-interest. It is in the best interests of all concerned that help, in the form of instruction, skill, ideas, or material resources, is mutually exchanged. Such interpersonal behavior produces high viscidity, hedonic tone, and *esprit de corps.*[19]

Collaboration affords the leader tremendous advantage. Many leaders encourage collaboration among their followers with the objective of improving performance, and such leaders will be recognized as having credibility in their organization. When individuals work in unison, and where there is mutual support, they begin to understand the need for each other in order to achieve success. Therefore, greater commitment to the purpose for which the leader stands will develop, greater rapport will be generated, influence will be enhanced, and those who follow should have a higher level of performance satisfaction. Leadership is vital when collaborative effort is in effect. Heterogeneous constituencies produce diverse opinions and sometimes conflicting attitudes, interests, and experience. The leader's ability to create a sense of team effort and shared values will result in a high degree of cohesion, cooperation, and trust in achieving any goal.[20]

Involvement. By seeking the counsel of others and encouraging them to share their knowledge and skill, leaders are assured that all participants are involved in the decision-making process affecting them. Of course, there is no certainty that any final decision will resonate well with everybody, but the likelihood is that resistance to or disaffection from the decision will be limited. Seeking information from others, or giving all concerned an opportunity to make their views known, providing an open forum, and not being judgmental about what is expressed will enable the leader to embody diverse ideas and interests for whatever action is undertaken. This, more than anything else, will probably demonstrate to the followership that their ideas are respected, given due weight, and used when appropriate to achieve group success. Naturally, the leader must explain why some ideas are used and others discarded. Adroit and truthful explanations may do much to assuage hurt feelings or egos while still retaining the individual's participation.

The establishment of rapport is the core around which human relationships develop. Simply stated, rapport is the mutual exchange of trust and confidence. Where there is trust there is great probability that information and resources will be shared equitably, problems and objectives will be subject to rational discussion, participants will seek various methods for solving problems, solutions will be jointly arrived at, and there will be closer relationships generated and higher satisfaction in the outcomes. Essentially, no one person has all the answers or skills necessary to achieve enterprise success.[21] Therefore, leaders openly make use of the talent, skill, knowledge, and experience available while providing input in terms of consultation or advice as needed. In this way a general feeling of comfort or ease is generated within the group, and participants do not feel the necessity to hide their light under a bushel. Instead, the sense of shared trust encourages further exploration of ways to further the enterprise, activity, or project. This results in more whole-hearted involvement in the situation and enhances cooperation.

The leadership demands of management

Management is concerned with obtaining desired organizational goals by effectively coordinating the human and material resources of the agency in such a way that economic, efficient, and cooperative effort is achieved without waste. The manager, necessarily, must define agency mission and then see that action to accomplish that mission is carried out. Managerial responsibility is to be certain that cooperative effort is produced to achieve fundamental aims while coordinating such endeavors to facilitate the work of the entire agency. Additionally, the manager will function as a catalyst, initiating innovative concepts and programs based upon employee expertise that can enhance the performance and the technical capacity of those individuals who compose the organization. It is at this junction that Blue Ocean Strategy may be put in play as a tool for effective management.

What is the manager's leadership role? When policy is determined and decisions made about any phase of agency operation, it is imperative that the decisions are communicated clearly and accurately to those who undertake their execution.

Managerial tasks

The manager has the responsibility of performing several different functions simultaneously. He/she must be able to conceptualize, analyze, and plan while also organizing, administering, and supervising. This poses a dilemma. To be an effective leader, a manager must understand the varied aspects of complex conditions and then reach a logical decision with regard to achieving the objective which has been slected. Asking for and receiving the available information, analyzing it systematically, obtaining diverse viewpoints for determining which alternative course will produce the most beneficial results, attempting to plan for future events, and implementing a reasonable procedure for accomplishment is a managerial task.

Planning aspects

There is the necessity for planning in order to formulate the procedures and then activate them. The manager must be able to work out the consequences of certain actions without actually having performed them. It is almost as if he/she were involved in the solution of some gigantic jigsaw puzzle where many possibilities exist from where almost any alternative selected could work, but where only one or a few will actually offer the most efficient, effective, and economical return. Because the managerial leader works with people as well as resources, he/she confronts the typical ambiguities which human nature develops. If it were only a matter of material resources the process would be mechanical. When one deals with people, however – both personnel employed within the agency and clients to be served by the agency – the intangibles of personality, need, and motivation must also be taken into account. This latter aspect is one which really requires leadership.

As a logical thinker, the manager must make decisions. In order to be most effective, however, weighing the objective data received against personal knowledge and empathy can also provide valuable insight into the people involved in the situation so that a rational decision can be reached. This process requires sensitivity to the problem and to the individuals concerned. Specifically this is true when materially-based information is inconclusive. To the extent that he/she deals with people and not things, the managerial leader needs to develop empathic tendencies so as to be able to perceive the viewpoint of those who will have to execute policy and those who are receiving services from the agency. Empathy endows the leader with an understanding of how others will probably react to some policy decisions.

In any leadership position, unless the manager is willing to support his/her own position, the likelihood of achieving goals along the lines which were indicated by objective reasoning and pertinent experiences is small. Once a manager has reached a decision and truly believes in its efficacy, it should be executed regardless of its popularity. If the manager has provided the kind of communication which is necessary, then the basis for his/her judgment will be well known, the conditions on which the decision was made will also be available, and his/her reputation for equity based on rapport should suffice to obtain support. It may sometimes occur that decisions will be made that create negative feelings on the part of some employees. It is unfortunate that this should be so. However, the manager should have the courage of his/her convictions even when they alienate others. The manager is probably in a better position to envision the entire situation, which other employees or specialists cannot appreciate. Under such circumstances, the manager utilizes a process of communication not only to transmit orders – if necessary, but also to educate. Even if he/she is not successful in persuading his/her peers of the rightness of the decision reached, action must follow. If one judges a situation and determines a course of action based upon knowledge, experience, diverse input, and analysis, then the individual must proceed with that judgment.

Managerial influence on personnel behavior

Managers are always concerned with ways in which leadership is exerted so that the needs of employees may be satisfied while they make effective contributions to their immediate place of employment and the entire system. The view of management as a process of weighing the activities of people who are engaged in accomplishing stated objectives elicits several leadership functions. Thus, the manager must assist others to achieve satisfaction in networking, reduce friction and conflicts between staff members as well as within the work situation, communicate praise and sometimes admonition, supervise, educate, encourage self-development of personnel, provide emotional support, define performance criteria, and stimulate achievement-seeking behavior. The management behavior inherent in such responsibilities is directly related to the willingness of personnel to cooperate in the accomplishment of organizational goals.

> The organizational task becomes one of first understanding the man's needs, and then, with him, assessing how well they can be met in this organization, doing what the organization needs to have done. Thus the highest point of self-motivation arises when there is a complementary conjunction of the man's needs and the organization's requirements. The requirements of both mesh, interrelate, and become synergistic. The energies of man and organization are pooled for mutual advantage.[22]

The ability of the system to achieve success as it operates is closely connected to leadership style personalized at the managerial level. Personnel cooperation and concern for responsibility rely upon positive interpersonal behavior between managers and other employees. The type of behavior most likely to elicit voluntary efforts on the part of personnel to effect the agency goals is one which heavily emphasizes satisfaction of individual needs and relies less upon the use of position or constraints, that is, headship to gain desirable ends. However, this will be shaped by managerial inclination and philosophy.

One of the basic needs of any affective leadership style is comprehension of the relationship between the satisfaction of human needs and performance. Perhaps the essential problem of all managers is not that their employees lack motivation, but that some managers are either disinclined or do not have the capacity to stimulate it. The normal course of the manager's behavior sharply affects the performance of those with whom he/she works. Personnel are extremely perceptive when it comes to detecting how a manager actually feels about departmental intent and institutionalized procedures. How the manager behaves, his/her deportment and activities, invariably convey significant signals to those immediately subordinate to him/her. The extent to which the leader espouses the achievement of agency objectives; the actions which are undertaken to advance personal professional development; the tendency to retain functions which are solely within his/her province to perform; effectiveness in handling departmental problems; and his/her earnestness and desire to provide support for co-workers, are all examples of managerial behavior that are observable by associates and other employees and which serve as a condition of behavioral responses of agency personnel.

The administrative process offers countless opportunities for leaders to exercise those behaviors which will stimulate employees to achieve at higher levels of productivity and, in effect, volunteer their active cooperation in the service of the enterprise. The kinds of leadership behavior that influence employee cooperation and willingness to perform are observed when re-lations are established on a foundation of reciprocity in terms of mutual trust and understanding. Individuals within the recreational service field and in specific agencies are involved in the cycle of employment. From recruit-ment and induction to the initial job placement and then throughout their respective careers, there is a continual need for appraisal and evaluation.

Because people are one of the essential components making up the resources of the organization, their behavior largely determines the effec-tiveness of the recreational service system. The responsibility of adjusting to the needs of the individual and the demands of the organization, and making them compatible is, perhaps, the chief function of the managerial leader. While it is true that the manager has no influence on some of the pressures which impinge upon the agency and its personnel, insofar as satisfying human needs is concerned, there are areas in which leadership has a profound influence. Among the methods the manager can use to affect personnel satisfaction and performance are the style of leadership employed and the development of rapport with associates. Leadership style and inter-personal relationships will be dependent upon the process of communica-tion, which is reciprocal. The interdependency of managerial–employee relations is well known – although some managers remain unconvinced of this fact of life. The success of the leader relies heavily on the performance of all personnel for whom he/she has responsibility. To the degree that the manager can gain cooperative effort he/she will be successful. The *quid pro quo* is to provide employee need satisfaction.

Managerial leadership requires a high degree of discipline and effort. Consistency in following the principles of recreational service among super-ior organizations is open and direct; but carrying them out over time is very difficult. The better agencies have bottom-up management. This means that personnel who actually interact with participants or are involved with operations, inform the executive, that is, the manager, what succeeds rather than the other way round. It essentially means delegating responsibility, thereby empowering subordinates.

The outstanding managerial leaders have domain knowledge. This means that they understand the field and are expert in their specialization. They have an immediate and intimate knowledge of the strengths and weaknesses of their own organization. It is this grasp of operations that enables these high-caliber people to make material incremental changes for improvement. There is no such thing as perfection, but managers who constantly strive for excellence in quality of service on an incremental basis will probably obtain the best results.

In the same sense, leadership growing out of the manager's position can be the greatest combination for the success of any organization. Administered techniques should insure innovation and productivity while leadership capability will maximize employee satisfaction and effort to see that the agency performs the tasks assigned to it in ways that bring approbation and support from a grateful public.

Focusing as it has on the leadership process, the idea of management as the repository of all that is going on is the inescapable outcome. This is hardly the truth. Managers are not super-beings. They have the same human failings as the rest of humankind. Nevertheless, the managerial leader attempts to overcome his/her biases and foibles by concentrating upon his/her skills, knowledge, experience, and talent in carrying out responsibilities. No manager can be all things to all people. At best he/she will be one significant influence on the behavior of others. To the extent that the manager can assist in bringing their latent talents, abilities, and experiences to the fore, thereby gaining a better perspective of their own functions and performing at a high level of efficiency and effectiveness, the manager will have done the job for which he/she is paid. In other words, the manager serves as a model for co-workers. His/her style of leadership will directly affect employee attitudes and become the basis for his/her instruction of them.

The managerial function is now concerned with human matters, rather than the traditional measures of output in determining organizational performance. Such factors as degrees of confidence and trust, loyalty, ability to communicate, and capacity to achieve sound decisions are the measures which more nearly coincide with managerial effectiveness. If co-workers feel that the manager is supportive of them rather than threatening, there will be a better pattern of interaction. To the degree that managers promote cohesiveness within their organization, so that each person feels him/herself to be a member of a close-knit and effective work group or team, it will be concomitant increments in the accomplishment of tasks assigned.

As Likert wrote:

> The units achieving the best performance are much more likely than the poor performance units to have managers who deal with their subordinates in a supportive manner and build high group loyalty and teamwork.[23]

The manager of the organization has it within his/her power to shape and guide the policies, philosophy, and employee behaviors in the organization. His/her concept of human relations and interpersonal development will become the pervasive influence within the system. If the manager is democratic in outlook and practices organizational democracy, there will be a corresponding attitude operating throughout all levels of the organization. It is the responsibility of the manager to develop and maintain the total human resource system within the department and to create an atmosphere that will stimulate this process to continue vigorously and imaginatively. The manager's work is made easier by a style of leadership which actually promotes collaboration in those phases of planning where consensus is essential. The manager recognizes individual and social needs as he/she works toward organizational goals. He/she controls the intervention of purely functional aspects; and encourages and rewards participation and effective contribution. As Heilbroner indicates:

> The preservation of democratic forms can only come about as a result of intellectually farsighted and politically gifted leadership. Paradoxically, it is only through leadership that authoritarian rule can be minimized, if not wholly avoided.[24]

One of the hallmarks of managerial leadership is flexibility of behavior. Different leadership behaviors are required in varying situations in order to gain effectiveness. It has been found that leaders have the ability to modify their approach to problem-solving when faced with changing conditions. There is every reason to believe that managers who display leadership will probably be more capable of adapting their behaviors as conditions warrant.

> Thus, the successful manager of men can be primarily characterized neither as a strong leader nor as a permissive one. Rather, he is one who maintains a high batting average in accurately assessing the forces that determine what his most appropriate behavior at any given time should be and in actually being able to behave accordingly.[25]

Flexibility is a necessary behavioral form if the manager is to survive the complex situational variables which typically confront any executive operating in societal domains. Management requires an adaptable person who has the capacity to cope with both the mechanical aspects of tasks and the subjective judgments that must be made in dealing with all employees, and the unknown quantity of personality. Of necessity, the manager's leadership style is integrally associated with the task-readiness and capabilities of co-workers to perform. It is the leader's responsibility to increase employee motivation by clarifying the behavior required for task accomplishment and accompanying benefits.

Managerial leadership is more than a contract between interested participants. It is not merely transactional, that is, something given for something received. Real leadership should be transformational. It involves the articulation of an ideal or vision that transcends the ordinary and compels the attention and action of those who listen and follow. In essence, it stimulates followers to outdo themselves insofar as their expected performance is concerned.

> In certain instances, the leader will invoke a vision of expectation that persuades others to see beyond themselves and become, at least for a short while, part of something greater in which they can involve themselves and for which they can make personal sacrifices. In this way the larger goal of group mission and success, with which the follower has identified, enables that person to achieve a sense of satisfaction and growth that previously might have been beyond the capacity of that person to perform.[26]

The single most important element in the provision of recreational service is the quality of recreationists employed within the agency. The next most important element is the quality of management provided throughout the system. It is through managerial services that facilitation of technical competences of all personnel is promoted. Furthermore, management is initiated to assist all efforts on the part of agency employees in providing effective and competent services through the program. The success of the recreational service offering will be in direct proportion to the quality of leadership available. The manager makes the difference between superior and mediocre results. The manager must maintain his/her professional competence and display those characteristics which enable him/her to sustain influence with others despite the position held within the department. There seems to be an immediate and positive correlation between a manager's leadership ability and his/her effectiveness as a manager; for leadership is the foundation on which the requirements of the organization and the demands of the individual worker are balanced.

Part II
Establishing recreational service

6 Development of recreational service

When governments at all levels finally recognize that a condition of life or a service is a necessity for their various constituencies, they typically pass legislation to ensure that provision. Most thinking people believe that recreational activity is necessary for a better quality of life. Such activity may be more important to the individual's self-expression and growth than any other social factor, except education. People everywhere engage in recreational activities – though these activities may be vastly different in nature, quality, setting, and outcome. The implications and consequences of recreational experiences for people are so vital that governmental support of recreational service has come to be expected. As has been stated:

> Life is dependent upon some factors so obvious that they are not seen at all by most of us. We can't live without food, air, and reasonably pure water, and we cannot have a full and healthy life without recreation.[1]

Such attention commences with control of anti-social forms of leisure activity and extends to measures which are designed so all of the people can avail themselves of the benefits of wholesome, developmental recreational experience, serving the purposes of the individual and the state.

Management and the law

Various laws impact the behavior of people and organizations of all types. Under the aegis of legislation, relationships between people, contracts, public, quasi-public, and private institutions are regulated and defined so that people's positive and untrammeled growth will be promoted and protected.

It is well known that democracies pride themselves on being societies of laws. Law is pervasive in a society that is devoted to the rule of law. It influences the daily lives of people from birth to death. In some instances, law is concerned with even the most personal activities into which people enter. The body of law guides and holds people and entities to certain standards of behavior. The law either constrains or extends how people act toward one another, how institutions can deter, palliate, encourage, or discourage social interaction, and the validity of contracts into which people enter. In short, all people are equal, or should be, in the eyes of the law and have certain rights, privileges, and responsibilities enabling them to function in the social order. This also pertains to agencies that are specifically designed to deliver recreational services. Broad interpretation of legislation has permitted a number of agencies to provide a more comprehensive recreational program. Various laws impact the behavior of people and organizations of all types.

Legislative philosophy

The rationale for recreational service under governmental auspices may be found in the American Declaration of Independence in terms of each person's unquestioned right to "the pursuit of happiness." This philosophical statement justifies governmental activity in public recreational service. Since governments are instituted with the express aim of ensuring domestic tranquility and enhancing the public welfare, no further justification is needed for establishing the public recreational service.

Law and recreational service

Laws control the operation and behavior of public and private enterprises and can have a profound effect on the plans and activities of managers.[2] Therefore, managers should be familiar with the legal precedents that have consequences for the duties and responsibilities that management comprehends. Managers must be aware of the current legal practices as well as the subtleties which legislation imposes. Of course, managers may be attorneys, but for the most part they will employ legal specialists to interpret the requirements of law as they direct the daily operation of the organization in which they serve.

The activities of government in the field of recreational service have not been undertaken for the purpose of interfering with the rights of individual citizens, but, on the contrary, with the aim of expanding the scope of recreational experience of the people in equalizing the opportunities for such experience. Certain activities recognized as of wide interest and value require cooperative effort beyond the ability of individual citizens. Some activities do not lend themselves to commercial enterprise and are still of such value that a beneficent government can ill afford to neglect them. Still others cannot be entrusted wholly to commercial agencies which sometimes disregard the needs and capacities of the individual. Some activities are of such general concern that public taxation appears to be the most economical and expeditious way of making them available to all. While recreational pursuit must remain largely a matter of individual initiative and a proper field for commercial enterprises, in many respects it is a legitimate field for governmental activity – not only in the regulatory and prohibitory sense, but also in a positive sense for the promotion of a state of general well-being and human development.

Governmental involvement

Because recreational service is closely embraced by government at all levels, the recreationist must have a sound working knowledge of the legal foundations for his/her agency and local ordinances and codes if there is to be conformity with the law, cooperation with governmental units, utilization of other governmental resources, and advancement of recreational service to the greatest degree possible. An understanding of governmental relationships, the attention that various levels of government focus upon recreational service in terms of legislation, finance, restrictions, and promotion are essential. Such knowledge is indispensable to intelligent, proper, and effective action in the planning and administration of public recreational service. This is valid regardless of the recreationist's position in the hierarchy of the agency organization. More significantly, such understanding enables the recreationist to learn about the basis of limits and source of legitimate authority. It also points the way to the development of a mission statement for the agency.

Establishing the agency

When the local governmental authority moves to implement a recreational service agency, the provisions for recreational service should be incorporated in the city charter, which can only be amended by vote of the people and approval of the state legislature. If the charter should lack suitable provision for recreational service (extremely rare in this day and age), the city may provide for recreational service enactment by an appropriate ordinance. Such ordinances may be amended or rescinded by the local legislative body which passed them. Thus, the department for the exercise of the recreational service function will be brought into being.

The extent of services to be provided by the department of public recreational service should be enumerated. The local ordinance or city charter should authorize the department to organize, promote, supervise, and conduct any and all recreational activities it deems advisable, either on property owned by the city or elsewhere. It should assign to the chief executive of the department the creation of necessary positions to carry out the work of the department in the fixing of salaries, unless these duties are already assigned to another local department, usually personnel or the department of human resources. In addition the executive is also given authority to recommend the selection, appointment, discharge, and suspension of all the employees. The ordinance will also probably authorize the establishment of rules and regulations governing public conduct in parks and other publicly operated recreational places, and for the control and management of the recreational program. These rules have the same effect, in theory, as ordinances passed by the local authorities, but they are in practice not as easily enforced because they do not include penalties for violation. They may, however, carry more moral force than ordinances and they have the additional advantage of being easily passed, rescinded, or amended.

Establishing legislation will also authorize the acquisition of real and personal property deemed to be necessary for public recreational purposes by purchase, condemnation, gift in fee simple or in trust, bequest, lease, transfer, and grant. The title to any property acquired should be owned by the city and not by any department. The power to acquire park property should be vested in the recreational service department if it is granted control of its own funds. If not, the legislative body will perform this function. Property set aside for recreational experiences should be dedicated in perpetuity to be used solely for park and recreational purposes. It should be specified that property may be acquired inside or outside the limits of the city. Although as a general rule the park and recreational properties will be within the municipal boundaries, there occasionally arise situations in which it is desired to acquire properties wholly or partly outside the legal limits of the city.

Such authorization may also enable city authorities to designate for recreational purposes any lands, buildings, or other structures owned by the city, regardless of the original purpose for which these might have been acquired. The department should be authorized to improve lands and to construct buildings and structures in a manner considered necessary or convenient for recreational purposes. More significantly the department should be granted authority to approve or reject plans for such improvement.

Local charter or ordinance

The ordinance or charter authorizes the department to establish, construct, maintain, operate, control, and supervise specific types of recreational places, but not to the exclusion of any others. These may include playgrounds, recreational centers, athletic fields, gymnasiums, parks, auditoriums, community centers, golf courses, museums, beaches, zoos, and camps.

Finally, the establishing legislation should authorize the appropriate governing body to make the annual appropriation of funds for the support of the recreational service department, and such emergency or additional appropriations as may be necessary. Financial support other than taxes may consist of fees or charges assessed for special services. The adoption of an annual budget of estimated revenues and expenditures is one of the primary duties of the executive.

All of these sources of legitimate authority constitute the basis for organizing and administering a department of recreational service. These essentials form the parameters that delineate the functions of the manager. They enable the executive to develop a mission statement and the policies and procedures necessary for executing them.

New functions are assumed by local governments in response to public demand. Sometimes the demand is expressed in unmistakable form through an initiative or referendum vote of the electorate. More frequently it is expressed by a minority group of citizens, of more or less influence, who are insistent that the government take steps to meet an obvious public need. So it has been with recreational service.

Municipalities have come to be associated with the most extensive operation and administration of all those services of a recreational nature which require the pooling of tax resources in order to provide a wide variety of indoor and outdoor programs, on a full-time basis, for the benefit of all the citizens of the community.

Control of civic disturbance

The social upheavals and anxieties raised in the aftermath of the Al Qaeda network terrorist attacks and assorted civil disturbances and violence prior to and during 2001 resulted in diametrically opposed feelings. On the one hand people reacted with fear while simultaneously expressing solidarity with the government. Some of this disorder could potentially touch the recreational settings where people gather in large numbers. What was once unthinkable, although a popular theme in the cinema, is now a distinct possibility under the influence of fundamentalist fanaticism. Acts of lawlessness and destruction costing the lives of innocent people have occurred and might continue to occur. The unprecedented security precautions taken during the summer Olympics in Athens, Greece in 2004 and the first International Rugby Games in Dynamo Stadium on July 24th, 2005, in Tbilisi, Georgia testify to this prevalent condition. Numerous other acts of terror where innocent people gather still happen. Recent outrages continue as disaffected persons persist in attempts to perpetuate their own brand of jihadism.[3]

Massive expenditures for the prevention of international terrorism, funds for clearing up the residue of destructive activity, and a turn away from normal activities enjoyed during leisure tend to impact the decisions that people make about what they want to do and how they want to do it. The diversion of taxes from public service functions to security needs has caused considerable upheaval in the way local governments act and how citizens expect their government to perform. When budget time comes around there is less support for public recreational service, which is considered a frill in any case, and a great allocation of resources for police, fire, and health protection. This might be considered logical in any circumstances, but it is of even more importance in today's climate.

Suppression of negative behavior

Many instances of riotous conduct at amusement parks, beaches, swimming pools, playgrounds, outdoor concerts, baseball and football stadiums, and other recreational facilities have been reported.[4] Although control of riots and civil disturbances is essentially a responsibility of law enforcement agencies, good management by park and recreational service systems can alleviate and often prevent such incidents. If appropriate measures are not taken, the consequences are often the closing of many facilities and the loss on the part of the public of the ability to organize and promote worthy recreational opportunities. For example, teenage dances have been banned; in other instances, swimming pools, golf courses, baseball stadiums, parks, playgrounds, and beaches have been closed to the public.[5] Vandalism is an ongoing problem.[6]

Preventive measures include planning the physical environment: decentralizing places where people assemble to participate in activities, lighting areas adequately, controlling ingress and egress, and regulating automobile traffic. They also include planning the program: arranging activities for groups of limited size, and assigning times for holding events. Public behavior may be controlled by a system of permits and fees for the use of facilities. Permits regulate the size of groups, specify facilities to be used at stated times, set forth regulations in general, and fix responsibility for compliance with regulations. The collection of fees usually requires that patrons be checked at a central point.

Nevertheless, it may be necessary to resort to law enforcement to preserve the peace and curb persons who are amenable only to police control. The content of regulatory ordinances is usually recommended by the governing board or the chief executive officer of the recreational service system to the local city managing authority. The ordinances are prepared by the legal department and adopted by the legislative body of the city. Prescribed procedure for enacting ordinances requires serving notice of intention to pass them, advertising their contents, allowing an interval between the first and final reading, and providing opportunity for the public to express its reactions to them. Deliberations should be free from hysteria and unenforceable rules should be avoided. Among the items usually covered by ordinances regulating conduct in parks and other recreational places are:

1. Prohibited:

    a. Posting of signs, commercial advertising, and the use of public address systems without permit
    b. Parades and demonstrations without police permit
    c. Removal of trees, shrubs, plants, and flowers
    d. Destruction, effacement, or willful damage to structures or facilities
    e. Misuse of equipment with intent to damage and destroy

    f. Use of explosives, firearms, fireworks, and fires except at duly authorized and designated facilities or areas

    g. Entrance to certain areas except during specified hours

    h. Disorderly conduct, annoying patrons of any age

    i. Gambling and solicitation of funds

    j. Vending and merchandising in, or in a stated distance from, the public facility except at designated areas

    k. Bringing animals into the area, unless otherwise permitted

    l. Molesting birds, fish, or other fauna

    m. Disposing of refuse except in designated containers, littering

    n. Inciting to riot

    o. Disregarding posted notices

    p. Causing hazardous conditions.

2. Permitted, subject to regulations:

    a. Picnicking at stated areas, usually under permit

    b. Bathing, boating, swimming, and winter activities in season

    c. Meetings, rallies, exhibitions, parades, and/or demonstrations

    d. Automobiles, bicycles, motorcycles, and other vehicular traffic

    e. Camping, use of tents and shelters, sleeping in areas at night.

3. Specified penalties for violations:

    a. Fines, not to exceed a particular amount in accordance with civic codes

    b. Imprisonment, in accordance with terms set by courts having jurisdiction in such matters

    c. Both of the above when warranted.

Government and recreational provision

The developmental and cultural implications and consequences of qualitative recreational experience motivate most governments to take positive positions in offering the public competently administered recreational services. But governmental enterprise in this field need not, nor can it, preempt private endeavor. On the contrary, it only exists where and when individuals, both alone or in voluntary association with others, are thwarted in securing the recreational experiences they want, need, and should enjoy as a human right. Thus, recreational service ranks with education, public health, and safety as a necessary concern of government.

Basic needs

Facilities and programs for recreational activity and leisure education should be available to everybody. Opportunity for recreational activity is essential for all, regardless of neighborhood of residence, social status, race, age, or gender. Therefore, as a supplement to the primary personal and home responsibility for the leisure of the family, a community and governmental responsibility exists. The former is exercised through voluntarily organized, but community-supported, agencies; the latter through public agencies within the structure of government. These responsibilities entail providing uniformly distributed spaces, facilities, and programs, with a reinforced supply in neighborhoods that are blighted, and of special or extraordinary social need.

Functions and divisions of responsibilities

In using their leisure, people seek four major levels of recreational facilities.

1. Facilities that people may use without the operating agency providing any group, individual leadership, or activity organization. Full freedom to use such facilities is permitted subject only to general oversight and the enforcement of reasonable regulations and laws. People want places to go to and equipment to use, their own or equipment provided by the place, for their own self-directed or self-organized recreational pursuits. For the vast majority of people, such opportunities are possible only at parks, beaches, swimming pools, picnic areas, golf links, tennis courts, museums, libraries, and the like which are established for their use.
2. Organized activity programs with leadership and equipment, including sports, music, drama, crafts, art, and social activities. People want opportunities to engage in a variety of activities that, by their nature, must be organized and, in many cases, require special places and equipment – playgrounds, play fields, activity buildings, meeting rooms, auditoriums, lounging places, game rooms, craft shops, natatoriums, and other spaces.

   Children need places to run, throw, climb, jump, and slide with protection and guidance. Adolescents need to acquire skills in sports, dancing, crafts, music, drama, and social interaction. They desire to learn; their motivation is to grow and develop their potential capacities. Even more importantly, they require guidance. Adults want to pursue their hobbies through self-realization, social experiences, and recognition. The leadership and organization of recreational programs, in addition to the mere provision of places and facilities, has now become an accepted public responsibility to be fulfilled by school districts and municipal agencies.
3. Smaller, continuing, self-determining groups require leadership and programs. People, particularly children and youth, want the satisfactions that come not so much from the activity itself as from close group association with peers. Citizenship, behavior, and life philosophy values are most satisfactorily developed in those responsible membership groups.

Group leadership and programming responsibility are foundations of both public and volunteer agencies. Public authorities, charged with managing and operating large facilities and a varied activities program, concomitantly organize and supervise many groups as part of the programs. The private, but community-supported voluntary agencies, without need to provide public facilities, focus on organizing, recruiting, and developing leadership and supervising their member groups.

4. People with special needs, that is, those who are physically disabled, emotionally disturbed, economically deprived, or individuals who are socially maladjusted need programs designed especially for them. It is possible that those who are not well adjusted can be directed to serve a positive social purpose through recreational participation. Their need is for socialization, understanding, and guidance. This responsibility is primarily a voluntary social agency function. However, the public recreational service agency function is able to identify problems and assist the voluntary agency in the use of public resources. When there is inadequate voluntary effort or presence concerning persons with disabilities, public recreational service authorities typically increase their attention to this function.

Priorities in allocation of resources

Neighborhoods, districts, and communities with special problems, such as rapidly changing populations, low economic levels, interracial tensions, inferior housing, and other social deprivations, require an intensification of services. In middle and upper economic neighborhoods and communities, families provide normal recreational spaces, outdoors and indoors, for children. Neighborhood playgrounds are essential in every neighborhood, but they are imperative in overcrowded, poor sections of the community where homes and yards are either non-existent or do not permit normal recreational activity.

All four recreational functions should be provided at the highest level in these problem areas, and special emphasis should be placed on the last two (special leadership for groups and guidance for persons with disabilities), because of prevalent social difficulties.

All citizens need and have the right to expect such opportunities for recreational activity and group living. Areas with greater social problems need more opportunities under superior professional guidance, leadership, and personal dedication to human welfare, including identification with people in the locale and the cumulative experience in their type of community living.

Priorities in facilities

1. Neighborhood playgrounds and play centers for children of kindergarten, elementary, and middle school age should be provided at their

respective public schools, with supervised programs after school hours, on vacation days, and during the summer. Well distributed in geographic centers throughout the city, schools should have ample sites that are adaptable as recreational centers. Public schools should be supplemented by parochial schools, when situated in neighborhoods of need. Non-school public recreational service agencies should provide neighborhood playgrounds in areas that cannot be served by the schools because of insufficient space and facilities, or for other reasons (pedestrian barriers presenting hazards to travel to and from the school). Full use of the neighborhood school should be exhausted before other neighborhood facilities, either public or private, are provided.

2. District facilities should be provided for teenagers, adults, and older adults. This is a joint responsibility of the municipal recreational service department and of the system of high schools and junior or community colleges, supplemented by voluntary agency centers.

3. Outdoor play fields and facilities for city-wide and sometimes regional areas are necessary for all types of physical activity, games and sports, and for outdoor education and environmental experience; these also need to be provided by the local municipal and county governments.

4. Indoor recreational facilities are required for social, cultural, and educational programs. Attractive lounges, meeting rooms, and social rooms are necessary for youth, young adult, and older adult programs. Vigorous physical activity can be carried on out of doors most of the time, but the social, cultural, and educational activities of the community require informal indoor facilities throughout the year. These community – as distinguished from neighborhood – facilities can be provided by the schools, by buildings situated in public parks, and by centers maintained by voluntary agencies.

5. Gymnasiums are basically a school responsibility to provide for the schools' curricular and extracurricular athletic programs. At other times they can be used by the community non-school athletic groups organized under the auspices of the school system, if it has espoused the community recreational responsibility, or by the municipal agency operating a city-wide recreational program. This extra-school use can sometimes also be accorded to voluntary agencies conducting community programs in sports and related activities. Outdoor gymnasiums provide similar facilities for less sophisticated play and should be maintained for use throughout the year and be equipped with lights for use in the evening.

6. The public provides swimming pools for recreational use and instruction. Instruction is a prime concern of the school system and facilities for this purpose should be built. When provided, pools can, of course, serve for recreational swimming, whether operated by the school system or by the community or municipal agency. School pools need to be supplemented by conveniently located community pools in public parks,

in which case they are advisably outdoor pools, since recreational swimming, for the majority of the population, is basically an outdoor summer activity.

7. Sites for day camping are important facilities in appropriate publicly owned parks or park-like places. They should be made available for school and other publicly supported youth-serving and voluntary agencies. A local recreational service department, which frequently has parklands suitable for the purpose, can best provide these sites. Overnight camping, requiring travel away from the city, is a proper service for county recreational service departments, state and national park systems, and state and national forest systems.

Managerial observance of law

Managers in the public and private sectors are subject to and influenced by the direct commands of the law as well as the more subtle nuances of legislation. Thus law can inhibit or enlarge managerial behavior insofar as infrastructure development, contracts, or interpersonal conduct are concerned. Law makes adjustments for the compelling needs of various groups and individuals, and requires conformity to the explicit regulations set forth or permits wide latitude and interpretation of obligations or expectations in terms of the wording of legislative enactments. Therefore, managers are compelled to be acquainted with legalities, use the offices of counsel when faced with questions of probity or conflict, and in general adhere to the spirit without breaching the letter of the law.

All managers, particularly in today's climate of affirmative action, entitlements, pressure groups, professional standards, political correctness, and a litigious population, must tread a fine line between personal common sense and the demands for equity of opportunity that sometimes use the bludgeon of victimization to achieve their ends. In this maelstrom of incessant conflicting claims, the manager's knowledge and experience must serve as a guide when a broad or narrow interpretation of the law is applied to the administration of recreational service.

7 Organizing recreational services

The management of recreational services is one of the most challenging and difficult tasks for local governments today. The problem lies in being responsive to the needs and insistent demands of a complex population; in planning for the future while grappling with present crises; and in persuading both budget examiners and politicians that recreational services are indeed a cost-effective means for achieving other social objectives, such as health promotion, youth employment, and the growth and development of all citizens to their full potential.

Contemporary society is experiencing conflict; this is particularly true in the urban metropolises where tight budgets, poorly prepared workers, and the headaches of maintaining and operating aging and deteriorated facilities abound. The field of recreational service may be thought of as all the opportunities provided through the marshaling of physical property, economic capability, and human resources in the delivery of recreational experiences. While this normally incorporates the elements of public, quasi-public, and private sector enterprises, it is primarily an outcome of public agency responsibility. This is so because it is the mandated function of the public recreational service department to offer, as its chief reason for establishment, a comprehensive and varied series of recreational opportunities to all the citizens residing within the locality's boundaries. Thus, the public recreational service department is the agency of last resort for those individuals who have neither the affluence, experience, nor physical means to gain recreational satisfaction without depending upon public sector offices.

Although the public recreational service department should coordinate its functions and cooperate with all other community-based organizations in the total provision of recreational services, it is the only legally assigned municipal agency, which is primarily concerned with citizen recreational performance. Everything that it does in order to fulfill its responsibility for providing immediate recreational opportunity, either of an organized or of a self-directed type, for people in the community is designated as a recreational service.

In contemporary society, there are so many different agencies and such a multiplicity of functions that the individual, as well as each agency, must have certain specialized tasks. It is this division of labor that prevents the tide of modern complexity from overwhelming us. The relationship between individuals and organizations is developed so that maximum output is presumably achieved with a minimum expenditure of time, money, and effort.[1]

The recreational service system has been established because public policy has determined that it is necessary to fulfill a desirable social objective. The nature of the agency, its form, and operation are designated by its initiators.

The recreational service function

The fundamental function of the recreational service system is the provision of recreational opportunities throughout the year to all of the citizens of the community, utilizing both indoor and outdoor facilities and activities which can best be supported by such places. The proper achievement of this function concerns the organization of the entire community and its resources.[2] Both personal and physical (artificial or natural) resources have to be determined, cataloged, appraised, and incorporated into the comprehensive organizational pattern. Physical resources are defined as natural, inanimate, and artificial such as land (space), water, structures, and other material assets. Supplies, material, and equipment will also be counted as physical assets necessary for the production of a recreational program. Personal resources are all of those human capacities included in individual skills, talents, interests, aptitudes, leadership qualities, and groupings of people to be found in the community.

The problem of organizing the community for recreational services may be viewed as having to do with coordination of people – both professional and volunteer workers – and with the establishment of recreational places. The latter requires the operation, maintenance, and administration of materials, funds, and activities. It must be remembered that material resources are of value only to the extent that they contribute to the satisfaction of human needs and realization of human aspirations through recreational experience.

The establishment of separate departments of recreational service in many cities has probably hastened the development of the function of the local recreational service system. Departments charged with a particular and well-defined function usually give its promotion more attention than those that have their primary interest in realms other than the provision of recreational service. Moreover, the specialized department is freer to experiment with new offerings, less bound to traditional ways, and more aggressive in the defense of its function during times of economic or political stress and retrenchment.

Where can the most effective and efficient service be attained? No one doubts that a variety of community agencies must be coordinated and maximum cooperation generated if optimum recreational service is to be provided. With past experiences as a guide, it has been determined that the most effective agency will be organized as an independent department charged with the sole responsibility for providing community recreational services. Relationships with other public, private, and quasi-public agencies will have to be worked out administratively for the benefit of the people who will be served.

It seems obvious that the problem of organizing municipal recreational services is extremely complicated. If all things that serve a common purpose were to be collected together in the municipal organization, then a single department specifically responsible for all of the services indicated would be effected. Such a possibility is often precluded because many of the resources are under the jurisdiction of agencies which have as their primary responsibility something other than recreational services.

Municipal recreational services are performed by designated agencies to serve all the people within a given city with programmed, organized, sponsored, and discretionary activities which offer the participants enjoyment, personal satisfaction, opportunities for self-expression, self-actualization, and life enhancement. Opportunities thus provided must be organized to allocate scarce resources of the community to satisfy social responsibilities and mandates. The use of every ethical means to achieve this goal, the coordination of disparate agencies, the encouragement of suggestions, advice, counsel, and the expectation of mobilizing the various elements of environment, capital, and people into an appropriate concourse to carry out this function is what the public recreational service system is all about.

What public recreational service management means

Public recreational service management is immediately concerned with the methods of providing effective recreational opportunities to citizens of a community at the least possible cost and without duplicating functions of other agencies. Organization, implementation, operation, and maintenance of all recreational services within any given system on any governmental level are part of management, as are the practices and methods of administration. Consequently, management emphasizes what the agency does and how it carries out the obligations assigned to it. Beyond these factors are those that attempt to stimulate the public through a dynamic program. The interrelationships existing between the recreational agency, other municipal institutions, and political and personal facets that duly represent the agency to the public are also important.

Public recreational service management is composed of three general categories:

1. Policy-making: local interest groups and political influence; legal establishment of the department; scope of agency function; and determination of purposes, policy, and plans.

2. Operations: internal structure, administrative organization, fiscal management and support, personnel recruitment and direction, program planning, and management.
3. Supervision: leadership, authority, responsibility, cooperation, coordination, conditions of work, morale, internal communications, in-service education, professionalization, and policy compliance.

There is no clear delineation of one area from another. Each segment of the major divisions influences the others, as they are interdependent for a most satisfying program of services.

Effective recreational services are achieved by:

1. Initiation, management, and retention of a legally constituted public recreational service system through permissive state legislation, enactment provisions in the municipal charter or establishment by local ordinances.
2. Activation, execution, and responsiveness of recreational policies through investigation of community recreational needs, financial posture, and balancing sound managerial concepts and principles with the expediency of public demand and political reality.
3. Administration of public funds in the operation of the recreational system. Instigation of sound fiscal policy clearly understood by local governmental authorizing powers for the financial support of the agency. Reporting obligation and transparency through standard public accounting methods accepted by the system for receipt and disbursement of public funds.
4. Administration of personnel practices and policies. Codes of conduct clearly established and explained in order to recruit and retain the best possible personnel. Line and staff functions precisely defined with the necessary authority and responsibility for performing the assigned functions.
5. Promotion of recreational experiences in the greatest variety and broadest possible range to assure the satisfaction of each actual and potential participant within the system's program. Continuous initiation of new activities designed to stimulate participation to fulfill personal needs and assure public support. (Properly conceived program management is the main function of the recreational service agency – the essential reason for the agency's creation. There is no justification for a recreational service agency other than to provide recreational services to the people of the community.)
6. Acquisition of land and development of facilities within the prescribed authority of enabling legislation, charter grant, or local ordinance and by due process. (Unless such acquisition and development are implemented and conscientiously carried out in terms of conservation and protection of such property, the program of services is greatly reduced and may be completely immobilized.)

7. Management of public relations. Transmitting and interpreting information to the public, analyzing the recreational needs of citizens within the community, and maintaining internal and external communications for the enlightenment and motivation of the staff.
8. Public planning management. This concerns providing the required spaces and facilities at logical places. Coordination of master planning with community growth to establish a priority in the development of a comprehensive physical plant enabling optimum use by the greatest number without impairing ecological balance or destroying traditional values.

Nature of public recreational service organization

Social needs require individual assignment to a particular role in order to function. This division of labor stems the tide of modern complexity. Although such arrangements will begin to change during the next few decades, individual relationships are developed this way so that maximum output is gained with minimum expenditure of resources.

Organization is inseparable from management. Organization involves the arrangements of personnel, materials, and money; management deals with the administration of these resources. Both suggest cooperation. Management is impossible unless or until organization is established. Within the structure of the agency, managerial objectives guide the organization. The purpose of a public recreational service system determines the structure of the agency. The organization of recreational services refers to all community resources; the process of directing and coordinating such resources and structure is management.

Because management is concerned with all patterns of organized effort, any participant in a cooperative endeavor with some set goal is engaged in management. This implies establishing the method by which cooperative effort can be facilitated and the arrangements required to initiate and sustain it.

Organization also means agency; that is, a formally designed agency created for some specified purpose or purposes and requiring the services of technically competent personnel to achieve that purpose. If organizations are to attain their mission and if the intricate relationships among individuals operating within the agency, those operating within related agencies, and those operating outside any agency are not to shatter under the pressures of modern life, then the organization – in terms of both agency and arrangement – needs to be understood. People who take part in and conduct the formal agencies need to know precisely what induces cooperative behavior and what disrupts it.

Establishment of recreational service

Recreational service agencies are created because individuals feel that such organizations are desirable. Conglomerate attitudes are transmitted to authorizing bodies and development ensues. The nature, structure, and operations of the agency are determined by the vision of its initiators.

Tradition or the established pattern of organization within the local legal subdivision will also determine structure of the recreational service department. If lay commissions operate other administrative or advisory departments, a commission will probably be formed for the recreational service agency. If the single executive plan is in use, it is likely to be the adopted pattern of organization for recreational service.

Rationale for a public recreational service system

Community recreational service systems in cities are generally two systems: the public recreational service system and the public school system. To understand the rationale supporting the whole, both systems must be considered separately; although they impinge on one another in many ways, they are also mutually complementary.

In spite of the fact that there is only approximate parity in the distribution of school and park areas and facilities for recreational use throughout the community, the whole has been established with a view to serve all residents in accordance with a rationale that needs clear statement and general applicability.

Comparison of school and city facilities and services

The overall responsibility of schools in a city is to educate children and some adults. Great dependence is placed on the public school system for after-school recreational activity, and especially to provide local centers and neighborhood services, because usually there are about three times as many schools as there are parks. Second, schools have many of the facilities required for a city-wide program of community recreational service and these are not regularly required for the educational function of the schools at all times. Any plan to duplicate centers and facilities already present must be dismissed as impractical and wasteful. Consequently, the city must accept a complementary role, even though schools are not ideally suited to all parts of a desirable community program in all circumstances. In some places an effort has been made to augment the facilities of each school in order to fulfill the neighborhood function more adequately. In doing so, care must be taken that clientele are not attracted and activities are not accommodated that would interfere with the education of those children attending each school.

From casual observation it might appear that the recreational areas, facilities, and programs of a public school and a city park are quite similar, but there are important differences.

Elementary school ground equipment is limited in kind, being selected, typically, for the physical education program of the school, if there is one.

Usually there are no slides, swings, teeter-totters, nor apparatus of unusual design; neither is there equipment developed for the teenage youth over the age of those attending the school. On the other hand, parks are equipped with a variety of apparatus, sometimes of exotic design and presenting a variety of challenges. Since attendance at parks is wholly voluntary, it is advisable to provide inducements to attend. Consequently, the criteria of novelty, attraction, diversity, and dimension influence design of the park and selection of equipment.

Parks more often have lights for evening activities and grassed areas that are necessary for some activities, whereas most elementary school yards in cities are paved from fence to fence and gates are often locked when there is no one from the school available to supervise the area. Parks are fenced only where the safety of players and others may so require, and, with a few exceptions, are open from morning until night. School security and particularly legal liability related to the public schools' custodial responsibility for pupils dictate the extra precautionary measures. Municipal liability is less restrictive; although the rising incidence of tort actions against municipal recreational agencies has recently made them more cautious.

Elementary school recreational programs and supervised activities usually occur from about 3:25 p.m. on weekdays and 10 a.m. to 5 p.m. on vacation days, with no planned use of the grounds on weekends or holidays. Obviously, there are many exceptions, particularly in small cities and neighborhoods of greater need. City parks and recreational programs extend through all days, including Sundays and holidays.

Although the use of elementary school grounds is not officially limited to children of the age regularly attending the school, in practice older children and youth are reluctant to attend. Equipment is specifically adapted to the younger age group and older youths view the school from which they have graduated as a place where restraints on their behavior are more restrictive than in public parks. School personnel often discourage the attendance of former pupils; they are regarded as a discordant element and are not made particularly welcome. The "freewheeling" operation of a park is more suited to the adolescents' fancy.

Interagency policy

The impingement of school and municipal recreational services in providing recreational experiences is such that public understanding and smooth operation require mutual adoption of policies and procedures, as well as priorities. Such an understanding or "division of the field" will be conducive to the fullest possible utilization of the resources of both agencies and will set the pattern for the future development of a sound system of public service. It is obligatory to state that this can only be carried out through mutual understanding.

8   The manager and the commission

The incipient manager needs to know about the power structure that enables him/her to function in a reasonably competent manner. This means that the manager must recognize where authority lies in the development of policy that guides the agency. This chapter is concerned with the relationship between the employed executive and the commissions which may exist as an extension of the Common Council or whatever legislative body controls the community.

As municipal responsibilities increased in number and complexity, the need for wider representation of the citizenry in public affairs arose. The plan of appointing commissions of lay-people to preside over the affairs of the separate town functions evolved. In essence, these commissions were appendages of the Common Council. Their members, presumably well-informed citizens in their respective fields, were deemed competent to advise the Common Council, city manager, and departmental executives, and to provide effective communication between citizens and their government.

Commission versus single executive responsibility

The council–manager form of local government has been rapidly accepted as the most effective type because of the need for professionalization of public service. Under this plan, a unicameral council is elected by the voters and the council selects and employs a municipal manager. The council also elects a mayor from among its own membership, usually the individual who received the greatest number of votes. The city manager serves at the pleasure of the city council, but the specialized field of management has developed such ethical codes applicable to appointments and dismissal that members are fairly well protected from political pressure and personal enmity.

The commission form of government has steadily lost its place of eminence over the past generation. Its basic defects include a lack of centralized responsibility for administrative assignment and, in some cases, incompetence of commissioners to assume the functions of departments regardless of their qualifications.

Clearly, the type of municipal organization plays a significant part in deciding on the structure of departments within the municipal family. The question almost always asked when establishing a new agency is whether it is to be headed by a single executive reporting to the managing authority of the community or by an appointed commission. In recreational service, there is support both for a single executive and for the commission type of organization, although the latter is steadily losing ground.

Why are lay commissions established? The underlying reason most frequently given to support the establishment of an independent commission is that such a body is less subject to political pressure groups. There is also a quasi-judicial aspect of the commission, and hearings before it are considered to be more impartial than appearances before an individual who might be biased. Unfortunately, the essential reason for establishing independent commissions is largely traditional. Commissions have not succeeded in keeping political pressures out of the management of departmental affairs and such bodies have tended to be influenced by vociferous groups which may have an interest in specific social, cultural, economic, or related functions of the department.

The single executive directly responsible to the chief executive (or city manager) is the form generally favored by secure administrators and by students of government who seek improvement of departmental efficiency. Advocates of this type of organization have generally presented two arguments: first, such an arrangement conforms to the premise of efficient administration; second, this plan establishes clear lines of authority and responsibility for success or failure in the administration of departmental efforts. It is therefore assumed, with some logical basis, that all administrative work should be performed by professionally prepared individuals capable of producing quality services within an organizational plan leading up to and in direct contact with the executive managing authority of the community.

It would appear that a combination of the best features of the single executive and lay commission forms could be applied to the municipal recreational service function. In effect, then, the commission would function in an advisory capacity only, bringing to the departmental executive the sense of the community which laymen are able to represent. Commissioners would still be selected and appointed on the basis of their interest and knowledge of the recreational service problems that confront the community, but their responsibilities would be limited to the area of advice and making recommendations to the professional in charge of the department. Thus, the best of two organizational forms would be placed most effectively at the service of the community. The commission would serve as the chief public relations medium between the department and the public while continuing to offer advice or suggestions to the recreationist/manager from a laymen's point of view. In this way, the department could function more efficiently, a sharply defined line of responsibility would be established, and the executive would benefit from the opinions and advice that the commissioners would offer. The commission would become an excellent sounding board for departmental policies and could serve as a buffer between disaffected citizens and the department. The commission would be in the best position to perpetuate the image of the department and develop goodwill between its personnel and the community. Offering a citizen's opinion of program or facility placement might prove highly beneficial to the community and to future activities and the provision of systematized recreational services.

Establishment of commissions

In discussing the organization of recreational services within the structure of municipal government and the role of lay commissions, it is necessary to distinguish between government as an instrument for the preservation of society, and government as a means for providing services desired by the citizenry. The view of government as an instrument for the provision of services is of comparatively recent origin and has been dictated largely by necessity, stemming from the complexity of urban living. Many services, presumably required by all citizens now, by common consent are administered by local government.

Some functions of municipal government can be performed best by ministerial agents (city treasurer, city clerk, city auditor) without the aid of commissions. Law enforcement agencies (police, fire, zoning, building regulation, sanitary inspection) may be provided with commissions, not only to advise but also to establish regulations according to legal authority and to hear appeals regarding decisions made by law enforcement agents. Their procedure must be formal and their findings recorded, because they are often put to the test of litigation. Commissions formed for the promotional fields (recreational service, library, arts, and cultural affairs) are valued for their advisory functions, having few or no law enforcement duties in the customary sense, although some of their policy statements do regulate behavior in public recreational places. Such commissions are rarely required to hear appeals. Although their proceedings may be largely informal, the need to substantiate policy statements or other regulatory guides may arise and, for this reason, it is sound to recall the work of the commission in minutes. Whether there will be commissions, how they should be appointed and organized, and what their responsibilities will be is set forth in the city charter.[1] The legislative duties are delegated by the Common Council; hence the Council must confirm their actions, for example, in setting the charges for amenity services, or fixing of salary schedules. Their administrative prerogatives may be prescribed by the charter or delegated by the Common Council or the mayor (in cities of the so-called "strong" mayor type).

For convenience, commissions are often differentiated according to whether they are advisory or administrative (legislative). In fact it is not an either/or situation; commissions may have limited or full administrative powers; in all cases their functions are advisory.

Heretofore, administrators of recreational service departments have preferred commissions, but this preference is waning. Commissions are often thought to be the most effective means for local government to learn of the needs of its constituent public, but in many instances this is no longer true. When citizens are appointed to commissions because of political affiliation, they may hinder efficient operations; when commission members have a high degree of interest and enthusiasm for public recreational service they may perform beneficially.

Up until 1940, more than three-quarters of American urban departments of recreational service were governed by commissions of laymen. Since then the trend has slowly been reversed; although commissions are still extant. Today, administrators are being made responsible to city managers or city councils rather than to recreational service commissions.

Appointment and tenure of commission members

When the local legislature believes that commissions are necessary, they authorize the establishment of a particular commission for service in the community. Recreational service commissions are appointed by the governing body of the community and are generally nominated for such appointment by the presiding executive. Commissions may have any number of members, but five to seven has been found to be the most feasible number. They customarily serve without compensation; however, the city charter or local ordinance may provide a per diem for each meeting. Commissioners may be appointed for indefinite terms, for terms coinciding with that of the appointing power, or for set terms. In the latter case, appointments are staggered so that only half the terms expire each year, so that several experienced commissioners remain on the board, thus providing continuity in policies. Under such a plan, commissioners need not resign when there is a change in municipal administration.

When a citizen is appointed to a recreational commission he/she is afforded many opportunities for unselfish service beneficial to the department executive, the recreational service system, and the city. Unless dedicated citizens with the ability to comprehend the function of recreational service and to exercise sound judgment in the public interest are appointed there is no advantage in having a commission.

Appointments to non-salaried commissions are not sought after as a rule. There are no emoluments of service to be had, but there is honor and satisfaction to be gained in rendering civic service. Usually, leading citizens respond generously when invited to serve on a recreational service commission because of their general interest in child welfare, education, city beautification, or because of a specific interest in an activity, such as amateur athletics, music, drama, or the arts.

Commissions usually elect their own presiding officer – a president or chairman. A secretary is required to keep minutes and other records of the commission and to certify its acts. Usually the secretary is an employee (the clerk of the commission) who may perform all the duties. It is not unusual for one of the commissioners to act as secretary. The department executive is rarely burdened with this duty. The executive should meet with the commission and be free to participate in discussions, but he/she should not be accorded a vote. A treasurer is not necessary, because the disbursement of public funds is made by the city treasurer or other financial officer of the city. If the commission is empowered in any manner to disperse private funds, another arrangement must be improvised.

Meetings are held as often as necessary (usually monthly) and sometimes, by legal requirement, in a public place, preferably the city hall or a local school auditorium; whichever is more convenient. The time and place of meetings should be published, and meetings should be open to the public so that all pending matters may be heard. If an internal matter arises during any public meeting, the commission is empowered to enter into an executive session, from which the public is excluded, so that unbiased solutions may be found.

Functions of commissions

The newly employed administrator must be cognizant of the required activities of the commission. This will save a great deal of conflict that might arise from a lack of understanding of the duties, powers, and functions of the commission insofar as the manager's responsibilities are concerned. Primarily, the chief functions of a commission are to formulate and promulgate policies governing the system. Commissions are responsible for the policies they adopt, but they may avail themselves of advice from the administrator and suggestions from the citizenry in formulating policies. The commission also endeavors to conform to the policies of the general municipal administration as expressed by the mayor, the city manager, or the city council.

The recreational service commission typically performs the following functions:

1. Approves the acts of the department. As the governing board responsible for the results of the work of the department, the commission receives work reports through the manager and records its approval of them.
2. Acts as a court of final appeal. Any disagreement arising from employees or between the public and employees, if not satisfactorily resolved by the manager, may be considered by the commission, whose decisions are final.
3. Advises the manager on problems of administration. All managers need advice in the performance of their administrative duties and in

carrying out the policies set by the commission. The advice of the commission should be sought by the manager but should not be interpreted as instructions or regulations, unless given such force by action of the commission as a whole.

4. Interprets the department and the general operation of the system to the public. The commission fulfills this responsibility by published actions, by public discussion and address, and by planned use of available means of public communication. The members of the commission often symbolize the aims and objectives of the department, for the character of the department is reflected in the members who are appointed commissioners no less than by the employees.

5. Represents the general public. Commissioners should conduct meetings that are open to the public and should permit individuals or delegations to address them on pertinent subjects. Most frequently the matter brought before a commission in this way is such that an immediate answer is not always possible or expedient. Often the petitioner is not in agreement with the commission. It should be remembered that the prerogative of the petitioner is only to state his/her views and not to participate in the action. The responsibility for the action, if any is taken, rests with the commission which, after giving a respectful hearing to the petitioner, makes its own decision based on the facts involved. The decision need not be made at the time the matter is brought before the commission; the subject may be taken under advisement and a decision announced in due course.

6. Represents the department at official occasions. Commissioners often act as spokesperson for the department at public ceremonies, public hearings on problems concerning the department, and conferences on recreational programs, policies, or other relevant issues.

7. Negotiates advantages for the department. Because of their individual and collective prestige, commissioners are often in a better position than the manager or others to negotiate advantages for the department with the local governing authority, or other public officials, and the general public. Among these advantages might be an adequate budget for departmental operations. The laymen who does not derive pecuniary gain from the appropriation for the department is usually more effective than a salaried employee in such negotiations.

8. Appoints standing and ad hoc committees. When the work of the department becomes extensive, the commission may appoint a special committee, usually consisting of only one person. A standing committee makes it convenient to assign to a commissioner, for further investigation and consideration, any matter on which the commission may not be ready to act. Committees will not have administrative powers in the matters referred to them. No committee or individual member has any authority except by referral to and through the entire body.

9. Separates managerial from policy-making activities. Execution of policy is delegated to the manager and the employed staff. Although there is no lack of interest in all phases of departmental operations by commission members, the creation of an administrative department to handle such matters provides for a sharp delineation between formulation and execution of policy.

Commission and managerial relationships

The relationship between the commission and the manager is a reciprocal one; they perform different functions, but are mutually dependent on each other. The commissioners must understand the functions and responsibilities of the manager and not trespass on them. The execution of the policies established by the commission, for example, is clearly a function of the manager. This clear-cut distinction is recognized as fundamentally important by municipal authorities and should be strictly adhered to. Encroachment by the commission on the prerogatives of the manager destroys good administration and tends to break down the system of responsible management.

The manager must also respect the prerogatives of the commission. There must be a feeling of mutual trust and confidence between the commission and the executive if they are to function together efficiently. Since the manager is selected by the commission, this confidence is present at the beginning of the administrator's service and should be cultivated and preserved continually.

Close association of commissioners and executive in the work which mutually engages them often results in personal friendships, but regardless of these personal relationships, the manager must be careful to treat all commissioners alike in his/her professional relations with them, and should certainly not presume on his/her friendship with any member or members.

There are many occasions when commissioners and manager do not agree on the matters before them. The administrator must reconcile him/herself to the decisions of the commission and must carry out its policies even when his/her own judgment is contrary to theirs. As in all group discussion and action, there must be a certain amount of give and take in arriving at conclusions. In the interests of harmony, minor differences should not always be asserted. However, on major matters material differences should be expressed and reiterated until the decision is reached. Such differences will be recorded when a vote on a motion is taken. The report of the manager should also be recorded, whether his/her recommendation is adopted or not.

Matters may be brought before the commission by any member, by the manager, by other city officials, or by citizens. In the interests of proper recording, referral of matters to the commission should be by written communication or report, but strict adherence to this rule is not always possible or convenient. Before a problem is fully discussed by the commission, the manager should be requested to give his/her report, thus encouraging his/her independent expression, unswayed by consideration of the views of any commissioner. The contrary practice would result in the cultivation of a "yes man" attitude on the part of the administrator. Such an effect nullifies his/her special experiences and skill. Having received the report of the executive, the commission is empowered to approve, disapprove, or modify his/her recommendations. The executive's duty and professional responsibility is to execute such decisions as have been made.

Selection of all employees should be made by the manager subject to the established municipal procedure affecting all departments. Only when the manager has the power of appointment can he/she be held responsible for the performance of the employees.

Any official dealings with employees by commissioners as individuals or as a body should be through the manager. Some employees may seek the ear of commissioners for one purpose or another, but they should be directed to bring the matter to the attention of the manager who will report on it to the commission if necessary. Most frequently such matters involve detail or questions of executive management which do not directly concern or fall within the purview of the commission.

Proper performance of the duties of the recreational service commissioner requires sound understanding and acquaintance with the recreational problems of the community and knowledge of the work being conducted by the department. A commissioner finds that more time is necessary to gain this background than is taken in official meetings. Visits to recreational centers, or attendance at recreational activities, inspections, and participation in conferences with professional and lay leaders are very helpful. Systematic planning of such occasions is advisable. Opportunities for conferences are afforded by the local, state, and national associations of workers and laymen.

One of the responsibilities of the manager is to aid commissioners in learning about the department, the work it performs, the manner in which it functions, and its traditions. Newly appointed commissioners especially are in need of assistance in these matters in order that they may assume their place in the deliberations of the commission. The manager renders this aid through conferences, correspondence, inspections of the work under varying conditions, and by furnishing reports and pertinent published material. The official meeting of the commission provides a good occasion to bring up matters for discussion. Participation of employees with the manager in discussion before the commission is sometimes helpful to the commissioners and stimulating to the employees.

Personality factors will always enter into any relationship between the commission and its executive. As long as the function and role of each is clearly defined, there should be little cause for friction. If the executive brings professional objectivity and empathy to his/her presentation, harmony and effectiveness must be the outcome in recreational service operations throughout the system.

The new manager requires a disinterested outlook concerning his/her relationship with the commission. This means that all commissioners will be given equal respect and consideration as they air their views concerning the operation and administration of the system. It is the professional obligation of the manager to clarify any misconceptions that commissioners may hold about the function of the recreational service department. This is not a forum for strident lecturing, but for simple explanations that are factually based and logically arrived at. In this way the commissioners will be in a better position to appreciate the information that they have received, as well as developing confidence in the rectitude and objectivity of the manager.[2] This shared information and mutual respect will go a long way toward building a sound relationship between the two parties.

9 Recreational service department structure

The form of a public recreational service system is largely determined by the social setting in which it is conceived and by the particular orientation of its founders. If the recreational service system is conceived in terms of children's playgrounds, one form of initial structure will be favored; if in terms of municipal beach, golf, swimming pool activities, organized sports, and adult hobbies, another form will be indicated.

Cities have continually experimented with different types of organization. However, the structure of community recreational services and the establishment of some branch of municipal government responsible for such provision have given rise to a modicum of confusion. The question is not simply: Where in the municipal setting shall the recreational service function lodge? The questions to be answered are: Which governmental agency will be responsible for recreational services in the community? Which agency is best able to supply the manifold activities of municipal recreational service? Which agency has the personnel with the most acceptable orientation for providing community services of a recreational nature? Which agency performs services most closely related to community recreational service? What additional personnel and managerial structure are required for the most effective and efficient performance of this function?

Park departments, welfare departments, school boards, quasi-public agencies, and private recreational agencies are all interested in the community's expanding need for adequate recreational service and are planning and organizing their facilities, personnel, and budgets to meet this need. Should an independent tax-supported recreational service department be created that will have control of all municipal recreational services? Can such as system adequately satisfy the recreational needs of all the people in the community?

Departmental structure

Recreationists formerly discussed whether recreational services were best administered under a special agency, park department, board of education, or some plan joining two or more agencies. All previous plans have had their advantages and disadvantages. Moreover, it was found that what was best for one community might not be viable in another. Essentially the structural plan will always depend on local conditions. Although each specific plan has something to commend it, some forms of organization are decidedly more advantageous than others, regardless of the size, condition, or economic ability of the community.[1] One type of structure will be found to serve the community best.

During the past century there has been an unmistakable trend toward more effective organization and integration of the several functions of municipal government, owing to a number of factors. The universal expansion of municipal functions since the beginning of the 20th century resulted in the establishment of so many new departments and bureaus that consolidation of some for efficient administration became inevitable. The First World War, the economic depression of the 1930s, the Second World War and all the subsequent clashes, the boom times and stagflation, as well as the insistent demand for reduction of property taxes dictated the necessity for more economic cooperation and limitation of duplicated services. The growth of certain agencies, notably those concerned with education, library, park, and recreational programming, has been such that a certain amount of overlap was created, pointing up the need for greater coordination of these services and a more effective organization. The spiraling costs of inflation, an unprecedented boom economy in the 1990s, negligible unemployment, and a proliferation of taxes did nothing to still the cry for less taxation. The municipality was caught between rising population, demand for more and better services, and insistence on lower taxes. There has even been a movement at the municipal level to privatize public services by farming some of them out to commercial firms.

The wars in Iraq, Afghanistan, and now Libya have cost the United States enormous amounts of money. The financial market collapse of 2007, the depressed housing market and the rise in the price of crude oil have caused an economic recession of unimagined proportions.[2] The outsourcing of manufactured products and even services overseas has added to a less than satisfactory economic picture. Because of the continuing money squeeze, standardized organizational structures have had to be defined.

The human services movement

The decline in urban fiscal resources has caused widespread panic among elected and appointed political officials. They seek ways and means of cutting down on their overheads. For the most part this has meant a diminution of human services to citizens. It has been manifested by layoffs or reduction in forces from departments serving a variety of clients both at the state and city levels. By reducing the number of employees it was thought that tremendous savings could be gained. Little savings have resulted, but welfare costs have risen and service deficiencies have grown in proportion to the number of persons cut from payrolls. Officials have begun to realize that simply cutting the workforce neither saves a great deal of money nor enhances the productivity of those who remain on the job. Rather, there seems to be a decline in morale and the service normally rendered by those retaining their employment. Other innovative methods must be sought to offer effective services to citizens who pay their taxes and have a right to expect such services in return. The current movement toward consolidation of urban departments is most clearly observed in the development of a super-agency – the human services department. This organization combines the personnel and functions of formerly independent line agencies (see Figure 9.1).

For good or ill, public recreational service departments have come to be seen as the repository of these combined departments. Thus, all human resource agencies within the community may potentially be placed within the organizational structure of an existing recreational service department, or an overhead agency may be established to administer the functions of several departments under the aegis of one chief executive. Instead of having five or six commissioners, superintendents, or directors there is only one. The heads of these former departments are downgraded to assistant manager positions. The current trend is to look to one of the managers of a line agency and select him/her as the new chief executive. Rarely is an individual not already employed by the city in some managerial capacity chosen to head the newly created department.

It may be valid to state that recreationists can be effective human services managers simply because the field of recreational service is one of the great humanitarian organizations and managers of such agencies have long practice in coping with the manifold problems which beset any complex urban department. However, there are numerous functions being thrust upon recreationists with regard to which they are ill-prepared to play a role. It seems hardly likely that recreationists will either want to, or will have dealt with welfare, health care, job placement, substance abuse control, personal counseling, family relations, child rearing, etc., which are part of the human services package. Nevertheless, it behooves recreationist managers to undertake these additional chores and perform to the best of their respective abilities. The entire question of making a conglomerate of the recreational service department and saddling its management with the heavy burdens of other human service functions is one that requires much study and evaluation. It is an area that may come to haunt the field of recreational service in the next few years.

The consolidated recreational service and park department

The plan shown in Figure 9.2 is oriented to a single, but comprehensive, purpose – rendering recreational services. Parks are not separated from other recreational facilities. All facilities under the control of the department

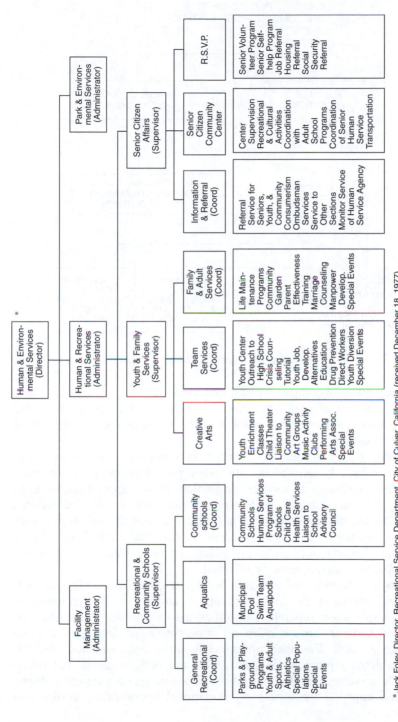

*Jack Foley, Director, Recreational Service Department, City of Culver, California (received December 18, 1977). Proposed Department of Human and Environmental Services, Human and Recreational Services Division

Figure 9.1 The human services department organization.

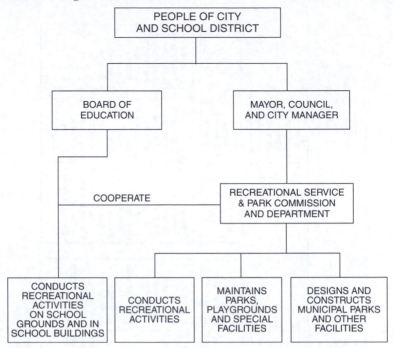

Figure 9.2 The consolidated recreational service and park department.

are interrelated to implement recreational services. This implies a modern, broadened concept of parks that views them as areas of both active and passive participation and enjoyment without denying the importance of esthetic landscaping.

This plan has long been in practice in cities in which recreational services were initially assumed by established park departments or commissions. When recreational services originated as an appendage to park functions, the two merged. Park services came to include recreational services. The use of the two terms is, in fact, an incongruity and in time may give way to the use of the functional term "recreational service" as inclusive of both, particularly since parks are places where recreational experience, in the broad and narrow sense, is achieved.

The major advantage of this plan is that it consolidates all municipal recreational service under one department and avoids the controversy that may arise when separate authorities are responsible for parks and recreational services. Thus it offers an opportunity for developing a more comprehensive and diversified program. It encourages and adds esthetic quality to activity programs in landscaped and buffered areas that otherwise would serve only limited purposes. It encourages economical administration and improves the quality of recreational opportunities available to the citizenry.

The plan illustrated in Figure 9.2 raises the question of whether park functions may not be seriously subordinated to recreational service. The likelihood of this is less, however, because the park function is more deeply rooted in municipal tradition than is recreational service. Then, too, the enlarged, enlightened concept of recreational service would normally encompass parks as essential for recreational programming.

The consolidated plan, because of its advantages, is commended to large or small communities. It is feasible even in the largest urban centers, where extensive systems of parkways and reservations, beaches, and other regional developments require extensive organization of material and personnel. Although these areas have little in common with the conduct of conventional recreational activities, they may serve as effective sites to produce major special events, which are an intrinsic part of the comprehensive recreational program.

In the largest urban centers, separate agencies may handle the development and construction of beaches, parkways, and reservations, but they should consult park and recreational planners. Some large park systems have their own police force; however, this is not a function of recreational service. Regardless of the size of the park system, the municipal, county, or state police force should be the agency of law enforcement. When uniformed personnel are necessary, they should be employed as attendants, custodians, rangers, or groundskeepers, not as police.

This plan offers no organic connection with the school system. The municipality may conduct activities on school grounds and in school buildings on a contractual or other agreed-upon basis. Questions of jurisdictional control of school facilities may arise if some written agreement is not made providing for the use of school facilities by the public department. Without contractual obligation, the schools are free to develop their own programs and facilities with or without the assistance of the public recreational service department, which can lead to duplication of service and competition for the same clientele. However, if close coordination and cooperation is maintained between the two systems, a more comprehensive service may be performed for the community at large. In some cities the school system either does not open its facilities at all for recreational activity or operates them wholly under school control. The schools are vital to the provision of community-wide recreational services.

There are numerous other plans in use in small cities and rural communities and in cities just beginning to organize themselves for recreational service. In most of these communities recreational service is a municipal concern only during the summer months; during the rest of the year there is little community recreational service except that provided by the schools through their adult education and/or extra-curricular activities programs. Such cities usually employ some personnel to direct the summer school playground and adult activities programming each year. Often the appointee is an elementary school teacher, a physical education teacher, or school athletic team coach. Typically, such programs center on sports and games and little else. These programs frequently serve as experiments; when successful, they grow into a more permanent organization and, with the passage of time, they become institutionalized for year-round community recreational service.

Internal structure of a public recreational service department

We are now concerned with the internal organization of a public recreational service department. Such a department should be large and should comprehend all community recreational services rendered by it. Thus, all relationships will be well illustrated in terms of areas, facilities, finances, and personnel.

Table of organization

Organization of a hypothetical recreational service department, including both park and recreational programming functions, is illustrated in Figure 9.3. This chart exemplifies the general principles of departmental structure but should not be regarded as an ideal plan. The organization must be adapted to the general structure of the municipal government, which is usually dictated by local traditions, procedures, and expediency.

The same principles of organization apply to smaller departments, but, in many cases, duties and responsibilities are consolidated and assigned to fewer persons than in the large department. Recording and filing may be combined with accounting and ordering; supervision of several generic recreational activities may be consolidated; direction and management of beaches and swimming pools or of all aquatic facilities may be combined.

Line responsibilities and relationships are indicated by ascending and descending lines, and horizontal lines indicate staff responsibilities. Several departments are large enough to require the subdivisions of structure shown here. The degree of ramification in organization and specialization in particular administrative and executive duties increases with the size of the department.

If the department does its own construction work, elaboration of this function will be necessary. Sometimes construction is consolidated with maintenance and planning. Special establishments (museums, art galleries, zoological parks, and botanical gardens) are shown for the sake of completeness. In certain instances, highly specialized facilities may have their own governing bodies and be completely separated from the recreational service department. Under each group of areas or facilities there may be a number of unit facilities and each of these will be under the supervision of a director. Some of the unit facilities require two services – maintenance and operation of the program. The director coordinates these functions.

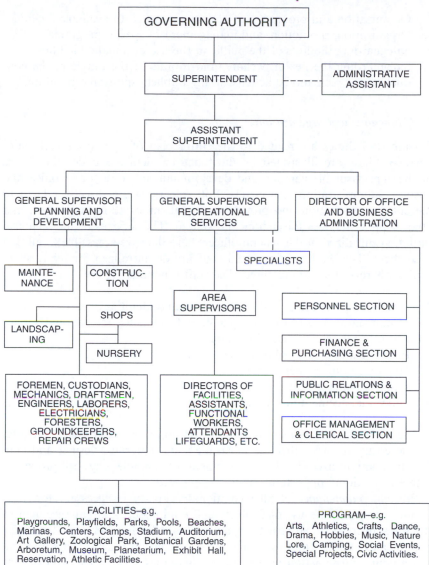

Figure 9.3 Organizational chart for a hypothetical recreational service department.

The chief executive is responsible for the general management of the department and for the efficient maintenance and operation of all facilities and the following line functions are typically found in large recreational service departments:

1. Supervision of the public in the use of areas and facilities.
2. Instruction of individuals and groups in certain recreational activities.

3. Organization and promotion of activities adapted to available facilities.
4. Organization, promotion, and management of special programs.
5. Safeguarding the lives of the public in the use of aquatic facilities.
6. Safeguarding the health, welfare, and morals of the public in the conduct of any recreational activity at any publicly sponsored program.

Staff functions and organization

Certain staff duties are related to the entire plan of operations and maintenance. These are illustrated by the functions depicted under the offices of the supervisor of planning and development and director of office and business administration respectively. Both positions are directly related to the entire organization and provide technical information, assistance, and other support services throughout the system. The services of the technical staff are centralized in the general office where they are accessible to all that need them. The services of the field staff are decentralized for ready availability wherever they are required. The staff functions are:

1. Planning and development of new areas and facilities.
2. Maintenance of all areas and facilities to enhance recreational service and other functions related thereto.
3. Public relations and public information.
4. Human resources management.
5. Finance management.
6. Office management and clerical work.

The *planning and development* of recreational places and physical facilities are necessary in order that the most adequate materials, design, and construction are utilized in the development of suitable physical properties where recreational opportunities may be enjoyed.

Efficient *maintenance* of all recreational property is necessary for maximum operation, safe use of facilities and equipment, and enhancement of the attractiveness of all structures and areas. Cleaning services, landscape maintenance, and prompt repairing and other related functions are essential to optimum participation in recreational activities. Convenient and orderly arrangement, attractive setting, and adequate equipment and space are important to the improvement of satisfaction in activities and enjoyment of participation and observation.

Public relations and public information are concerned with the development of goodwill between the public and the system, and with the dissemination of information concerning the policies, programs, and function of the department. This is distinctly a staff function and related to all the facilities and services of the system. The person in charge of this should be close enough to the superintendent to know the regulations and policies of the system and to be aware of any modifications.

Financial management includes custodianship of public funds, control of such funds, and records of purchases, receipts, and other fiscal transactions for the guidance of the executive. Every department has a certain amount of accounting to perform and, in some instances, will audit its accounts to ensure their correctness.

Office management and clerical work refers to recording, computer operating, clerical custodianship of supplies, and the maintenance of inventory. These services are incidental, though necessary, to the efficiency of the system's work.

Modern office practice favors consolidation or centralization of these duties as far as is practicable. Maintenance of supply depots or a storehouse and a current inventory of supplies or equipment, indicating quantities and location throughout the system, are essential to the discharge of accounting responsibilities and for buying purposes.

Internal coordination

In a large organization in which functions are departmentalized, there is always the danger that coordination between divisions may be lacking. The fact that the work of the system is conducted at widely separated facilities contributes to this tendency. Joint projects in which all parts of the department must cooperate, such as city-wide events, intramural competitions, pageants, parades, or special projects requiring cooperative endeavors, assist in correlating the several parts. Divisional and departmental meetings, supervisory conferences, regular bulletins or a departmental newspaper dealing with every aspect of the recreational system and its affairs, sound personnel practices, and social occasions for employees are also useful devices to promote mutual understanding and coordination.

Part III

Management functions and responsibilities

10 Human resources management for recreational service

Current organizational theory and practice recognizes the importance of both interpersonal relationships and the structure of administration. Rather than presupposing that people are made for organizations, this enlightened concept negotiates between the extremes of organizational necessity and individualization. This management orientation is clearly observed from efforts to develop a human resources organizational contract as a coordinating process in which neither aspect can be truly intelligible without the other. This chapter concerns the human factor in management and the principles and practices that have been utilized for dealing with personnel working in an enterprise governed by public policy.

Personnel employed by a public recreational service department perform duties related to three more or less distinct functions: (1) organization, promotion, supervision, and leadership of the recreational program; (2) planning, construction, and maintenance of recreational facilities and places; and (3) business administration, clerical duties, and other office work. Employees in the last two categories are recruited from the general labor pool of mechanics, laborers, office workers, and other functionaries available to all agencies and enterprises. Their titles are generally similar to those of their corresponding numbers in other businesses and governmental agencies. Their preparation is not necessarily slanted toward recreational service. The adaptation of their skills to the requirements of the recreational service department is a problem of in-service education and staff development. Of course, there are employees who have been prepared for the planning and development specialization for employment in recreational service agencies. These individuals may have studied park planning and design or architectural design with major emphasis on recreational places and structures. Such individuals may have been indoctrinated with concepts of recreational resources. These people would not be recruited from the general labor market but would be selected from institutions of higher education where such specialized programs exist or from the field.

Employees engaged to perform duties and undertake responsibilities directly concerned with recreational service operations are either generalists or specialists who may be presumed to have had professional educational preparation. The uniqueness of the recreationist lies in his/her general orientation to recreational service and in his/her special knowledge, appreciation, and skill in specific recreational activities. The abilities necessary for the organization and management of recreational service, whether in the public or private sector, contribute to his/her stature as a specialist and as a member of a discipline aspiring to professionalism.

Management of any organization depends on the persons employed in it. The success or failure of departmental activity is based on the soundness of human resource management. Human factors must be considered as the vital source for analysis, research, and scientific formulation of policies and principles. In the overall picture of public service administration, the management of human resources is the most important function.[1]

Functions of human resources management

Although the basic activities depicted by the term *human resources management* vary with the locale, they comprise a body of responsibilities and functions that must be carried out by one or more individuals in almost every organization.[2] The major services generally performed are:

1. Position analysis, classification, and specification: a rendering of the nature of the work to be performed in any given position so as to establish requirements for recruitment practices.
2. Recruitment, screening, induction, orientation, and placement: the procedure by which individuals are identified in terms of skills, interests, talents, and knowledge coincidental with position requirements.
3. Appraisal, assignment, and promotion: the methods utilized to recognize and reward achievement so that individuals may be placed to the greatest advantage for the organization and themselves.
4. Remuneration: compensatory plans by which monetary scales, increments, and schedules are equitably distributed for the type of work performed.
5. In-service education, development, supervision, and conditions of work: the process by which competence, efficiency, effectiveness, high morale, and organizational devotion are stimulated.
6. Disciplinary activities: the techniques utilized to discourage incompetence, disaffection, misfeasance, malfeasance, nonfeasance, or any negative behavior by an individual.[3]
7. Evaluation: the process by which employee efforts are compared with previously set goals to determine whether they have been met.[4]
8. Records, reports, and research: the maintenance of all records concerned with the employee's hiring, work productivity, appraisals, evaluations, compensation, leaves, and any psychological testing performed to match the individual with his/her position.

These activities and the fundamental beliefs characterizing them have developed over a considerable period of time. The assumptions are undergoing continual scrutiny and are subject to modification as changing situations and conditions are brought to light by research into the processes and practices of organizational behavior. The staff activity of human resources management is generally concerned with the recruitment, selection, induction, in-service education, staff development, promotion, motivation, and disciplinary practices of all employees for the most effective coordination of work performance.[5] Human resources management carries out general policies established by the community in question or the company of employment, and, more specifically, the policies adopted by the particular recreational agency. In accordance with the needs of the system, human resources management initiates basic rules governing requirements in education and experience, examinations pertinent to the several specializations, recruiting for available positions, reference of eligible applicants for selection and ultimate placement, and the keeping of official personnel records.

The human resources function also includes the classification of positions by direct analysis, typically performed by the central employing agency of the city with guidance from the department, or by the personnel department of the private agency. The application of the position classification process to individual job descriptions which were formulated after proper analysis, and the establishment of compensatory rates by legislative enactment in the public sector or the going rate in the private sector is undertaken. The position classification process is, perhaps, the primary responsibility of human resource management,[6] but other functions include provisions for the health, safety, and welfare of employees; salary schedules; hours of work; leaves; vacations; overtime; salary increments; disciplinary actions; ratings; research; and final separation from the department.

Management aids

Four basic procedures facilitate the selection, education, rating, and direction of personnel: (1) formally adopted rules and regulations that guide personnel in agency operation, purpose, and jurisdiction; (2) a handbook of personnel procedures listing in detail the steps to be followed in fulfilling the duties and responsibilities of different positions, conduct required of incumbents, rules and regulations for employees, and technical information required by employees to execute their respective assignments effectively; (3) forms specifically designed to record all pertinent information relating to the employee's personal, education, professional, technical, medical, and/or health qualifications; and (4) personnel folders containing data sheets and records of relevant information about each employee.

A merit system

The decision to employ any individual in a municipal or governmentally operated department of recreational service should be based on that person's competence to render the indicated service and to hold a position.

A system based on individual merit does much to offset nepotism or nefarious political patronage. A logical merit system should encompass the following factors: (1) a sound and enlightened policy established for all municipal employment; (2) a human resources section adequate to handle the details of classification procedure; (3) position classification concerning duties, responsibilities, requirements, and relationships; (4) a uniform grading and salary schedule; (5) open competitive examinations; (6) promotional examinations; (7) a probationary period following appointment; (8) merit ratings used in counseling and promotions or transfers; (9) uniform regulations for leave, retirement, hours of work, vacations, disciplinary actions, and separations; (10) arrangements for pooling personnel for seasonal or emergency conditions; and (11) group medical, hospital, life insurance, or general health plans.

Specialization in recreational service

Within each organization is an intricate series of events for which the work of the system is performed. These complex tasks are divided into components for effective management. This division of labor into specialized spheres determines position analysis and classification. Administration, in part, organizes and groups duties and responsibilities so that the work of the agency may proceed unhampered, and this aspect of human resources management requires examination.

Generally, division of labor or specialization consists of sequential activities beginning with the original purpose for establishing the system and the primary objectives of the organization; organizational planning based on position and methods utilized in obtaining the agency's goals; development of job descriptions and position analysis for tasks to be performed; position specifications comprising education and experience; development of performance criteria for appraisal and evaluation of each position; and establishment of general and specific policies, rules, and regulations governing the work to be performed and the method by which it is to be performed. Although each of these segments emanates from the one directly preceding it, there is considerable interdependency and reciprocity in the process. Thus, the process of job specialization is based on organizational goals, organizational planning, position descriptions leading in turn to job analysis and specification, performance criteria, human resources policies, and regulations governing performance. Specialization may therefore be divided into organizational goals, position delineation, position analysis, and specifications.

Organizational goals

Identification of organizational goals stems from managerial oversight and precedes all other organizational aspects. The aim of identifying organizational goals is necessary if the work of the agency is to satisfy community needs. Essentially, all recreational service agencies have one basic goal – to provide experiences that can meet the recreational needs of all residents of the community during their respective leisure.

The public recreational system has a comprehensive task of fulfilling recreational needs for all of the people in the community in which the department is situated. Therefore, its aim is not only focused on present residents but also on transients and future citizens of the community. Additionally, there are sub-goals which every recreational service department desires to achieve. These sub-goals deal with the development of the most efficient and effective personnel possible through the enhancement of individual talents, skills, and capacities of professional and technical employees; the development of an established and dedicated workforce; and the creation of a community climate of goodwill, which can foster better service through increased public support of the system.

Organizational planning and position delineation

When organizational goals have been clearly defined, the structure of the system can be planned. The aim of organizational planning is to separate the components of the task to be performed into feasible and practical segments and to provide for their effective correlation. Through this process, the entire system is broken down into manageable units, such as individual positions, sections, and divisions within the department or system. Not only is there a division of effort throughout the system, with various tasks being undertaken by specialists (linear subdivision), but there is also a longitudinal subdivision of work that forms an organizational hierarchy. Thus, at each succeeding level within the organization there is greater responsibility for the supervision of more employees, the coordination of a larger proportion of the work being performed, and more intricate and comprehensive planning. The use of improved technological processes (systems analysis, computer technology, and the like) is a basic part of organizational planning. In a modern recreational service department, systems technology, particularly as it concerns informational displays, work simplification, retrieval, and reporting, must be considered as a constituent part of organizational planning in order to avoid conflict in executing the work to be performed.

Organizational planning and position delineation, originating from the basic goals of the system affect the desired levels of performance in a variety of positions created to carry out the goal-dictated tasks. Furthermore, this expectation identifies position specifications, the educational preparation and in-service staff development required, the complete compensation schedule, and the motivation of employees. Organizational planning and position delineation necessitate some formal classification procedure.

The position classification system[7]

The development of position classification is a consequence of the increasingly technical and specialized duties that employees perform in the field of recreational service, and the need to fit personnel with specific skills and abilities to specified jobs. Position classification is more than the process of arranging functions into groups for facilitation of management; it is part of a process whereby the whole task of recreational service is rendered more susceptible to effective management.

A *position* is a specific role or job calling for performance. The duties, responsibilities, and relationships it requires are set forth in a job description. The employee is appointed to the job described and is presumed to perform no other job. Positions may be short- or long-term, full- or part-time, occupied or vacant. Employees may come and go, but, once created, the position continues until abolished.

A *class* is a group of positions whose duties and responsibilities are similar enough to require personnel to have comparable education, experience, skill, and knowledge, and whose level of responsibility and difficulty are sufficiently alike to justify similar or identical remuneration, promotional practices, orientation, and in-service education.

A *vertical* or *longitudinal classification* or *series* includes all positions that are related to a specific technological or professional group, but which differ in degree of difficulty and responsibility. Hence the work involved; the kind and degree of supervision or authority emanating from the position, and the kind and degree of supervision governing it; and the responsibilities, qualifications, prerequisites, and capacities necessary for employment in that position indicate the level that has been obtained within a service series.

A *horizontal* or *linear classification* or *grade* groups positions according to levels of similar requirements and responsibility, supervision given and received, and difficulty of the work. Grades cut across vertical series. Routine positions that carry little responsibility and require little technical skill are classified at the lowest level or grade. Positions are graded correspondingly higher as the work becomes more difficult and responsibility greater. Wages and salaries usually are assigned by graded schedule.

The *classification plan* is a system of classes of positions, series, and grade definitions and descriptions, and a procedure by which job descriptions may be kept up to date. Each position is carefully analyzed and all tasks necessary to accomplish agency goals involved with the creation of that position are thoroughly detailed. The requirements of the position, in terms of education and experience, as well as the duties and responsibilities, are recorded. Illustrative examples of the work to be performed are also provided.

The value of the plan is its impersonal objectivity and ease of administration in dealing with personnel problems, conflicts, or questions. The plan provides a sound basis for formulating equitable salary schedules and assists in the recruitment, selection, induction, and orientation of personnel; it encourages the use of common terminology or position nomenclature; facilitates appraisal and the value of techniques for performance, promotions, demotions, transfers, or separations; aids in the identification of specific duties and responsibilities; and tends to avoid inconsistencies by clarifying human resources practices.

Once such information is collected, each position is placed in a series. Series are then broken down into classes which then may be described by title, functions, responsibilities, illustrations of the work, and required qualifications. The allocation of individual positions within the classification series is the final step in the plan.

Requirements for and duties of recreationist positions

Although organizational goals and planning identify and determine almost exclusively the duties, range, and status of individual positions within the system, jobs are also delineated through the development of descriptions, specifications, performance criteria, and policies, rules, and regulations. Not only do these instrumentalities tend to qualify the essence of such positions, but they clarify the behavior and special features required. These instrumentalities are not only significant facets of the specialization process but units of other personnel procedures as well.

Position descriptions

Position descriptions are summaries of fundamental tasks, assigned to one employee, performed on a given job. The description has a title or label. The basis for a position description varies from a mental picture the prospective employer has to a comprehensive investigation of the actual position. This procedure, called *analysis*, is typically the basis for the title and description. Position descriptions have several usable functions: (1) for the development of job specifications, that is, qualifications required to perform the work; (2) for recruiting a staff; (3) for orientation once the position is filled; (4) in developing performance criteria, that is, quantitative and qualitative performance to be achieved within a specific time.; and (5) for evaluation procedures to determine the proximity of performance to stated objectives.

It is necessary to differentiate between requirements for and the duties of various types of professional positions in departments of recreational service. Obviously, the duties of a chief executive of a department employing only two or three recreationists are different from those of an executive of a department employing a staff of a hundred or more. In the small department the executive performs duties of all descriptions. In the larger department the executive's duties are more specifically managerial. Although the latter requires preparation and aptitude of a specialized nature, the chief executive must also be well grounded in the basic operations of the department.

Wage and salary administration

Salaries in public recreational service, as in all governmental services, are established by legislative act and are basically a matter of legal review. Local governmental policies dealing with the salaries of public employees are subject to the normal circumstances of administration. Managers may recommend salary schedules, but they must be fixed by enactment of law. Typically salaries are paid to recreationists having responsibilities that are not routine or that do not have fixed hours. Wages, on the other hand, are normally paid to individuals representing the trades, manual labor, or semiskilled work. Several factors usually influence managerial wage and salary and practices:

1. *Salaries of comparable positions in public service jurisdictions and in private organizations.* Competitive salaries of comparable positions have a marked influence on any public service agency in its efforts to attract and retain competent personnel. Dedication to public service and the advantage of a governmental position (such as security, earned vacations, compensatory pay, leave, medical allowances, or other fringe benefits) are not enough to attract and hold individuals with the necessary talent and preparation for the position. Salaries constitute roughly three-quarters of local governmental operating budgets and are carefully adapted to the services to be performed. Although monetary compensation is not the primary reason for entering public recreational service, so many positions are available to qualified workers that competitive salaries must be maintained if recreational service positions are to be filled effectively.
2. *Salaries of comparable positions in the private sector.* Supply and demand for personnel may boost wages and salaries for certain specialties. Often, companies engaged in the provision of recreational services in terms of popularized experiences, such as golf, shooting, aqua slides, skiing, boating, rafting, or the rental of material and equipment for such activity, may produce a climate of competitive wages and salaries that draws competent personnel away from the public sector.
3. *Legal limits for professional positions in the jurisdiction.* The fixed ceiling for salaries in municipal positions will often affect the amount that can be awarded to anyone employed by the municipality. Whatever the salary

of the chief executive officer of the city is, all of the positions within the city government usually are scaled in a descending series below that sum.

4. *Financial ability of the municipality.* If the city cannot afford adequate salaries, the amount and quality of municipal services necessarily must be restricted. The ability to compensate adequately is largely based on the willingness of the citizenry to be taxed or bonded for the essential governmental services for their health, protection, and welfare; the economic capacity of the community; and the financial aid available from county, state, and federal sources.

5. *Advancement.* The lack of opportunity for continual advancement occasionally forces some personnel to resign in favor of more lucrative or prestigious positions. When a position does not allow the employee to progress beyond a certain rank, incentive or longevity pay may be provided as a device for retaining qualified personnel. Such salary increments may result in a higher rate than would otherwise have been provided.

6. *Fringe benefits for public service.* In fixing local governmental salaries, the value of the additional benefits accruing to the incumbent should always be appraised in addition to the real money compensation. These benefits include retirement and disability programs; prepaid hospital, medical, and group life insurance; liberal vacations with pay; and allowances for room, board, transportation, equipment, and clothing. These benefits also should be taken into account by employees in comparing governmental compensation with that available in quasi-public or private enterprises.

7. *Duties and responsibilities.* The type of position, degree of difficulty, relative responsibility, necessary qualifications, and other factors weigh heavily in salary determination. The entire salary schedule or plan of compensation rests more on an effective analysis of positions and on a sound position classification plan than on evaluation of the individual employee's merit, which tends to be more important when promotion is being considered.

The salary schedule and plan

In the establishment of the salary plan, a financial value must be placed on performance or personal services so that comparable positions have equitable compensation.

When the position classification plan has been implemented, the salary schedule may be initiated, which usually involves: (1) the identification of positions according to classes, comparison of present salaries with salaries of similar positions in the public jurisdiction and in private enterprise, and adjustments required in recruitment to fill vacancies; (2) an examination of the community's ability to satisfy requirements of a compensation plan; and (3) the establishment of minimum and maximum salary limits for each class.

Entrance salaries for special professional positions for which there may be no comparable data must sometimes be determined on the basis of competition for such services, the preparation and experience required, and the need of the system.

Salary range

The maximum and minimum salaries of any given class of positions are known as the *salary range*, consisting of an entrance salary (usually at the minimum point) and two or more annual grade increments toward the maximum rate. The basic objective of a salary range is to provide incentive and remunerative reward for efficient performance. Advancement within classes by increments is usually automatic but subject to a satisfactory performance rating. Acceleration of advancements by increments is sometimes granted as a reward for additional education or superior performance.

The complexities of modern life and professional requirements in recreational service have deepened the need for individuals of extraordinary education, talent, skill, and intelligence. To attract and retain such individuals, salaries should be equal to those of other professionals in the public service. Realistically, salaries of public service personnel are paid in relation to the esteem in which the services are held by the public. Only recently has recreational service had any impact on the general public. During the past decades a noteworthy trend toward higher salaries for recreationists has been observed. This rise, in part, may be due to a cost-of-living increment in an inflationary economy. However, there is good reason to believe that recreational service is entering a new period of recognition and value. The services that recreationists provide to the general public may be making more people aware of their need for the service. In consequence, compensation to recreational service personnel almost tripled within the decade of 1990 to 2000. Although there are executive positions that now call for salaries of more than $100,000 and there are many salaries being paid between $50,000 and $85,000, in many communities compensation for recreationists is still not comparable to salaries in allied fields, that is, education, public health, police, and fire.

In large cities, chief executives of the recreational service system should be remunerated at a level closely approximating that of the superintendent of schools. Subordinate employees of the system should receive salaries at least equal to those of their hierarchical counterparts within the school system. Equitable compensation for recreationist positions should compare favorably with that of school personnel everywhere. In instances in which degree of difficulty and job responsibility are of greater intensity, the salary should reflect the added burden of educational and experiential requirements. There is little question that recreationists' salaries at all levels will rise dramatically over the next few years when the economic recovery strengthens and as public demand for recreational services becomes more intense.

The incidence of higher salaries, although gratifying, is still not sufficient to attract and retain outstanding individuals. The highest salaries paid may be encountered in the giant metropolitan areas in the country. In too many instances, recreationists are grossly underpaid for the position, the degree of difficulty it entails, required educational preparation, and experience that they must have to perform competently, effectively, and efficiently.

Grievances

Imagined and real employee grievances arise in all organizations and ways must be found to express them and to have them satisfied or adjusted. They are usually related to compensation, advancement, work load, physical environment, treatment by supervisors, and sometimes purely personal matters. It is important for employees to know that a mechanism for the expression of grievances exists and that all grievances will be heard with tolerance and understanding and without resentment or unjust recrimination. Imagined grievances often can be dispelled by frank discussion. Real grievances frequently may be adjusted by simple administrative action.

Unless there is a union representing employees, it is usual for contracts to contain a clause dealing with arbitration. However, in most cases negotiation of grievances involves logical employee–employer discussion of a complaint (generally filed by an employee) at successively higher levels in the system. The grievances may be ameliorated at any level, but, if not, the problem may be submitted to the chief executive or to an impartial third party for final mediation. The main purpose of all grievance procedures is to achieve equity for both parties regarding a complaint or problem without deterioration of service or personnel morale. It should be noted that where arbitration is the technique used, the two parties to the disagreement submit their cases to a neutral third party expert whose decision need not be agreeable to both sides, but whose findings must be accepted if the initial agreement called for binding arbitration. Secondarily, the grievance process is a communicative device reaching from the line workers to the highest managerial levels within the system. It is surely the simplest and most direct link between line and staff, between functional employees and top management. The entire grievance procedure provides an ongoing opportunity for morale appraisal by the executive of the staff of the system, indicating where and what types of difficulties are present or potentially present.

Finally, the grievance procedure almost forces some concept of justice to be maintained within the system through performance standards and compensatory practices. There must be uniform application of human resource policies and regulations when similar jobs are concerned. Within the recreational service system, particularly when there is no direct check by an organization representing employees, the administration of justice becomes extremely important. Managers and supervisors must take a professional view of all employee grievances. Being sure to maintain absolute objectivity and mature deliberations in hearings about complaints and problems will produce an atmosphere more conducive to high morale, goodwill, and effective service to the community.

Day-to-day treatment of subordinates requires consistency of action over time. Systematic procedures for determining decisions about the allocation of rewards and discipline are of inestimable value in the administration of equity within any organization.[8] Systematic planning, sympathetic understanding, and consistent application must be part of the established criteria of position and employee value. Scrupulous attention to standards must be maintained, with an equal opportunity for review. The quality of human judgment is an essential aspect in the grievance process. Systematic procedures assist in refining judgment.

Employee organizations and management relations[9]

Until a few years ago, there was general resistance on the part of recreationists to join trade union organizations. This reluctance has now given way to a very real inclination, on the part of subordinate line and staff personnel, to become represented in collective bargaining units. During the past 30 years an upsurge in the number of public recreational service employees seeking affiliation with independent employee associations or labor organizations has been manifested. There are numerous reasons for this noticeable trend and an ostrich-like attitude on the part of managers, who hold that this movement will vanish if they ignore it long enough, can only compound problems. The desire on the part of employees to seek collective bargaining should not be viewed as a direct assault on the executive or as a sign that subordinates are attacking the manager personally. Rather, employee requests for bargaining units must be seen as a logical outcome of both legislation and court decisions regulating public employee relations.[10] A majority of the states now have laws which require management and subordinates to meet, confer, negotiate, and otherwise bargain collectively. It is only natural that recreationists in the public sector should avail themselves of this condition of employment.

Changes in the law and directives issued by the attorney general have led to a revised labor–management environment. Whereas recreationists at all levels formerly identified themselves with management and resisted unionization, for the most part, several significant influences have contributed to increased recreational service personnel union activity in the past ten years. First, are the profound frustrations which program recreationists felt, arising from a relatively authoritarian concept of superior–subordinate relationships pervading the system. This is reflected in the type of department where policy statements are issued from the executive's office as fiat, without any input by those who must execute such policy. Second, there has been a disinclination on the part of local government to be responsive to the demands of departmental employees for salary improvement and other fringe benefits. Finally, there has been the feeling that public recreational services are merely a frill and therefore can be chopped with impunity. The question of job security for competent work performed was either ignored or thought to be unimportant. Little wonder, then, that line recreationists began to turn to those organizations which appeared to be able to offer relief from these circumstances.

Community taxpayers who reside within the city have a right to expect a variety of services, including health, education, and protection, as well as the opportunity for leisure activities provided in a clean and safe environment. All of these city services must be delivered at a price which is within the community's ability to pay without undue stress. In the same way, employees should be able to expect competitive salaries and fringe benefits. Unfortunately, equitability between the expectations of community residents and municipal employees frequently are denied when tax rates zoom or employee demands become too burdensome. The largest cities in the United States are faced with economic shortfalls and are limited financially or have actually approached bankruptcy.

In the public sector, the chief concern of elected officials is re-election, rather than economic self-sufficiency. One result of this political tunnel vision is to make elected officials susceptible to pressure tactics by members of labor organizations. Labor lobbyists continue their influence attempts by making politicians assume positions or promise financial commitments prior to any consideration of the effect that such assurances will have upon the provision of community services. For this reason, professional negotiators who deal in labor–management relations almost always advise elected officials to remain aloof from the collective bargaining procedure. The distance which elected officials maintain permits the necessary disinterest so that they may formulate policy that is effective for the diverse aspects of local governmental performance.

In many instances, public employees seek better wages, working conditions, and hours. Sometimes employees become concerned about the kind of supervision imposed upon them, inappropriate job assignments, and inequitable selection for advancement, poor in-service education, unsafe working situations, unfair disciplinary procedures, and cronyism – to list but a few of the reasons for employees becoming militant. The significance of and corresponding reaction to such practices as they relate to employee satisfaction, stimulation, and output should neither be overlooked nor emphasized too much in determining employer–employee relations. Perhaps the most important objectives of employee associations are the basic items of a fair salary and conditions of work. Additionally, recreationists want to be a part of the decision-making process within the agency. As professionals, they will want to have input into the practices which critically affect them. On the other hand, managers want to control the operation of the agency in all respects, particularly in terms of specified powers and responsibilities which have been delegated to them. Specifically, executives desire unshared authority in the following areas:

1. to recruit, induct, assign, transfer, and promote employees;
2. to take appropriate disciplinary actions against employees for just cause, including: suspension, transfer, admonishment, demotion, or discharge;
3. to devise the procedures and practices for human resource management insofar as numbers, responsibilities, and supervision are concerned for the efficient operation of the agency;
4. to regulate the departmental budget;
5. to take whatever steps are required during crisis situations in order that the proper functioning of the department is maintained.

Collective bargaining

Free collective bargaining is a process whereby organized employee associations and management negotiate the terms and conditions of employment which are then incorporated in a collective bargaining agreement. All of the collective bargaining process is conducted under adversary arrangements; but there are certain common ends towards which both management and labor strive. These shared interests comprise the following:

1. offering and maintaining high-quality services to the citizens of the community based upon financial considerations which will not place such services in a threatened position;
2. promoting superior performance among employees while enhancing efficiency and economy;
3. providing in-service education and maintaining professionalism among employees;
4. maintaining the appropriate supplies, materials, and equipment as well as the places where recreational services are to be carried out so that personnel may perform their duties most effectively;
5. retaining productive personnel through competitive remuneration and conditions of work;
6. establishing and sustaining a labor–management relationship based upon mutual trust and respect;
7. establishing and maintaining a positive and impartial *modus operandi* for the resolution of departmental problems.

Departmental executives should be familiar with the applicable legislation as well as the development of labor–management relations as they have matured in cities of similar size. In negotiating with employee associations they should request assistance from city staff experts, if the community operates its collective bargaining procedure on a departmental basis, or obtain assistance from professional consultants on a fee or contract basis. When the bargaining process is transacted professionally, there is greater likelihood that employee interests will be served while managerial authority will be preserved. Any concessions made will be appropriate to the situation and in areas that are helpful. Professional expertise brought to bear should enable the process to be conducted on a logical, problem-oriented basis rather than through subjective, personality-centered approaches.

Collective bargaining is an evolutionary process and, therefore, it should prevent management from simply meeting demands by offering everything for which it is asked. When this occurs, management is reduced to a rubber stamp because it often has nothing left with which to negotiate. Recreationist executives have become cognizant of this fact. To forestall any poverty of position, some managers are developing plans to more nearly equalize bargaining outcomes. The following statement deals with productivity measures resulting from negotiating with employee organizations:

> Historically, employee organizations have annually made demands on governmental agencies for increases in salaries, fringe benefits, and improved working conditions. Many times the demands have been linked to the reduction of management prerogatives. At this juncture in time, when we are considering how we will be able to deliver effective services to the public in a period of austerity, it is important that we give adequate attention to the development of counter demands which we can present to the employee organizations at the bargaining table. These management demands should focus on recapturing the various management prerogatives which were given away at previous negotiations or as a result of past practice which can help us increase the organization's productivity. Also, it would be valuable at the time of negotiations to present our new program directions and manning patterns which we would like to introduce to increase productivity and to cope with the attrition situation. It would be our objective to gain acceptance of these directions as part of the salary negotiation process.[11]

By developing negotiating positions before any actual bargaining occurs and making plans to present managerial demands, rather than assuming a defensive stance and reacting to employee demands, executives can take a more successful posture. Where negotiating issues are worked out well in advance there is more latitude for the give and take of bargaining, where each side's desires are worked out to the satisfaction of all parties concerned. The entire process of good-faith negotiations should end in a mutually agreed upon contract containing all of the provisions which were discussed and ratified. Neither party to the process can be compelled to agree to any proposition, unless there is binding arbitration. Moreover, neither party must concede its position by virtue of any proposal which is brought up.

The process of collective bargaining proceeds through several stages from an initial point when the employees want to organize or gain representation for future collective bargaining through negotiation, and final contract administration. It is not the intent of this section to summarize the collective bargaining process. However, there are some tactics from which executives can profit.

Avoiding past errors

Learning from past mistakes is indicative of managerial precaution. Only a fool repeats mistakes and these inevitably prove costly for all concerned. By studying the history of previous collective bargaining sessions it is likely that excellent insight into how future negotiations should be conducted will be acquired. In planning negotiations, the following observations appear to be important:

1. How well did the previous negotiating team perform? Unless the agency's negotiators have the authority to reach definite decisions, nothing can really be accomplished. The best settlements are those which leave both parties satisfied.
2. It is important to come to the negotiating table with a well-thought-out position plan, including a logical comprehension as to what expectations the opposing side has for a contract settlement. The worst fault that executives reveal is an embarrassing lack of information as to what the other side will give or expect because of supposed "inside information" which proves to be erroneous.
3. It is always dangerous for management to interfere in local employee association politics. Generally, it is beneficial for management to adopt a policy of avoidance of local union politics completely and prepare for negotiations despite any opposition.
4. The use of misleading or falsified information should be scrupulously avoided. Unless factual data are properly utilized the material will be ineffective to support issues which management wants to discuss. More importantly, future statistical representations will be greeted with skepticism and have little impact on negotiations.
5. The timing of proposals has an important influence upon negotiations. Modified demands presented too early or too late will obviously lose the intended impact. Proper timing is something which develops with accumulated experience.
6. In developing appropriate bargaining units, management should remember that its supervisory personnel need to be closely allied to managerial postures and represent management on a day-to-day basis. If members of the supervisory level are permitted to affiliate with the collective bargaining unit, the administration has lost a significant part of its ability to deal with human resource problems that arise in the

course of daily operations. Far better for supervisors to have their own bargaining unit, if they feel that they too must organize, than to have middle management personnel in association with those whom they normally have to direct. If the administration can successfully maintain its management personnel as a separate bargaining unit, they will have reduced the likelihood of uncontrolled service breakdowns.

7. It is undesirable to present so many demands that they cannot possibly be worked out during the current negotiating session. One of the more useless tactics used by parties to a negotiation is to present too many demands and end up with few, if any, obtained. The adversary will probably discount many of the demands in advance and not seriously appreciate what the opposing party actually wants. It is far better to propose what is really wanted together with a few additional demands abhorrent to the employees' association to be used for trading purposes.

8. Negotiating subjectively or permitting one's emotions to become involved in the oftentimes delicate matters of contract agreements can lead to disappointment and dissatisfaction with the results. When emotions are allowed to hold sway, the several persons who are party to the negotiations may make statements in the heat of the argument which come home to roost later. Every attempt should be made to cool tempers, offer dispassionate debate, and, at the conclusion of negotiations, to smooth out any hurt feelings that may have developed. Everyone will not be absolutely satisfied with the negotiated contract, but if negotiations have been conducted in the objective atmosphere of economic reality, rather than having dwelt upon personality factors or aroused emotional feelings, acceptance of the end product is usually assured.

Experienced professionals realize that at the negotiating sessions the members of the bargaining teams play out scenarios. The sessions permit each person to act out some latent fantasies. With the bargaining table as the stage there is an opportunity to make speeches, curse, debate, and take the limelight. All this is part of the negotiating program. Some employers might object to large employee negotiating committees without realizing that there are both political and substantive reasons involved. A large committee provides the audience to play to; a larger group can more easily disseminate information to the rank-and-file; and, most importantly, a large committee comes under less suspicion from other employees. Bargaining strategy requires patience and recognizes the need for permitting the other party to state their position and reveal whatever knowledge has been acquired about the issues. The climate in which negotiations are conducted should be relatively informal without rigid rules of procedure. However, certain minimum rules can help. It would be both unseemly and disorderly to have everybody shouting at once. Finally, it behooves management to clearly understand what has been determined upon before the signing of any contract. That is another excellent reason for having professional consultants or permanent staff personnel undertake the collective bargaining process. The language of the contract should be clear and the parties to the contract should be absolutely certain that they understand all the ideas which have been formulated. This can be the basis for saving the taxpayers' money in the public sector.

Professional conduct

In recreational service, the conduct of employees on and off the job remains a matter of official concern. Appropriate behavior during and after working hours reflects not only on the employee, but also on the public system that employs him/her. Exemplary conduct is expected of personnel in this field of public service equally as much as in public education. Recreationists, like all public employees with professional interests, affiliate with a variety of organizations for mutual benefit. In recent years, some attempt has been made to establish one master professional society by which the discipline might gain unity and status.

The continuing expansion of the field and the increased demand for qualified, competent, and professional practitioners have given rise to the adoption of certain principles of professional conduct by professional societies or associations of recreationists, to raise the standards of practice and maintain the ethics of professionalism.

11 Financial management for recreational service

All organizations, whether in the public or private sector, must have enough money, secured routinely, to maintain its operation. How funds are obtained, where they are located, controlled, and accounted for constitutes the formidable responsibility of fiscal management.[1]

Financial management comprises three major facets.[2] Fundamental to such management is fiscal policy definition, which deals with the political aspects of setting guidelines for public programs and appropriating money to execute them. Fiscal policy concerns taxation, revenue, and allocation of money. The second component is responsibility, that is, of certifying that the allocation of public money is spent in conformity with legal criteria and in the most efficient manner to give the greatest return to the public. The third aspect relates to the duties and responsibilities of fiscal structure and the budgetary process.

Financial policy

Members of public recreational service boards and/or commissions, where they exist, are responsible for advising on and supervising the expenditure of funds for recreational service, and to advise on and assist in the procurement of funds for recreational service in their jurisdictions. Otherwise, that function belongs to the manager of the department. Fiscal policy is determined by political leaders and is the outcome of adjustment to diverse factors, including the condition of the local economy, the availability of revenues for public programs, the monies expended on current programs, and the demand for additional programs. In relation to such elements is a complex of basically normative powers: the economic orientation of political leaders and their immediate advisers and their concept regarding the function of government, and the vociferous requests of lobbies and the importance attached to these lobbies by legislators, executives, and managers. The following discussion attempts to illustrate how fiscal decisions are reached and the kinds of factors that intrude on financing recreational service systems.

Fiscal administration

Fiscal administration is the management and control of all revenues received by the recreational service system from taxes, fees, grants, private donations, or other sources that are utilized in the operation of the department. The custody of such finances is delegated to specific officers who are responsible to the public for protecting such monies from misuse, embezzlement, and fraudulent misappropriation, and for expending them prudently.

The purposes of fiscal administration are to supply pertinent data about how public funds are acquired, safeguarded, allocated, and used; to determine whether the fiscal system is performing adequately; and to discover ways and means for reducing expenditures while receiving greater returns on facilities, equipment, and programs. Money is the basic tool of management and is a primary resource for agency operations.

In public work a specific finance bureau or department is usually constituted by law and charged directly with the responsibility of compiling and recording the financial transactions of the department and of preparing essential statements interpreting the financial facts. Such bureaus are headed by an official known variously as the auditor, controller, comptroller, or director of finance. Other fiscal officials of the city include the treasurer, who invests, disburses, and safeguards the public funds; the tax collector, who collects all taxes levied; and the assessor, who places a value on all taxable property.

The several line departments of the city perform certain accounting and auditing duties to provide original information to the finance director and to avail themselves of more detailed and accessible records than those kept by the controller. The form of such records may be prescribed by the controller and the records are subject to verification. All original accounts, which require detailed verification, are inspected periodically and audited. The accounts of the auditor and, if necessary, of the several departments are subject to further validation, sometimes by state auditors or by private auditing firms engaged by the governing body of the city on contract.

Fiscal management within the recreational service system is assigned to the chief executive of the department, but responsibility is shared with other employees, including the assistant executive, accountants, auditors, clerks, and employees at facilities where fees are collected and transmitted. All are responsible to the chief executive of the system who in turn is responsible to the city manager, the mayor, or other governing body, and ultimately to the public.

Financing operations

The development and operation of the municipal recreational service system may be financed from any funds accruing to a general fund or from an earmarked fund supported by a special tax levied on property and established by ordinances. After consideration of requests and recommendations from department executives and the chief executive officer, the governing body adopts an ordinance fixing the budget for the ensuing fiscal year. The expenditures budget may not exceed the revenue budget, which is an estimate of the revenue from all sources classified according to the several sources. The proposed budget is published in legally approved newspapers for a stated number of days. Prior to final action the citizens and taxpayers have an opportunity to be heard. The foregoing practice is customary but there are minor deviations. Once a budget is adopted, the administrative officers are empowered to expend the funds accordingly throughout the year.

Revenue to support municipal government is obtained from many sources. The general property tax yields by far the greatest amount. Revenue is also collected from commercial, industrial, and corporate enterprises. Federal, state, and county governments contribute grants for specific purposes: urban renewal, public health, homeland security, purchase of open space, and road building. Taxes on gasoline, cigarettes, sales, licenses, franchises, and fines, forfeits, fees, and donations are also revenue sources. Some cities assess income and payroll taxes.

Financing recreational services

The financial ability of the city to sustain a recreational service system from ordinary tax and other sources depends on the share of the tax burden carried by commercial, industrial, and other corporate enterprises compared to the burden carried by individual property owners and residents. The ratio of population to assessed valuation of property subject to local taxes is a fair measure of the financial capacity of the city. This ratio varies from a median on either side of approximately $1000 per unit of population.

The dependence of city government on the general property tax for general revenue (including recreational services) is perhaps an important reason why community recreational service has not been funded better. Functions of the municipal government have greatly increased in number and the cost of traditional functions has also increased. This increase in cost has been charged against the general property tax. Thus the claims of the public recreational service must be evaluated in comparison to the claims of the numerous other municipal functions, and, because it is a relatively new function, the recreational service department is somewhat at a disadvantage. The longer-established functions are cared for first and then small appropriations are doled out to the newer departments and bureaus. Recreational service has just begun to achieve sufficient recognition to command insistent support. Many other jurisdictions are finding – to their alarm and dismay – that public recreational services are coming to be considered as an essential requirement, especially among inner-city residents and concerned teenage and adult populations in small towns and cities.

Recreational service departments do endeavor to procure a fair share of the budgeted revenue of their city for their support. The amount is determined, however, not by any set formula as to what may constitute a fair share, but rather by a careful estimate of the needs of the city in respect to the many functions it must perform. Recreational services do well if they are allotted about 12 percent of the general fund revenue.

Taxes

General property tax. The general property tax is levied on real and personal property. Each year valuation is placed on all such property by the municipal assessor. The total assessed valuation of all taxable property is divided into the amount of required revenue in order to determine the exact tax rate. The rate is expressed in mills per dollar of assessed value or, for convenience, in cents per hundred dollars of assessed value. Thus a tax of one mill per one dollar is equivalent to a tax of 10 cents per 100 dollars.

The determination of true or cash value is difficult because there is no scientific manner of computing it. Values fluctuate, and the value of property is largely a matter of judgment. Theoretically, a true or cash value is considered by assessors to be the price the property would bring in a sale by a solvent debtor to satisfy a debt. Except by actually selling the property, there is no exact way of confirming this estimate. Comparisons of assessed valuation of taxable property in different cities and of the tax rates derived from them are of little significance unless the variable bases of valuation are taken into consideration. These vary from 20 percent to 100 percent of true or cash value. In many states, the basis is determined by state law.

The maximum tax rate is usually fixed by the governing body of the city. Cities with charters may set their own maximum tax rate which, however, does not apply to any rate that must be fixed for payment of interest on municipal bonds.

Sixty-five years ago property taxes produced over 90 percent of the general fund revenue raised by cities for municipal functions and for support of the public schools; present property taxes scarcely produce more than 25 percent.

Capital improvements by bond issues. Although there have been some improvements within the last 35 years, most cities are far behind modern standards in acquiring and improving recreational spaces, places, facilities, and structures. Capital improvements (purchase of land, construction of buildings and other structures, and general infrastructure improvements) can be financed by the issuance of municipal bonds for general purposes or particular projects. Capital improvements for public recreational services are only meagerly financed from annual municipal operating funds. Cities have frequently resorted to borrowing by issuance of bonds with 20, 30, and 40 years' maturity.

With few exceptions, bond issues must be submitted to the electors at a general or special election and usually require approval by a two-thirds majority of the electorate. Since such bonds are a lien upon property, the two-thirds majority has become most difficult to achieve. The legality of the two-thirds rule has been challenged in various suits and the basis of the "one man, one vote" decision of the United States Supreme Court. Blocking a needed public improvement by a decision of one-third or more of the electorate is held to be a denial of a constitutional right.

Once approved, the retirement of the bonds and the interest paid on them are a charge against the assessable real property of the taxpayers, although the tax rate is computed and listed separately on the individual tax bill. State laws regulate the amount of bonds that any city may issue for general governmental purposes, including recreational service, and this limit is typically about 3 percent of the assessed valuation of all taxable property. This limit does not apply to bonds for non-governmental purposes (as for self-liquidating public utility enterprises, which carry a considerably higher limit). The reasonable limits of bonding capacity, independent of statutory limitations, are also influenced by the rating computed by large bond-buying houses. If a city overextends itself, it may be difficult to sell the bonds and the city will have to pay a premium or offer prohibitive rates of interest.

Sinking fund bonds and serial bonds. Sinking fund bonds and serial bonds are classified by the method of payment. Sinking fund bonds require complete payment with accrued interest at maturity. During the life of the bond, the municipality makes payments into what is called a *sinking fund.* These funds are then invested and the monies accruing from them are finally used to amortize the bond. This method has the advantage of flexibility. However, a major disadvantage is the difficulty of administration owing to the required computation of actuarial rates and the accounting and investment of city funds. On the other hand, serial bonds are amortized in annual installments, which eliminate the complexity of sinking fund operations and saves administrative charges.

General obligation bonds and revenue bonds. General obligation bonds are issued in amounts not in excess of constitutional or statutory restrictions. If city revenue proves insufficient, taxes may be increased to the statutory limit in order to meet payments on the interest and principal. General obligation bonds are those having the faith and credit of the community as support. Interest and risk are lessened with this type of bond.

A revenue bond, on the other hand, may be defined as an obligation of a revenue-producing activity or property, payable completely from revenues derived from that activity or property. When cities have approached the legal limit of their bonding capacity or when the enterprise is clearly profitable, the utilization of revenue bonds may be indicated. Although use of revenue bonds has not been a general practice of municipalities for the development of recreational structures and facilities, some communities have resorted to this type of bonding for marinas, auditoriums, stadiums, swimming facilities, or golf links.

Many people object to financing municipal improvements by borrowing and issuance of bonds. The cost of such improvements is increased because of interest payments and the burden of repayment falls on future generations. These objections are less applicable to bonds for recreational places and improvements because new values are created, and the investment, especially in the land, is of permanent worth. The benefits continue to be enjoyed long after the bond issue has been paid off, and, since future generations will enjoy the benefits, they may justifiably be called on to pay a portion of the cost. Perhaps the most distinct advantage of the bond plan is that it is the only plan under which a large comprehensive program of improvements and acquisitions can be undertaken and accomplished in a few years.

Pay-as-you-go plan. Some cities prefer the "pay-as-you-go" method of financing improvements, scheduling a series of desired improvements in several fields over a period of years according to a priority estimate of comparative need. In using this method the city may draw on its general funds or levy a special tax above the statutory limit for general purposes. Some states authorize special levies, the proceeds of which are then deposited in a special fund for the particular purpose.

The advantages of the pay-as-you-go method, under which additions and improvements are made yearly out of current funds, are obvious. Such a plan requires payments to be made out of the annual tax levy or through the utilization of a reserve fund which is built up through annual accumulations to meet anticipated expenditures. In the long run, this plan is less expensive than bonding, since it eliminates the need for an expensive debt service. All cities endeavor to employ this method to some extent, but in the area of recreational service it has generally been used only for comparatively inexpensive improvements.

In most instances, the city cannot afford to finance large capital construction on the basis of current revenue. If the pay-as-you-go method were the only means for providing improvements and acquisitions, the major portion of such needed development and construction never would be accomplished.

Special assessments. The special assessment plan for financing the acquisition and improvement of lands for recreational purposes has been used in several cities. The cost of the project is assessed against the property in the district that presumably will benefit from the project. The assessment may be paid in cash or, if it exceeds a specific sum ($25, $50, or $100), it may be permitted to go to bond; then its principal and interest would be paid in annual installments over a given period (usually 10 years). In principle, this is the same method as that used for many years to finance the opening, widening and paving of streets that are purely for local benefit.

The special assessment plan seems eminently fair at first glance because those who desire and are willing to pay for the improvements and services may have them. If the plan is generally applied, however, the less well-to-do neighborhoods suffer and this is not compatible with the principles of democratic government. If community recreational service is a general governmental function, it must be provided for all and financed by the same means that other governmental functions are financed.

Other objections to the plan arise out of the difficulty of administering it. The determination of the district including only those properties that will benefit by the improvement is almost impossible to assess and must, in the last analysis, be arbitrary. Grading of assessments according to proximity, those residing close to the improvements paying more and those residing farther away paying less, present another difficulty. Moreover, the plan is costly to administer, particularly in the computation and collection of each assessment. For comparatively inexpensive local recreational improvement involving many small assessments, the total cost of the project is often exorbitant.

Other financial resources

Private monies channeled into the public treasury and earmarked for public recreational service purposes are a considerable resource for the support of these services at the municipal level. The resources are of three kinds: first, fees and charges paid by individuals as users of public facilities and services; second, gifts of funds or materials to support stated programs and events; and, third, grants or bequests of real or personal property, improved and unimproved. Leaseback, rents, and concessions also bring money into the department.

Fees or charges. It is common practice among public recreational service departments to charge individual and group fees for certain services, admittance to some public recreational places, use of areas and facilities, instruction, and administration of athletic competitions. The practice of charging fees arose primarily from a desire to augment the meager appropriations obtained from tax sources. The once frequently made objection that fees constituted double taxation has now been fully dissipated.

Not all recreational services should be self-supporting and public recreational service should never enter into profit-making schemes. If the service can be rendered commercially it is better left to private enterprise.

Policies governing fees. In general, authorities are agreed that recreational services should be rendered free provided sufficient funds can be obtained from other sources to make such a policy practicable. The question of policy, therefore, becomes one of economics.

If it is necessary to levy fees for recreational and related services, the following rules are suggested. Fees should be charged:

1. when the particular service is relatively costly to render and few persons participate at one time, although the demand is great;
2. when the particular service is demanded by a comparatively few persons and the cost of providing the facility is relatively high;
3. when services are offered in competition with private business. Many believe that such services should not be rendered at all; however, if offered for some special reason, they should be offered at a fee. Dancing instruction is an example;
4. when the services are primarily for adults, since adults are better able to pay for special services than are children;
5. when participation in the activity is limited to an exclusive group, a charge for the utilization of a public facility is justified for the special privilege accorded to closed groups;
6. when the service is enjoyed by a considerable number of non-residents. The justification for levying fees is based upon self-protection; either by making the visitor pay a share of the cost or by reserving the service to local people;
7. when collection is practical. Frequently a fee seems justifiable, but the cost of collection is greater than the revenue that would be collected, or the revenue does not exceed the costs sufficiently to make a system of levies practicable.
8. when levying fees does not create poor public relations. Any fee tends to arouse public opposition, especially when it is established after service has been rendered free. Probable revenue should be weighed against the public ill-will which might be created.
9. when the fee deprives persons of limited means from the benefits of necessary community recreational service it should not be established. *Activities that are universal in appeal and that serve a universal need should be free.*

Fees for services or privileges. The charging of fees for particular services or privileges has been justified on various grounds. Special services are enjoyed by comparatively few persons, thus those enjoying them should pay directly so that the costs of the services are not a burden on all the taxpayers. Without fees, some costly services could not be offered. Fees permit higher-quality services than would be available otherwise. Some recreationists believe the practice of charging fees favorably affects the behavior of persons taking advantage of the service. However, it may be that those who can afford a fee may be more amenable to control.

Fees for use of recreational areas and facilities. Fees are sometimes collected for the use of areas and facilities:

1. Basketball, football, soccer, hockey courts, tracks, tennis courts, and basketball courts. Usually the use of these facilities is free; occasionally, when the facilities are maintained in a manner desired by the most

skilled teams, a flat fee is levied. The fee is collected from the group to which a permit is issued for a given period.

2. Archery, golf driving, skeet, rifle and pistol ranges; handball, horseshoes, badminton, and volleyball courts. These facilities are used by individuals rather than by teams, consequently the problem of collecting fees is complicated. Usually the fees are on an hourly basis, per unit of equipment, or imposed as an entrance levy.
3. Golf courses. With few exceptions a fee is levied. The fee is collected from the individual when he/she reports for play or a season ticket is sold. When no fee is charged, the course is usually inadequate.
4. Bowling greens. Sometimes a fee is levied; usually a membership fee is imposed for a month or a year; depending upon use.
5. Ice-skating, skiing, tobogganing. The use of areas for winter sports is usually free, but equipment required by the individual often must be rented.
6. Bathing beaches. The use of public bathing beaches is usually free. A few cities with small beaches and great demand levy admission fees.
7. Swimming pools. About as many cities levy admission fees for the use of swimming pools as offer the service free. When a fee is high, it usually includes the use of locker, towel, and soap.

Fees for instruction. Fees are also levied for individual or group instruction in specific activities, especially when the undivided attention of the instructor is required:

1. individual golf lessons
2. individual and group swimming lessons
3. individual and group scuba diving lessons
4. individual and class tennis lessons
5. sailing lessons
6. individual and class instruction in arts and crafts
7. dramatics classes
8. class lessons in dancing, instrumental music, twirling, gymnastics, horseback riding, and the like.

Fees for administration of athletic competitions. There is increasing tendency to levy fees for the administration of adult athletic competitions. Fees are charged to cover drawing up and publishing schedules; services of umpires, referees, and linemen; trophies; and incidental expenses. A forfeit fee to guarantee appearance of teams and a registration fee for individual athletes are also frequently charged. These fees are often collected and dispersed by extra-official agencies, such as municipal athletic associations, which operate on public facilities and are subject to varying degrees of control by the public recreational service departments. However, many departments now handle all details of administration of athletic league competition. This is most desirable when dealing with funds involved in athletics and in promotion of other activities.

Amounts of fees or charges. Fees should not be so high that persons with limited financial resources will be unable to avail themselves of the services. Public recreational service may be the last recourse that many inner-city dwellers have for participation in worthwhile recreational experiences, and, if such services are closed to them because of exorbitant fees, the entire public system should be called into question. To permit economic discrimination to interfere with the provision of recreational service undermines the essential principle that public recreational service must meet the needs of all the people regardless of their social or economic level.

The amount of fees for recreational services must be determined by local conditions:

1. The fee may be determined on the basis of the actual cost of rendering the service, including interest on and amortization of the investment.
2. The fee may be computed on the basis of direct operating expenditures, disregarding capital items.
3. The fee may be determined at the rate that would represent the costs of rendering the service over the normal cost of other services taken together.
4. The fee may be computed at the rate that will result in efficient use of a given area or improvement.

Gifts and other benefactions. Money and real property are sometimes received from a philanthropic agency, private organization, individual, or group for which the contributor expects no repayment or special service. Donations and bequests are not infrequent and often assist in expanding public recreational services. Outright gifts of cash or materials to public agencies are small in comparison to total revenue from fees. Such aid is frequently contributed for a special and limited program that appeals to the donor. Sometimes the contribution pays for prizes, or non-returnable costumes for which public funds may not be expended. It should be added that when the gifts for such "private" purposes are received, they should be accepted by non-official agents, for once deposited in the public treasury they may not be permitted to be expended for their intended purpose.

Grants or bequests of real and personal property. Park and recreational service systems often receive valuable properties from private donors, dedicated in perpetuity, usually by terms of the grant or will. It is a curious fact that no other function of cities is similarly benefited, not even the public school system. Advantage should be taken of this disposition of citizens to convey to the city a gift of property for park and recreational purposes, and perhaps systematic procedures should be employed to encourage this practice, but how to do it is difficult to state.

Concessions. Many recreational service departments and park agencies have adopted the practice of granting concessions to private operators to offer services and to sell commodities to patrons of parks and recreational centers. The most common service concessions are parking automobiles; renting boats, horses, and various kinds of equipment; conducting boating excursions; operating amusement devices; commodity concessions or refreshment stands, vending privileges on grounds and in grandstands, and stores for sale and repair of sport equipment.

When the problem of providing certain services and commodities first begins the question inevitably raised is whether or not the municipality should enter into merchandising in competition with private businesses. The current view is that public businesses should not be inaugurated unless private business is unable to render the required services. The justification for the public business is not primarily to make a profit but to render a needed service and this point should always be kept foremost. If the needed service cannot be conveniently supplied by private business on its own premises adjacent to or outside the public area, then the services must be rendered directly by the municipal agency or through the granting of a concession.

The concession plan is open to serious objections: (1) It permits making private profit from public investment. (2) It encourages use of political influence to gain private advantage. (3) Concessionaires apply commercial standards to their operations and may not be inclined to uphold the high standards of public recreational service, particularly when these conflict with profit-making. Accordingly, public park and recreational service authorities have recently assumed more direct responsibility for this type of business. Full-time specialists may be employed by the department, not for their recreational service skills or knowledge, but for their merchandising effectiveness. In this way the department may set the standards for safety, equity, quality, and service while making the patron's experience more enjoyable.

Accounting and auditing

Accounting concerns the computation and use of financial data.[3] It has a real and specific function, broadly stated, control over finances and revenue. Control over personnel is a consequence of employees' responsibility for handling finances. Accounting involves the examination of operating effects and the resultant financial condition, as well as budgeting. The functions of accounting may be detailed as:

1. Capital:

   a. Determination

   (1) of the worth of each asset
   (2) of the amount of all liabilities
   (3) of net worth.

   b. Protection

   (1) of all capital to prevent monetary corruption through the mishandling of funds, misappropriation, or improper use of funds.
   (2) through the utilization of appropriate accounting methods to determine depreciation and required repairs.

   c. Examination of financial situations as a reflection of changing conditions.
   d. Management of the financial condition in compliance with the budget.

2. Revenue:

   a. Calculation

   (1) of each revenue item by specified periods
   (2) of each expenditure or loss by specified periods
   (3) of profits and loss
   (4) of revenue from segregated capital items in the statements and financial records.

   b. Protection

   (1) of revenue to ensure the receipt and correct accounting of each item
   (2) against incurring or paying of improper items.

   c. Examination of the consequences of departmental operations during stated periods and the comparison of results between various periods of time.
   d. Management of revenue and expenditure items and operating effects in compliance with the budget.

   The functions of accounting are executed through a system of accounts, records, procedures, and statements.[4] The accounts are the means by which necessary data are collected for the preparation of accounting statements which are the formal summaries used for administering the enterprise. Statements are the bases of policy formulation and substantive managerial action. Thus, the functions of accounting are enacted by means of recording transactions, verification of records by audit, operation of internal control methods, preparation of fiscal and operating statements, examination of statements, and budgeting of operations and financial condition.

   Governmental accounting is based on the same concepts and practices as is private or commercial accounting. The orientation, however, is quite different because of the problems that governmental agencies encounter. A governmental agency is established for the benefit of the citizens, and sources of funds are vastly different between public and private enterprises. The benefits of citizens are received at cost. A governmental unit, through legislative action, installs funds and appropriations and requires strict accountability of its personnel.

Accurate and complete accounting records and auditing procedures in governmental administration are necessary for a number of reasons, chiefly the pervasive requirements of the law:

> There is no phase of financial activity which, in some manner or other, is not controlled and directed by the law. The law determines the manner in which money received is to be allocated to specific funds for expenditure, the law dictates, through formally adopted budgets, the purposes for which money may be spent. The routine requirements for controlling money received and its deposit (are) many times formally stated in the law. The duties and responsibilities of administrative officials are stated in the law. The submission of claims by vendors for payment in the manner of approval by governmental officials is another phase of financial activity which is subject to legal requirements. The foregoing are only a few of the ways in which legal mandates directly or indirectly influence the fiscal operations of local government units.[5]

Other reasons for thorough systems of accounting and auditing are to make a permanent record of financial transactions; to guarantee that public funds have been received and disbursed according to proper legal authorization and restrictions; to fix responsibility definitely on authorized individuals and bodies; and to facilitate the transaction of public businesses generally.

Accounting also indicates the financial condition of the system and its operating services during a specific fiscal period as well as the day-to-day position of the department with regard to the receipt of various revenues, and the kind and amount of services engendered as a result of the appropriation of funds.

Accounting records

Financial statements contain information taken directly from the accounting records which consequently should be designed in such form as to enable this to be done without additional computations. In other words, the classification of accounts, the terminology used in the accounts, and other details should conform to the requirements of the statements. A distinction should be made between memorandum records, which any employee or executive might find expedient in the conduct of his/her work, and official records. The former are mere aids to management. Official records register the official transactions of the city and must be of standard form and accurate. A falsification of them may constitute a crime. All entries are part of the official records which become instruments for internal control.

Cost accounting

Cost accounting is the analysis of costs for services produced. Therefore it may be defined as a system of accounting that attempts to evaluate the benefits of services received by the public in terms of the cost of measurable units. Cost accounting is used as a basis for determining fees to be charged for services. It facilitates the evaluation of the efficacy of departmental activities and actually promotes it. Cost accounting is utilized in the preparation of budgets of those departmental services that can be estimated in terms of measurable units. Accurate cost accounting is valuable in determining the feasibility of constructing facilities with the agency's own labor force or through contractual means.

Analysis of unit cost data is of special interest in observing a proper balance between different phases of a department activity. Such data may reveal that too little is being expended for supplies in proportion to the expenditure for supervision; or that a highly expensive activity is being maintained in one quarter to the detriment of an inexpensive yet extremely desirable service elsewhere.

The customary accounts compiled by a central financial office cannot supply the essential information required for a thorough system of cost accounting. It is necessary to install systems of field reporting that will show personnel services, supervision, materials, supplies, equipment, and the overheads which are applicable to separate jobs. Such field records usually cannot be handled easily by the general accounting and auditing department of the city, but they can profitably be assembled in each department or bureau concerned.

For routine, continuous operations, cost checks can be made from time to time by sampling. The cost of separate items of expense in operation may be computed and compared with the cost of rendering such a service at similar recreational centers.

Auditing

Auditing is an official examination and verification of accounts to determine whether or not an agency has spent or is spending appropriated funds in accordance with the budget.[6] It has a deterrent effect upon misuse, but it reveals evidence only after an act has been committed. Auditing relates to the collection and disbursement of money, the certification of its deposit, the payment of funds for contracts, and the receipt of the goods and services for which the money was used.[7] An internal audit is made systematically by designated employees of the department or city; an external audit is usually made by an outside agency, such as a state auditing bureau or a private firm of auditors.

The accuracy of an internal audit is assured by the controllable financial stationery and by the assignment of auditing duties to persons other than those charged directly with the duty of making invoices, or charges, or collecting money. An internal audit also includes an inventory of all supplies in the central storeroom and a check of the supplies received on purchase and of withdrawals by requisition.

A new technology has been developed that includes user-friendly audit tools and work paper solutions. Computer assisted audit techniques (CAATS) are used to analyze data stored in large systems. Other useful tools are those which include question and ad hoc report writing systems, spreadsheet packages, and application developmental tools. Additionally, work paper software converts the usual paper-based audit process into a more efficient, automated procedure.

Control

Control is also called *concurrent auditing*. It is an appraisal procedure that takes place prior to the expenditure of public funds or during the process of spending money.[8] Control acts as an administrative check since it not only inquires into the correctness of expenditure, but also into whether the policy guiding the expenditure is wise.

In public work, a pre-audit of disbursements and receipts and a post-audit of all transactions are necessary. The pre-audit of disbursements checks original documents, such as invoices, receipts of deliveries of commodities, payrolls, and purchase orders, to ensure that each expenditure is made by proper authority and in accordance with law. The pre-audit of income checks duplicate receipts and other evidence of the collection of funds to determine the proper amounts to be deposited in the treasury.

Control has the distinct advantage over the post-audit in that it greatly assists in the minimization of possible invalid expenditures for purposes not consistent with the legal instrument dictating the allocation of public funds. In other words, it helps to alleviate the problem of unauthorized shifting of appropriations.

12 Budget management

The technical intricacies of budgeting almost never receive the attention of the mass media even when public attention is focused upon national, state, or local presentations of the executive budget to the respective legislatures. Usually, public interest is directed toward several controversial items and those projects which represent radical or significant departures from typical government policy. The media and public may be concerned with why more funding is recommended for some programs and others are curtailed, but they seldom inquire as to how such decisions are made and the kinds of information on which budget formulations and governmental decisions are based. Consequently, there appear to be few public matters that are more untranslatable for the ordinary citizen than the methods used for determining program expenditures. Nevertheless, the policies and programs of every agency are very much an outcome of the procedures utilized for collecting and analyzing the spending requests made by managers and their subordinates at every level.

The fact that a great deal of the budget-making process is conducted in a give-and-take atmosphere of trade-offs and desired policy implementation as opposed to or in accord with political decisions cannot diminish the importance of the process.[1] The business of budgeting is inextricably tied to complex accounting and administrative techniques which are vital for professionals to understand.

As the public sector has developed in size and scope, the public has also grown increasingly concerned about the sufficiency, effectiveness, and efficiency of the methods employed for determining public expenditures.[2] In the past 50 years, broadly based attempts have been made to improve the budgetary process used within the public sector. In the 1950s the concept of performance budgeting was put forward. During the 1960s the concept of Planning Programming Budgeting System (PPBS) was developed. The objective of performance budgeting was to inform budget makers more completely concerning the work and services of a given agency. PPBS has a considerably broader purpose – the utilization of the budget process for analyzing the goals and predictable results of public programs, and for assessing the degree to which programs actually achieve the objectives they are designed to satisfy.

Performance budgeting measures whether or not management is delivering expected financial performances; it also measures whether income from all sources and expenditures incurred are in accordance with intentions informing budget development; it also assesses whether management is really delivering expected administrative performance.[3]

Budgetary uses

The budget has as many uses as there are users. It is a vital factor of the economic, political, and managerial machinery of every modern government. This is also true in the private sector.[4] Budgeting practice has been endowed with a variety of administrative applications directly related to the control of agency spending, the management of public activities, and the direction of agency objectives. Every budget improvement transforms the uses to which the budget is put, and it is these applications that are most pertinent to the achievement or failure of the innovation, the method of implementation, and the attitudes of those concerned with the daily function of budgeting.

It demands compliance to the allocations imposed by centralized authorities. The performance budget was developed for efficient managerial activities. Management concerns the use of budgetary authority to gain economical and effective utilization of human and other resources necessary for the conduct of the agency. Performance budgeting focuses on agency production; that is, what is being performed, for what price, and a comparison between actual performance and budgeted objectives. In PPBS, the budget process is looked upon as an instrument of policy and program planning. Planning deals with the methods by which public objectives are determined as well as the appraisal of alternative programs. In order to make maximum use of the budget for planning purposes, central authorities require information concerning the objectives and effectiveness of programs. Additionally, information concerning multiyear expenditures and of the connection between spending and public benefits must also be known. The planning orientation emphasizes the pre-preparation of the budget or the analysis of policy prior to the submission of budget estimates.[5]

The budget, in a very real sense, focuses attention on intelligent policy decisions as well as effective management.[6] The budgetary process is closely identified with every phase of planning, from the original concept and formulation of objectives and goals to the selection of priorities for immediate practice. It is concerned with the operation of current enterprise; without it the consequences of operations cannot be determined. It sets forth the manner in which monetary resources are allocated among competing requirements and how effectively such monies are utilized. In significant ways the budget of local government, particularly that of the recreational service department is the fundamental instrument for identifying the major purposes of the system and achieving public policy.

The budget form

Control[7]

The recreational service department budget is a managerial tool for fiscal policy and financial administration. The budget reflects and shapes the system's economic capacity to perform and maintain those services deemed essential for its existence in the community. The departmental activity described in the budget will mirror the estimated recreational requirements of the community and the projected action by the system responsible for meeting its needs. Budgetary control is concerned with the functions of collecting, analyzing, and categorizing data; recording such data in a prescribed manner; and presenting them to the governing body for approval in compliance with relevant policies.

The budget format is such that it is intelligible to those who read it. To facilitate understanding of the needs which its estimates attempt to satisfy, the budget is divided into specific parts. It should contain the following subdivisions and headings:

1. A general statement giving the major financial aims which the department executive hopes to achieve during the approaching fiscal year. This statement is made in terms of recreational service needs throughout the community and points out particular projects which are vital to the provision of such service. This statement may indicate the number of new facilities to be developed and constructed, employment of additional personnel, purchase of new equipment, specific programs to be initiated, and the general aims of the system.
2. A schedule of estimated revenues from various sources available to the operating department. This may include fees, charges, rentals, leases, concessions, grants-in-aid expected, probable donations, or retail sales which the department collects during its operational year.
3. A detailed itemization of expenditures in terms of functions and objects, or by performance or program.
4. A balanced statement for each separate fund which the recreational service department maintains and administers.

The recreational service system budget cannot perform its proper functions unless it is based upon a well-formulated plan of departmental activity. The budget is but an instrument designed to effectuate a plan of service. Thus, the plan of service is a carefully worked out program for providing the public with the service that it requires within the limitations defined by available and anticipated revenue.

The financial plan

The budget, as a fiscal plan, has three elements which must be present. It must strike a balance between revenue and receipts, be inclusive of all the financial requirements of the system, and incorporate annual requests for appropriations. In theory, a budget should correctly reflect and match anticipated revenue and expected expenditures. In practice, such a precise balance may be obtained by recreational service departments only when contingencies impinging upon modern government can be offset either by accurate forecasts or the luxury of taking in a larger amount of income than was anticipated. In some instances, the department may actually show an estimated surplus of income. Practically speaking, however, most departments tend to count upon contingency funds, by which they plan to offset required emergency expenditures which were not foreseen. Unlike a profit-making organization or business within the private sector of society, it is not the aim of public recreational service systems to become profit-making enterprises for the municipality. The service performed by the system is as necessary to the health and well-being of the community as are other public services. It is not generally observed that municipal functions, such as fire and police protection, public health, public works, or homeland security, forecast anticipated revenues to balance expenditures. Normally, the expenditures of departments are equal to the anticipated amount of revenue taken in by taxes, fines, licenses, and/or forfeitures of various kinds. It has only been within the past 25 years that covetous eyes have viewed the public recreational service department as a municipal profit-making enterprise and have thus demanded that the system pay its own way. That this is an error of philosophy cannot be denied. As a political expedient it is surely a devastating piece of business because the essential reasons for the existence of the public recreational system will become subordinated to the profit motive. Eventually, the taxpaying public will begin to question the reasons why additional payments, after taxes, must be made to enjoy the services for which they are already paying through those same taxes. Nevertheless, there are legitimate sources of revenue which the public recreational service department may utilize. To the extent that these are readily forecastable, a balanced budget may be generated.

Inclusiveness indicates that the budget comprehends all revenue and all expenditures of the municipality, and, hence, the department. It signifies that the budget incorporates all the financial requirements of the local government and its several departments. It is a definite statement that means that all monetary requirements are at their appropriate relation to each other, so that a budgetary balance may be struck. Except for those public recreational service departments which administer ear-marked or special funds separate from the common or general fund of the municipality; most departments pay their expenses from a general fund through a system of checks, vouchers, and receipts. In this way all money received by the municipality is paid into a single fund and all expenditures are disbursed from this fund. In order for the financial plan to be practical and comprehensive, every item of revenue and expense is listed. This makes the entire monetary process of local government more convenient and controllable.

The concept of regular voting of the budget safeguards the public purse because it requires that monetary disbursement for a given year must be met out of income for the year, and revenue must not be left to accrue from year to year. This really means that revenue and expenditure should be equal in every year.

Formulation of the budget[8]

The initiation of the budget involves the preparation and collation of estimates, revenue and expenditure, the review and revision of such estimates, and the development of the financial plan. The work of gathering the budget estimates and compiling the data required for the preparation of the budget necessitates a staff whose size is directly associated with the size of the government. This staff is considered when there are permanent municipal employees, as well as political figures, who are directly responsible for the actual performance of the financial system of the government.

The information necessary in the development of a financial plan is as varied and extensive as the functions and responsibilities of the municipality.[9] It involves current jurisdictional policy; forms of taxation and other sources of revenue; the discharge of existing financial obligations or the assumption of new financial obligations. It touches every phase of community life insofar as such aspects may have some connection with the income and outgoings of community economics. The information thus generated comprises quite specifically the immediate fiscal needs of the local government, sources of all revenue, expenditures due to payments and purchases, and all cost data indicating functional performance and probable trends. From the facts and supportive documentation the budget process is systematically worked out and financial plans for individual departments are finally expressed as a budget for the municipality.

Budgets must be devised and considered several months in advance of the fiscal year to which they apply because of the involved procedure which is usually prescribed and also because the final budget estimate is the basis for determining the revenue-raising plan and the tax rate for the year. The tax rate must be fixed before the tax bills may be computed. A time schedule is stated for submission of department estimates to the budgetary authority of the municipality, for transmittal of the recommended budget to the chief governing body, and for its adoption by that body. This may be the body politic as in the case of town meeting communities, a duly elected finance board or commission, mayor–council form or other extant corporate bodies that have authority to adopt the financial plan. The adoption of the budget is by local ordinance, which requires time for publication, hearings, and debate. If the city operates on a fiscal year commencing July 1, it is not uncommon for preliminary department estimates to be submitted as early as January. These estimates, after careful study, tabulation, and comparison, may be found to be in excess of the estimated available revenue and are referred back to department heads for revision. In this process there is a good deal of give and take. Compromise is not unknown. Further revision may also be necessary when all budgets have been submitted by the budget-making authority to the chief governing body. These revisions may be influenced by public opinion, departmental propaganda, the mass media, or other vociferous groups as they manifest interest during the period of consideration.

The preparation of the budget theoretically proceeds in the following order:

1. *January to March.* The process of budgeting is initiated in order that preliminary estimates may be culled to provide the basis upon which the departmental program requirements will be transformed into budgetary figures. During this time the finance officer makes preliminary estimates of the coming year. If the size of the department does not warrant an accountant, the chief executive, his/her assistant, or some other designated employee performs this assignment. Although such estimates leave a wide margin for error, the prior commitments or obligations contracted by the department provide a fairly reliable platform on which to build. After such estimates are gathered the accountant for the department confers with the line and staff executives and discusses preliminary figures.

2. *March to April.* The accountant confers with the chief executive officer of the department after preliminary construction of the departmental estimates has been made. At this time the tentative ceiling for the system's expenditures is conceived as relayed to the chief executive by higher authority. The ceiling figure is transmitted to the line and staff managers as the basis for preparing final estimates.

3. *April to May.* During this period line and staff managers adapt their estimates to the chief executive's ceiling figures. They not only submit a budget that stays within the limits imposed by the chief executive, but they also forward for his/her consideration any items that are over the restricted figure for further scrutiny. Detailed analyses for personal services and other items are prepared.

4. *May to June.* The detailed estimates from the various divisions and sections of the department are compiled and reviewed by the accountant or chief executive. Appropriation propositions are considered and the budget document is developed. There is a detailed review of the document and the divisional managers are called upon to defend or justify their estimates and proposal for expenditures.

5. *June to July.* After internal departmental hearings and reviews have taken place to determine the rationale for expenditures, the final

budget document is compiled, edited, and submitted to the fiscal officers of the municipality for their inspection, amendment, emendation, and approval.

In the first year of operation of a newly established department there would be limited budget-making preliminary procedure. Either the department estimates the expenditure needs for its operation or the governing authority simply appropriates a certain sum, which may or may not be adequate, based upon a specific per capita figure. If the department finds it cannot operate effectively on such an appropriation, contingency funds might be available for use. In those instances where the monetary allocation to the department falls short, the recreational service to the citizenry must, of necessity, also fall short. This will be reflected in the following budget message which the department prepares.

Incremental budgeting

This type of budgeting is probably best used for newly established departments. It means exactly what it says. It concerns the annual planning and provision of small increments (or sometimes decrements) to the previous year's budget. The supposition of incremental budgeting is that the priorities of the last year(s), cumulatively represented in the present budget, remain suitable. A more sophisticated approach to incremental budgeting is symmetrical incrementalism. Here, every increment that is proposed, both the activity and the budget required to support it, must be compared to an activity of equal or relatively equal cost already in the budget. Therefore, the highest priority increment must be comparable to the lowest priority decrement; then the next highest priority increment with the next comparable dollar-level decrement continues until a certain percent of the previous year's budget or base is reached. Supporting a higher priority proposal within current budget levels by eliminating a funded lower priority activity is referred to as growth by substitution.

In any event, the budget process for the second year of operation would begin during the first year of establishment. Estimates would most probably be borne out by the third year of operation. There is greater probability that more valid comparisons between expectations and accomplishments would also be available.

The formulation of plans for raising revenues from taxation for the support of public work is a duty performed by financial officers and departments of the municipality and does not directly concern the chief executive of recreational service. The raising of direct revenues from sources attributable to recreational and related services is, necessarily, an immediate concern of the executive in charge of recreational services and particularly so if these revenues are credited to a specific recreational service fund and not deposited in the general fund of the city.

The budget of revenues

The revenue budget is typically considered to be the estimated income that will supply the necessary financial resources for the local government to perform its varied services. It is the most significant because it is the medium for fixing the amount of the tax rate. The revenue budget should not in itself be used as the instrument for determining new policy, such as the inauguration of new services, expansion of current programs, or the development of capital projects. All policy decisions influencing the budget should have been settled prior to its adoption, although operation of such services guided by new policy cannot be activated until budgetary allocation is made and authorized.

Even if the revenue budget is not the means for establishing new policy, it most assuredly gives effect to it. It is through the budget that local government decreases or enlarges borrowing and spending according to prevailing economic conditions. Factually, a rational long-term policy can scarcely be attained unless there is a concomitant budgetary management and advanced planning. The municipality may carry out its intent to acquire potential recreational land, develop recreational centers and other facilities, repair and otherwise maintain present recreational places without borrowing by carefully planning for revenue budgeting over several years. A good revenue budgeting procedure is quite valuable to local government in the formation of policy. It permits a guide for subsequent work to be performed as well as a means of control. There is a need for a methodical approach in compiling and assessing data which in turn encourages a sense of responsibility. The budget also requires all of the line agencies of the municipality and the officials who have been charged with the responsibility to review their aims and objectives, at least once during the year, and, perhaps more importantly, the methods by which they hope to achieve goals. Finally, the practice of budgeting not only assists in managerial functions, it is extremely helpful in educating both municipal officers and the public in understanding the programs and performances undertaken as well as the financial implications of whatever budget policy is in effect.

Operating revenues are earnings resulting from fees, charges for special recreational or related services, income from sales of commodities, income from concessions, and the like. In the whole scheme of municipal finance these do not bulk large, but from the standpoint of the departmental operation and control they are of great importance. Currently the trend is to produce more revenue as a result of fees and charges for a wide range of commodities, rentals, instruction, or use than has been done heretofore. Many public recreational service departments are getting into business operations in order to offset insufficient support received through tax base sources. For these reasons, it is quite as necessary to maintain control over such practices and to regulate operations which produce revenues as it is to control expenditures. Eventually, there may be a violent public reaction to the continuation of user fees and charges, although legitimate sources of revenue for amenities will continue to flourish.

Form of budget estimate

After discussion of revenue budgeting, consideration must be given to long-term capital and the annual capital budget. It has been determined that periods of from three to five years are significant enough to provide realistic bases for the development of capital projects. Beyond the five-year figure, estimates and projections no longer have any meaning, but become wishes. All capital programs should comprehend the capital expenditures which are projected. Thus, the ordered plan of capital programs can be utilized to determine borrowing policy. Plans comprising the capital program must be adequately classified. Therefore, plans being developed, plans on the way, plans approved by the local authority, and plans awaiting approval should illustrate the annual estimated cost of the program. A comprehensive report to the local authority should make perfectly clear the demands which long-range programs will make upon the financial resources of the community.[10]

Annual capital estimates concern a single year and incorporate expenditures on projects under way and plans which will be undertaken during the forthcoming year. To be of maximum benefit, the annual capital budget should define the result of each program on revenue in the current and first complete year. Annual capital budgets are worthwhile because they draw the attention of the local authority to those plans already fulfilled, and focus attention on those plans contemplated for immediate development.

Detail sheets or supporting schedules showing how the several estimates are built up should accompany the department budget. For example, the detail sheet for "Services, Personnel" should show under "Salaries and Wages, Regular": (1) the classification of position; (2) the names of incumbents; (3) ordinances fixing salaries; (4) the compensation for the current year; and (5) the compensation for the coming year. Wherever practicable, unit costs of all items enumerated in the budget should be shown together with the number of units that make up the total request.

The functions and objects budget

A municipality performs several kinds of services which may be differentiated as to function. The classification of functions of the government is reflected in the organization of departments. The work of the department usually entails a single major function which often consists of two or more subordinate functions. For example, the major function of a recreational service department is provision for public recreational experience through planned and spontaneous activities conducted at public recreational or ancillary places. The subordinate functions may include operation of eating places, parking lots at beaches, or the maintenance of a nursery for public park beautification. It is desirable that expenditures be differentiated according to subordinate functions for which they are made.

Under each major function of the city and under each subordinate function of the several departments expenditures are made for similar objects: that is, personal services, supplies, materials, equipment, and purchase of property. A high degree of standardization in the classification of objects of expenditure is possible and is urged by all authorities. This enables comparisons of expenditures for like objects to be made between departments and between subordinate functions within departments, and often reveals inequalities in salaries paid for similar services and in prices paid for the same commodity.

The budget classification of expenditures should, if possible, parallel the classification of accounts used by the city comptroller or auditor. For the purpose of making and controlling a department budget within the department itself, it is often desirable to classify expenditures in more detail than is required by the fiscal officer of the city. A simple expenditure classification that is already in use in more or less modified form in a number of cities is as follows:

1000. Services, Personal
    1100. Salaries and Wages, Regular
    1200. Salaries and Wages, Temporary
    1300. Other Compensations
2000. Service, Contractual
    2100. Communication and Transportation
        2110. Postage
        2120. Telephone (fax)
        2130. Internet (e-mail)
        2140. Freight and Express
        2150. Traveling Expenses
        2160. Rented Vehicles
    2200. Subsistence, Care and Support
        2210. Subsistence and Support of Persons
        2220. Subsistence and Care of Animals (zoo operation)
        2230. Storage and Care of Vehicles
    2300. Printing, Binding, and Public Relations
        2310. Printing
        2320. Word Processing and Copying
        2330. Binding
        2340. Public Relations
        2350. Engraving and Stamping
        2360. Photographing and Blue Printing

4240. Official Bonds
4250. Employee Liability
4300. Refunds, Awards, Indemnities
4400. Registrations and Subscriptions
4500. Taxes
5000. Current Obligations
    5100. Interest
    5200. Pensions and Retirement
    5300. Grants and Subsidies
6000. Properties
    6100. Equipment
        6110. Office
        6120. Furniture and Fixtures
        6130. Instruments and Apparatus
        6140. Tools
        6150. Recreational and Park
        6160. Motor Vehicles
        6170. Nursery
        6180. Animals
        6190. General
    6200. Buildings, Infrastructure, and Improvements
        6210. Buildings and Fixed Equipment
        6220. Walks and Pavements
        6230. Sewers and Drains
        6240. Roads
        6250. Bridges
        6260. Trees, Shrubs, Flowering Plants
    6300. Land
7000. Debt Payments
    7100. Serial Bonds
    7200. Sinking Fund Installments

The code numbers which appear opposite each segregation in the classification of expenditures are for convenient identification of each item. For example, in the classification given above, a requisition for postage would have been noted at the number 2110. This would indicate that it is classified as a contractual service because it is in the 2000 series, and is classified under *communication and transportation* because it is in the 100 series. If it is to be charged to a particular place, further elaboration of the code may be made by using the unit digit, or by adding letters.

Quarterly estimates

To prevent premature dissipation of funds and resulting embarrassment toward the close of the year, expenditures under the several segregations should be estimated by quarters or by months and only that portion of the total budget should be made available as is estimated to be required for that part of the year. The quarterly or monthly "split" should be based upon the work program. The several parts estimated for each quarter or each month will not necessarily be equal, but will be adjusted to the seasonal requirements of the department. Quarterly or monthly estimates should not be exceeded without explanation, and overdrafts should be made up in subsequent periods.

Budget savings

Adoption of the budget should not necessarily commit the department to actual expenditure for the items which were used as a basis for determining the amount of funds required. Conditions may alter the necessity for a certain expenditure, and if any expenditure proves to be unnecessary, funds set aside for it represent a saving. If a contemplated expenditure should prove unnecessary or should be deferred, the funds originally appropriated for it should not become available for an item that failed to be approved when the budget was first drawn up, nor should such funds be used to meet a need not initially anticipated without the approval of the higher executive authority.

At the end of the fiscal year unexpended balances usually exist in several segregations. These balances arise either because certain expenditures were not made or because the actual cost of certain work or commodities prove to be less than was estimated.

The chief executive of recreational service would probably prefer to be permitted to expend funds as he/she saw fit with no curbs except the injunction not to exceed a specific total for his/her department. With municipal government becoming increasingly centralized, however, financial control has come to rest with the chief executive of the municipality (mayor or city manager) rather than with department heads. Accepted theories of municipal government assign to an elected or otherwise authorized body – usually the city council or finance commission – the responsibility for determining how the city funds shall be spent and for conducting the affairs of government within the available income. Some measure of responsibility must be assigned by the chief executive officer in the governing body to department heads and other subordinate officers, but final control of expenditures must not be relinquished. Likewise, control must be retained without hampering good and convenient management. The budget plan, if wisely administered, accomplishes both these objectives.

Flexibility in the budget

Good management requires a budget that is flexible so that minor adjustments may be made without delay and difficulty. The appropriating body should adopt a budget differentiated only by departments and principal objects within the departments. This permits the chief executive officer, who is responsible for budgetary control, to make minor adjustments throughout the year so long as the total for any principal object is not exceeded.

There has been a resurgence of highly detailed budget documents as a means of insuring expenditure of funds for specific purposes for which the money was originally intended. Responsibility is assigned to one or a few responsible executives who are held strictly accountable for carrying out the plans of the appropriating body. Occasionally the total appropriation for a principal object will prove insufficient to accomplish the program of work contemplated under that object. Relief in such a contingency is usually afforded by the judicious transfer of funds, by authority of the chief executive, from an unassigned appropriation made for contingencies when the original budget appropriation ordinance was passed, or from an "unappropriated balance." The latter is the difference between the total amount appropriated and the total estimated revenue.

Control of expenditures

The budget has too often been recorded merely as an instrument for obtaining appropriations, to be filed away and forgotten once appropriations are secured. Actually, it should be considered a controlling financial plan for accomplishing a program of work and departments should be held responsible for completion of the work indicated under the estimates. Failure to complete such work should be excused only under the most stringent circumstances. (In many communities a work program based upon the approved budget is drawn up after the appropriations have been made.) The work program of a recreational service department may include, among other things, the number of recreational centers to be maintained and operated, periods and hours during which they are to be supervised, recreational activities to be initiated and conducted, improvements to be added, supplies to be consumed, and contracts to be entered into. During the year, and especially at the end of the year, the actual accomplishments of the department should be checked against the work program to encourage adherence to a plan and assist in making more accurate the estimates for subsequent years by comparing actual costs with estimated costs.

Authorization of expenditures

When the budget has been finally adopted, the auditor, comptroller, or other designated financial officer sets up in an expenditure register all appropriations by principal objects. Expenditures of all kinds, as specific authorization for them is formally requested, are entered in this register against their proper appropriation. When an expenditure is requested, only its estimated cost can be entered; when the actual cost becomes known, a correction can be made. The requested expenditures are said to "encumber" the appropriation. An *unencumbered balance* is carried forward for each segregation of the appropriation, from which it can easily be seen what part of an appropriation remains to carry the department for the rest of the financial year.

Since the auditor's expenditure register will check expenditures only against principal objects, the chief executive of the department should establish a departmental register in which expenditures are differentiated by subordinate objects or segregations, and by centers or activities to which they apply. Similarly, the director of the center, if it is of sufficient size and importance, should have his/her own expenditure register to guide him/her in management. This process should be carried on as far down the ladder of administration as practicable. One of the difficulties in the management of a large organization is that the higher executives are inclined to think too much in terms of costs, and those in charge of operating units too much in terms of needs. Sharing by all managers in the procedure of budgetary control aids in bringing about a more balanced consideration of both costs and needs.

An essential budgetary principle is that no estimate may be exceeded without authorization. To exceed the total department appropriation or the total estimated for the few principal objects should require the approval of the chief executive, usually the mayor or city manager. To exceed subordinate segregations should require the approval of the departmental executive.

13 Budget types and formats

A budget is a planned quantitative allocation of resources.[1] This may be for budgeting funds, human resources, supplies, time, or space. For the purposes of this chapter we will be addressing the budgeting of financial resources. Budgeting formats selected for use have reflected particular intentions of budget officers. There are a number of budget formats that have been developed to accomplish both planning and control activities. There are single-purpose budgets that are used to control the single project as well as a budget to control the standing plan which can be reused. The single-purpose budget is often associated with Program Evaluation and Review Technique (PERT) and other similar programs that control the coordination of the timing of the execution of the various elements of a project by coordinating the rate of budgeted expenditures with a projected schedule of completion. These techniques will be explored later in this chapter.

Historically when budgeting officials decided that central office management was required for controlling expenditures, an object or line item budget was introduced. This was useful to prevent administrative abuses by listing all objects of expense and controlling the expenditures by limiting them to the purchase of the item or service specified. Unfortunately, object or line item budgets can also hamper innovative thinking and stifle managerial ingenuity.

The necessity of having an effective budgetary system is increasingly clear insofar as governmental management is concerned. All public institutions must cope with an environment in which the allocation of resources offers a continual contest between increasing demands and service costs along with diminished capability to pay for such services.

The master budget process[2]

The master budget process requires three elements:

1. *Revenue plan*. The revenue plan has become of greater importance as ever more portions of public tax-funded agencies' budget expenditures are offset by entrepreneurial involvements of the operating agency,

insofar as both the projected revenue and the costs associated with the activity are concerned.

2. *Operating budget.* The operating budget projects the planned expenditures of expendable materials and supplies and human resources to perform a mission over a stated time; typically, 12 months.

3. *Capital expenditure budget.*[3] This is the financial plan to fund the major replacement or refurbishment of structural elements or non-expendable equipment that is to be amortized over several years. Budgeted funds for this purpose are placed in a reserve account to be used as required. The amounts appropriated for this purpose, on an annual basis, are a cumulative projection of the replacement cost necessary to be available to fund such replacement or refurbishment of non-expendable elements at the end of their expected useful life.

To create a capital expenditure budget, each non-expendable item in the agency's inventory is cataloged and then assigned estimates of its useful life and current replacement cost. A representation is made of the needed amount to be placed in reserve each year to fund the replacement at the end of its useful life. An inflation factor of 2 percent on average is used, or the past year's inflation rate is added each year to accommodate that issue. For example, a pickup truck is estimated as having a useful life of 10 years, and has a current replacement cost of $30,000. Each year $3000 plus 2 percent for total of $3060 would be included in the comprehensive budget for this purpose and placed in a reserve account to be used to replace the truck at the appropriate time.

Operating budget

There are several formats used to create an operating budget for an agency. The most common is the historic budget because it is the least labor-intensive to create and is simple to justify. However, it does not provide a meaningful tool for management purposes. This budgetary technique assumes that the previous year's allocation was sufficient to enable the agency to perform its mission in an adequate matter. The amount allocated for each budget category is the same as the previous year with a percentage added to accommodate an increase for inflation.

Line item budget

This budgeting format is often used along with the historic budget technique. It was introduced to control expenditures by the item to be purchased without any relationship to its programmatic purpose. The detail employed would reflect the need of the budget official to exercise control of the organization's expenditures. In this budget format, administrators are authorized to make expenditures within present categories that have set expenditure limits. The categories may be broad, such as salaries or office supplies, or narrow; exemplified by salaries broken down by job description or office supplies listed as #2 pencils. This format provides excellent control for the budget officer. Unfortunately, it does not offer any relationship to agency goals or desired outcomes.

Program budget

This budget format segregates the costs associated with a specific activity, program, or unit. This gives administrators the ability to evaluate the effects of the program on the agency's mission and to make adjustments accordingly. It is often used in conjunction with a line item budget. This allows administrators to justify expenditures for a specific program or, when retrenchment occurs, it allows the discrete cutting of the funding allocated for that specific program.

Zero-based budget (ZBB)[4]

This budgeting technique does not assume that incremental funding of previous years' budgets is a basis for future years. Zero-based budgets are focused on the agency's mission and the particular goal set for the year ahead. It is the most labor intensive of budget formats as it requires the budget officer to build and justify each element of the budget from scratch. It would be appropriate to employ zero-based budgeting in times of rapid change in the operating environment or when establishing new programs.

Program Evaluation and Review Technique (PERT)[5]

PERT is a project management technique designed to analyze and catalog the tasks and especially the time involved in completing a project. The timing and dependency relationships for completion of the specific tasks are expressed as the critical path of the project. The tasks are presented in chart form in a logical sequence and no activity can begin until its immediately preceding task is completed. The costs of a project are controlled by allocating the projected expenditures for the completion of each phase of a project. PERT is normally applied to non-routine complex infrastructure projects.

Fixed budget expenses versus discretionary budget expenditures

All budgets have both fixed and discretionary elements in them. Items that are set by contracts negotiated with labor unions, salaries of classified employees, costs of utilities, federally or state-mandated services would normally be considered costs that leave little room for flexibility. The discretionary portion of a budget is the only area in which an administrator can exercise his/her skill and authority to better achieve the agency's mission or its objectives.

Planning Programming Budgeting Systems (PPBS)[6]

The program budget is one in which expenditures are primarily based on programs of work and, second, on category and object. This is a planning oriented approach to developing a budget. It is a transitional type of budget between the traditional character and object budget on the one hand, and the performance budget on the other. The major contribution of PPBS lies in the planning phase; that is, the process of making program policy decisions that lead to specific budget and specific multiyear plans.

An example of this type of examination was undertaken by Los Angeles County after the passage of Proposition 13. This was a ballot measure that severely reduced the county's ability to raise revenue to support the public programs. The consideration of privatizing various maintenance responsibilities of the Parks and Recreation Department was explored as an alternative to lifting the hiring freeze and bringing on new civil service employees. The costs of new hires was compared with contracting out services previously performed by county personnel and the outsourcing of certain tasks was found to have favorable cost comparisons.[7]

PPBS utilizes four basic practices: (1) budget alternatives are to be made more reflective of public objectives instead of needed resources for agency activities and operations; (2) the multiyear costs and effects of public programs are estimated, not just the subsequent year; (3) structured inquiry is mandatory for various means of achieving public purposes, not only based on the sole method supported in the budget estimates; (4) evaluation is undertaken to determine the benefits of agency expenditures.

PPBS attempts to mix an analytic thrust into budgeting by accommodating those with knowledge and systems analysis in policy-making positions as well as by moving the budget process closer to central planning and program development activities. Essentially, PPBS classifications deal with the basic purpose or mission of the agency. They are joined to the process of decision-making and policy implementation through the allocation of agency resources. It is this emphasis on the systematic appraisal of alternatives in deciding what activities should be authorized which characterizes PPBS.

Basically, the procedure followed is described as budgeting up the ladder. It is a bottom-up approach where field personnel are deeply involved in developing the product. This may be indicated by formal policy statements or in other ways. The process is influenced by devoted partisanship during the early stages when divisional managers make their presentation. This requires program review and appraisal. The budget of any department should encompass and stimulate continuous analysis of problems of resource allocation among competing needs and programs. Hence, all factors in the budgetary process should combine to formulate departmental aims that are consistent with the municipal goals and aspirations, translate aims into program and performance, obtain authorization for proposed programs, execute authorized programs, and evaluate performance in relation to established goals.

Forms of the budgetary process

PPBS conceives a special connection between planning and budgeting, one that does not reflect the ordinary budget process. In actuality, planning comes before budgeting. Both ZBB and PPBS have come to be seen as distractions from other management responsibilities due to the labor-intensive activity to produce and maintain them. However, there are occasions when a modified ZBB approach can be useful: when fundamental changes (reorganization) occur; when the manager is employed to oversee a new strategic plan; or when competitive bidding for contracts is intense and awards are made on the basis of cost.

The program budget

The program budget is designed to offer information according to the objectives for which the recreational service department was established. There will still be lines of classification of objects and functions for control and management purposes, but this may be easily undertaken if the step over or transposition method is employed.

Performance budgeting

In the process of refinement of budgetary procedure by municipal finance offices the technique termed performance budgeting[8] that has come into use is basically a method whereby money is budgeted for the accomplishment of specific measurable units of performance. This requires the preliminary development of the system of units of accomplishment for each of the functions to be performed, with estimates based upon prior experience of the costs of accomplishing a single unit. It then becomes a matter of simple arithmetic to estimate how many units of accomplishment it is desired to achieve during the budget year and the amount of money necessary to achieve this total. During the year, the estimated performance operates as a discipline upon the managers of the function by providing an incentive toward efficient performance and improved economical operation.

The performance budget permits the management to interpret to the public what service is to be rendered during the budget year, rather than solely how much money is to be spent. It also helps in the interpretation to the public of the role of costs of different types of services, thus rendering more intelligent the pressures brought to bear upon public officers for improved and expanded services. When fees are to be charged for special services, it provides a basis for the assessment of a fee commensurable with the actual cost of rendering the service.

Performance budgeting does not preclude budgeting according to a classification of functions, sub-functions, and objects of expenditures. It merely complements the conventional system and needs and better estimating programs of work and of accounting for the outcome of expenditures.

Detailed description of functions and activities

One of the elements of the performance budgeting system is a detailed description of the functions, sub-functions, activities, and sub-activities of the jurisdiction or department. In a comprehensive recreational service system these might be stated as follows:

1. Administration and business management
2. Construction, planning, and development
3. Maintenance of recreational places
4. Operation of playgrounds
5. Operation of pools and beaches
6. Operation of camps, golf links, parks, and other recreational facilities.

This breakdown function obviously is not a detailed one; each could be further subdivided.

Work units by functions and activities

Another element is development of appropriate units of work measurement for the activities and sub-activities and the systematic recording of them day by day. It is relatively simple to break down into measurable units the work of the street maintenance group, a rubbish collection squad, meter readers, receptionists, or cashiers. But the work done by employees who render service to persons is more difficult to describe in meaningful work units. The director of a playground or center performs different services which vary according to daily needs. Recreationists also have difficulties in expressing units of their service in any meaningful way. Class enrollment may be suggested as one unit, but conducting classes may be only incidental to the basic core of the professional's responsibility, whose service might well be his/her physical presence to supervise people and to preserve order even on days when there are no classes. To measure his/her work by class enrollment would be similar to measuring the work of the police officer on the beat by the number of arrests made, when his/her duty might best be measured by the lack of arrests – in other words, by the influence of his/her presence in preventing conduct requiring arrest.

Work units can be developed for maintenance functions: but even these must be applied and interpreted with caution. Formulae may be developed as to how many square feet of space one ground caretaker should maintain satisfactorily, assuming a normal division of the space into grassed area, asphalt walks, and play apparatus. This sounds very simple, but local parks may vary in size from half an acre to 20 acres. Moreover, the space devoted to several elements varies greatly. The most complicating element is the wear and tear resulting from use. Greater use requires more service.

Preparation of work programs

An additional element is the preparation of departmental work programs and budget estimates applicable to the programs in accordance with standard forms and instructions. The work program might be stated in terms of the following:

1.   Parks maintained (acres)
2.   Playgrounds maintained (acres)
3.   Buildings maintained (square feet)
4.   Beaches maintained (acres)
5.   Camp operation (camper days)
6.   Playgrounds operated (visitor attendance)
7.   Swimming pools operated (total attendance)
8.   Beach lifeguard stations manned
9.   Special structures and facilities (paid admissions or attendance).

Delegation of budget formulation and responsibility

Performance budgeting encourages delegation of authority and responsibility down the managerial ladder. The proposed budget is a compilation of units of performance translated into costs and consolidated by activities and functions. It seems to have the effect of promoting cost-consciousness among those who participate in it, especially line supervisors. Cost-consciousness is a valuable attribute to develop among recreational service personnel, for it promotes employee cooperation toward greater productivity in the use of the employees' time and may permit savings to be applied to the range of services. Performance budgeting, on the other hand, provides top management with more effective means than previously to control the activities of all divisions. This is, of course, one of the reasons for its development. The drive to introduce performance budgeting in a city came not from separate department managers or the performers within the division of a department, but from top city executives and from legislative bodies who make the appropriations.

Budgeting for service benefits and capital improvements[9]

Allotments for service innovations and capital improvements must be considered separately from the budgeting of funds for continuation of established services. Suppose, for example, it was found in the public interest to offer fireworks at a dozen parks both to discourage the use of fireworks in the street and to provide public entertainment. The pyrotechnical displays might be provided by donations, but the presence of supervisory and maintenance staff would be required and probably (since fireworks are usually set off on holidays) on time-and-a-half pay. Presumably, under the performance budget, the staff is already assigned to capacity on other days, hour by hour. This innovation, then, would present a considerable additional cost. It would have to be studied months before the event and would have to be included in the budget. Recreational activities and the needs and habits of people or events for which program adaptations should be made, cannot be predicted and planned with the exactitude desired by strict adherence to the performance budgeting system.

Park and recreational service executives traditionally have been effective in the creation of architectural effects, horticultural displays, and pleasing vistas in the parks. Most of these creations have been accomplished without formal plans and specifications. Personnel and materials budgeted to maintenance were used for capital improvements. Use of personnel in this matter is invariably prohibited by the performance budgeting technique. A budget request for an extra crew to be used at the artistic whim of the park manager receives cold treatment when it competes with "practical" proposals involving prosaic and established service functions or critically needed capital improvements such as bridges and storm sewers.

14 Information technology diffusion in recreational service

Information technology (IT) is a method for dispersion of information within and between organizations. It has the capacity to facilitate the exchange of goods, services, money, and knowledge on a digital basis. It is the automation of transactions, communication, and interaction using computer and exchange technologies for whatever purposes those who are participating intend.[1] It includes inter-organizational systems such as e-mail, iPod, Skype, and telephone. The most significant aspect of IT is its effective distribution within the organization, that is, the process by which IT spreads throughout an organization and is extensively used or adopted by the various organizational units.[2]

Among the technologies currently available, the computer has gained significance in the field of recreational service, particularly in the public sector, because it processes information quickly, precisely, and economically. Surely, this implies that there is information which needs to be processed. The generation and diffusion of knowledge about things, people, and resources has assumed a proportion and rate that is important to the well-being of society as a whole, and, by inference, to all sectors in which recreational service operates.[3]

Each succeeding year sees an increasing amount of time, money, and effort in producing, processing, translating, recording, and eventually retrieving information, while simultaneously there is relatively less investment in dealing with the material products of our technological society. This obviously holds true for service-based fields of endeavor. Recreationists have traditionally provided services that required no physical product other than the supplies necessary for the participant in an activity. However, the need for informational services from which direct leadership services can be programmed is now growing at a faster pace than ever before. Recreationists are now beginning to understand that the way they perform their jobs may hinge less upon their direct expertise in the activities programmed than upon the way a variety of resources – physical, personal, environmental, fiscal, or time resources – can be brought together, transformed, examined, reduced, and translated into the kinds of recreational services necessary for the satisfaction of people's needs.

It has been justly stated that the most vexing problem confronting society is learning to appreciate and adjust to complexity. In many fields this perception is almost axiomatic. Computers are one means whereby people can readily and rapidly cope with complex and interacting situations such as those increasingly facing the field of recreational service. Under the circumstances, electronic data-processing (EDP) and machines, which perform the computations, have become more prominent in assisting managers to do their human jobs more swiftly, accurately, and effectively.[4]

Despite enormous advances in computing power, IT could become inundated with data generated by interconnected devices, processes, and people. Fortuitously, new technology is accessible which can process, store, network, and apply a new level of system intelligence, or service management. The new model, termed *cloud computing*, makes it possible to secure, confirm, customize, and keep abreast of the onrushing flood of data complexity and volume. To maintain technological proficiency, IT producers must enlarge their base so that service management systems are made available to those agencies that require increased capabilities while having access to only limited resources.[5]

Acquiring and assessing data are basic aspects of the administrative process. In fact, such procurement and appraisal are the objectives toward which the entire process of management moves. Electronic digital computers are having such a phenomenal effect on the collection and processing of data that managers have developed great insight into what computers are capable of doing and what is concerned in their utilization. Therefore, managers have a significant role in the extent to which the specific practice, strategy, or new technique is diffused within the organization. Technology use will probably reflect several attributes, for example, the manager's perception of the usefulness and facility of IT, the degree of centralization insofar as organizational structure is concerned, and the number of employees staffing the organization.

Centralization and formalization

Centralization is the degree to which legitimate authority is concentrated and controlled by one or a relatively few individuals. To the extent that centralization characterizes the structure, technology diffusion will be limited.[6] Along with centralization there will also be found formalization. Formalization emphasizes rules and procedures to be followed by all personnel in terms of performance. Initially, formalization may inhibit the early stages of IT, but it can become effective insofar as technology dissemination throughout the organization is concerned because it lessens ambiguity and conflict. Of vital importance to technological innovation in the organization is continuous and intensive collaboration and interaction within the professional staff.

Information technology requires well-developed lines of communication among and between bureaus and divisions of the department. Inter-departmental relationships through a network of communications among organizational members will probably ease the way for new ideas or technologies to enter, thereby initiating a favorable climate for effective diffusion.[7] The advent of EDP and its consequent capacity for IT diffusion is an opportunity for change management to occur. This means special scrutiny of the way things or actions are performed within the agency. Typically, the most common reason for IT failure is that custom-made systems are built to fit existing ways of working. In order to avoid such pitfalls, managers should regard the installation of new software as a magnificent opportunity to re-engineer the way the agency operates in light of both the internet and how to project the work to be carried out in the future. The necessity for total automation is of vital importance. Therefore the purchase of business applications that are designed to work together from the outset is a matter of common sense.[8] With an internet-based system, important information can be stored in one place, and managers can retrieve it, as need dictates.

Computers in the workplace

Recreational service agencies are presumed to desire the most effective patron satisfaction possible. To this end, the use of IT will only enhance the ability of the department to serve its constituency better.

The rapid growth of computer terminals within the United States has placed this electronic marvel within the reach of every recreational service agency which contemplates rapid data-processing. Modern organizations have their own computer work stations, laptops, smart phones, and other devices with which information may be processed. The use of applications or "Apps" that deliver customized or specific content to end users is gaining adherents.[9]

Some agencies are connected with computer systems serving a network of clients. It is almost inconceivable to imagine a recreational service department without computer facilities and just as hard to contemplate an administrative situation in which the department could not profitably benefit from one of the diverse computer applications now in use.

EDP applications

Today, technology concerning data-processing is approaching a point where departments of recreational service find it economically necessary to introduce IT as a tool for the rapid solution of the manifold problems confronting management. Factors which should be considered in determining the potential of EDP machines are the volume of repetitive tasks, present clerical costs, costs of machine installation, and the availability of formerly unobtainable management control information. The determination of how computers may be put to the best use in the solution of local managerial problems must be analyzed in terms of the costs incurred by such operations, as compared to operations that are carried on without machines.

Successful EDP application has been found advantageous in every aspect of recreational service. Used for record keeping, the planning of material requirements in a system, controlling materials or inventories on hand, land-use planning, storage and retrieval of information, or programs handling detailed bits of data from which facility planning may be made and conclusions drawn about public needs can really be performed only by computers. The ability of computers to show schematics, diagrams, and 360-degree pictures of buildings, areas, and the placement of facilities and apparatus from any angle enables the viewer to select the plan most likely to satisfy the needs of the agency's constituency.[10] This signifies that computer users at every level may have information at their disposal, which enables them to reach conclusions concerning departmental operations. Essentially, this means that organizational structure can be decentralized to the extent that professionals on the lowest levels of the department may make informed and accurate decisions designed to increase efficiency and effectiveness.

The EDP challenge

The potentialities of EDP make possible, through their application to vital functions, a greater recreational service at less cost and with minimum error than any other available workforce.[11] The use of EDP in planning, research, and decision-making, public and private jurisdictions, particularly those systems that are concerned with the general welfare, education, or health of people, can help in many of the difficult choices which face policy-makers and/or managers. EDP must be used to delineate purposes, assist in making acute value judgments, help to refine plans, inform the user with regard to making more appropriate allocations of economic, material and natural resources, aid in clarifying the proper roles of the public, quasi-public, and private sectors of society, and perform those functions which can revitalize local government, private agencies, and the management of both.

Computer impact

Mastery of the techniques dealing with advanced data-processing methods can result in a highly efficient operation at lower costs and a sharpening of the decision-making process whereby the art and science of management can be improved.[12]

Continued production of knowledge can no longer be handled by the archaic methods of yesteryear. New concepts, the future development of materials and systems for the control of products will continue only through the application of technological innovation. The rapid obsolescence of information makes impractical any planning without the use of EDP.[13] There are now so many alternatives from which to choose that it is beyond the powers of managers to cope with the volume of information and the complexities which modern life produces. The fundamental assignment of all managers is to select the best possible alternative from a complex mass, to make such decisions swiftly and accurately, and to be correct. Such a task appears to require powers far above those of human ability. There is a need, therefore, for the production of planning, organizing, and decision-making systems that can tackle the complexities of contemporary affairs with optimum effectiveness. Management, in alliance with knowledge gained from the behavioral sciences, offers the technical assistance necessary.

IT and innovation

The ability to satisfy patron needs is the ultimate measure of success for the effective exploitation of IT and consequently the allocation of resources. This is particularly true in large recreational service agencies where collective activity requiring frequent communication among specialists and functions is routine. Successful management of technology requires the ability to coordinate and integrate functional and specialist staff for the implementation of innovation. To do this, necessitates continuous questioning of the appropriateness of existing organizational structure and skills for the effective use of technological opportunities. Finally, responsible management with experience in all functional activities involved must be willing and able to take a comprehensive view of technological accumulation within the department, combining this with the skills and élan to have realistic expectations concerning the implications of ongoing technological developments.[14]

Human/machine interface

The confrontation of society with computer technology is important for recreationists everywhere. We have now had 50 years of experience of EDP. Eventually, if not sooner, the emergence of automation will finally free most people from the drudgery of repeated tasks. Of course, a radical change in economy, education, and social organization is to be expected, but the result may well prove beneficial beyond the wildest dreams of those who look to the future. Almost everyone sees the computer as a common tool to assist processing the simple routine jobs of payroll checks, inventory control, personnel records, and the like. Certainly the computer can do these functions, but it is wasted if these are the only tasks for which it is used. There is a better understanding of the use of computers for a great variety of functions. Computers are being used in operations concerning shaping of human decisions, once thought to be the sole province of the technician and executive. Access to the internet opens a world of information on almost any subject the user needs or wants to explore. There are software programs, for example, which deliver real-time visibility and accountability to every level of the organization. This could mean that every employee could be held financially accountable for decisions made at his/her respective level. In other words, all recreationists have visibility into their own financial environment within the agency. With embedded cost controls, online procurement, and real-time alerts, every professional is empowered to make the right decisions. In turn, top management can achieve the results they are counted on to produce. Moreover, specialized software is not only concerned with financial management solutions but also with human resource management, patron or participant relationship management, supply chain management, and application infrastructure. The instantaneous availability of material that provides accurate information for the resolution of problems, or assistance in reaching conclusions based on fact, enables all personnel with computer stations to participate in the decision-making process.

Computers are of basic significance primarily because they comprise so much communications and guidance technique, and also because, in order to operate at maximum efficiency, they require sharply defined ideas and associations. Ultimately, when facts, ideas, and relationships are identified and made clear, the machine accomplishes the swift and accurate calculations of a logical nature that are beyond human endurance or capability. In many instances, computers permit acuteness in making choices or accuracy of control previously unimaginable. Until recently it was inconceivable to compare extensive possibilities in order to resolve a problem or find the most beneficial alternative. Now, through the utilization of aids such as linear and dynamic programming, critical path analysis, factor analysis, network analysis, and simulation, decision-making with precision and rationality has become available.

Computer graphics[15]

Utilization of computers for the presentation of films, animated drawings, and other graphic displays can be a tool of immense value to planners and managers. Animation of static drawings, whereby individual images, with small, controlled differences in their outlines or position, or photographed frame by frame so as to provide the appearance of movement can be used to instruct personnel in the handling of unfamiliar equipment. This technique might also be employed to simulate landscape features and the development of recreational areas and facilities within a given planning period. Such information could be useful in determining which areas should be developed, and which should be maintained in their present form or modified in some way. Moreover, the computer could offer alternative plans based upon potential user capacity of the property, cost–benefit ratios and other variables.

Both animated and motion pictures, particularly insofar as time-lapse photography is concerned, would be capable of informing the general public about future recreational developments within the community as a sound public relations device. When people are shown how certain plans will affect their environment as well as provide for their own recreational opportunities they may react with greater support for the department and the planning program. Visual stimuli seem to have a greater impact upon the receiver than does an oral presentation. If lay-people can see the animated or photographed project developing before their eyes, rather than being subjected to maps, drawings, and models, there may be a better understanding of what the planner is attempting.

One of the advantages of computer graphics is that the display can show modifications, different views or perspectives, and probable benefits both to the potential user and the environment before any attempt is made to turn the first shovelful of earth. There is little doubt that computer animation is perfectly suited to scientific planning, and that its application could be justified in terms of scientific research alone. However, there are other ways in which computer techniques can be used. These are in the areas of public relations, personnel instruction, and the most economical and efficient methods for determining recreational sites, constructing centers and other facilities, or assisting in the development of safety procedures necessary to ensure the health and welfare of patrons of recreational service systems. Animated pictures coupled to computers may offer information about faulty equipment, unrestricted access to areas, potentially dangerous facilities, and the means for preventing or forestalling such dangers.

With the availability of miniaturized computers capable of operating more economically than ever before, more artists and planners will gain access to them. This expansion of electronic cinematography might do much to provide the correct answers upon which decisions can be made for the greatest possible recreational service at the least cost in time, money and personnel effort.

PERT (Program Evaluation Review Techniques)

One of the many applications of computers is PERT[16] or, as it is sometimes known, the critical path method (CPM).[17] The initial action in PERT is to carefully analyze whatever process, activity, or project is involved in the provision of recreational service to the community, and then to chart the sequences which must be executed if the system is the carry out its function. The PERT chart is typically drawn as a complex diagram. Circles and arrows represent time periods and processes respectively. Each circle has arrows running to it or from it. These depict the various processes which either depend upon it or which must be performed before it can be initiated.

For the development of a particular recreational program involving physical resources, for example, facilities, equipment, supplies, materials, personnel, transportation, public relations, and so forth, the graph will contain many circles and arrows. Actually, as with a flowchart, there is no single final level of detail, only levels of detail that support different purposes. It is possible, therefore, to expand one PERT chart into sub-PERT charts illustrating options in greater detail. For example, the construction of a beach facility, which contains a pavilion to house administrative personnel, eating places, and essential lifeguard stations, can become a chart showing the development of the pavilion in the process of constructing the beach.

Once the PERT chart is graphed it is then necessary to obtain accurate estimates of the time required for carrying out each process that is depicted on the graph. A PERT chart contains numbered circles and time estimates for each process that appears on the graph. With these data programmed for the computer, together with the desired completion data, that is, the last circle on the graph, the computer can scan the entire procedure from the last circle to those immediately preceding and, from the time estimates of the associated processes, determine and assign the date at which each of these earlier activities has to be finished. These earlier activities can be scanned back to their preceding circles. When two or more process lines originate from the same circle, a not infrequent occurrence, then the process having the earliest time is used to assign the time at which this circle must be completed if the entire program is to be accomplished at the desired date. In this manner, the time to be linked with any circle can be determined, especially when all those processes that depend upon it have their respective times assigned, by selecting the earliest date necessary. By utilizing this method, the graph is arranged with the times each circle (or completed process) must be reached if the entire program is to be carried through successfully and on time.

Additionally, the limiting path or paths are designated. This critical path is the one that needs the most time to travel. If any process on this path is lengthened, then the total program will require more time. The critical path provides the manager with information dealing with the entire program and indicates which segments must be carefully followed up while checking the whole program. The manager needs to monitor the procedure to make sure that each process on the critical path is on schedule. Other processes, not on the critical path, must also be monitored, to ensure they are not delayed.

Often, the consequences of having managers check the critical path is that processes on that path are accelerated while other parts become slower. At routine intervals, those processes that are completed are listed and old parts of the chart are filed. Also, due to early preparation of some of the processes on the critical path, and sometimes others, the time estimates for the different processes may be extended or reduced more than originally calculated. Therefore, the critical path will have to be recomputed. The new critical path will focus the manager's attention on what to look for. This interaction between reshuffled charts and the manager's locus of attention maintains emphasis approximately on where it is most required. The entire program moves more rapidly than it would otherwise, and the terminal date for program operation gradually moves up. This simple decision instrument, the determination of the critical path by computer with regular search procedures for the critical path whenever there are revised data or new time estimates, is an extremely valuable managerial device. Of course, PERTs can be done by hand, but this is time-consuming and may not be as reliable as computerized PERTs.

An example of a PERT chart is presented in Figure 14.1. In developing a PERT chart certain information must be obtained: the number of activities necessary to complete a given project, the length of time required for each activity completion, and the sequence of activities to be performed:

1. Activities A and B begin the project. Both activities are independent and may be concomitant. A requires 4 time units and B requires 3.
2. C requires 6 time units and D requires 4. D cannot begin until A is completed.
3. E requires 5 time units and cannot begin until B is completed.
4. F requires 2 time units and cannot begin until A and B are completed.
5. G requires 1 time unit and cannot begin until D and F are completed.
6. H requires 2 time units and cannot begin until E is completed.
7. I requires 7 time units and cannot begin until A is completed.
8. J requires 5 time units and cannot begin until C and G are completed.
9. K requires 1 time unit cannot begin until C, G, and H are completed.
10. L is terminal and requires 4 time units and cannot begin until I, J, and K are completed.

Activity	Event	Duration (units)	Least time (units)	Maximum time (units)
A	1–2	4	20	20
B	1–3	3	15	15
	2–6	0	12	
C	2–4	6	16	16
D	2–5	4	15	
I	2–11	11		
E	3–8	12		
F	6–7	2	12	
G	5–7	1	11	
H	8–10	2	7	
J	9–10	5	10	10
K	10–11	1	5	
L	11–12	4	4	4

PERT Diagram (Initial)

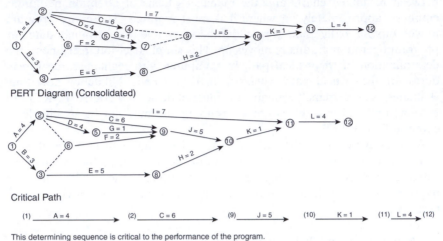

PERT Diagram (Consolidated)

Critical Path

| (1) | A = 4 | (2) | C = 6 | (9) | J = 5 | (10) | K = 1 | (11) | L = 4 | (12) |

This determining sequence is critical to the performance of the program.

Figure 14.1 PERT diagram and time chart with critical path sequence.

Obviously, the shortest possible time which can elapse between all of the activities and events starting at point (1) and finishing at point (12) is determined by that sequence of activities which takes the longest time and is therefore known as the critical path. This determining sequence is critical to the performance of the program.

Computer applications in management

There must now be understood the human–machine relationship which is really the use to which machines may be put for human value. The machine is nothing more nor less than an extension of human capability subjected to human control. The computing machine is already affecting the social existence of people, methods of education, political control, relationship to the social and physical environment, and may eventually radically reorder all existence.

With the utilization of computer technology, managers now have at their disposal data that are composed of extremely reliable facts. High-quality data in quantity permit decision-making that must be more efficacious than that which is based upon attitude, prejudice, or supposed knowledge. It is at the point of decision that the manager alternately confronts the results and interactions of his/her managerial, political, and behavioral activities. The manager's effort is best made in terms of specialized knowledge or expertness and high-quality data. Under such circumstances, the system that relies upon EDP will probably be more efficient, effective, rational, and capable of correct responses to the variable needs of the constituency.

The recreationist, in an executive position, has the opportunity to begin to increase the utilization of computer technology for the benefit of the recreational service system and the people that it serves. It may be as an outgrowth of public administration use of automation for fiscal matters, human resources matters, or land usage. In whatever way the computer is introduced within the jurisdiction for which the recreationist works, there is currently available technology that can advance the services that the department can perform. Computerized budget making, payroll processing, statistical data collection for all divisions within the system, the development of recreational activities for literally every individual within the community, planning new recreational places, selection of types of facilities, apparatus, design of areas, equipment as well as inventory control are all well within the most simplified use of the computer. Centralized data banks are being established which will provide administrative information in a centralized location. The retrieval of these data is made more rapid by simple methods, which include tabulations of specific units having common characteristics. The recovery of this information is based upon the parameters, which are indicated as required. Additionally, data banks also include storage files, and record maintenance for updating and modifying information.

The power of computers is of such immensity, and the capability of programming a computer is so broad in scope, that in almost every field where a mass of data is to be processed, EDP is applied. How may the computer be of specific assistance to the recreationist/manager? The following samples are just some applications of computers and data-processors in the field of recreational service.

Departmental finance factors

1. Forecasting revenues from whatever fees and charges are levied.
2. Forecasting expenditures for all operations including human resources, maintenance, construction, program, office management, and other services.
3. Budget formulation, either line item, program, or project.
4. Budgetary and appropriation accounting.
5. General ledger and fund accounting where required.
6. Supplies, material, and equipment inventory.
7. Property inventory.
8. Motor vehicle equipment retrieval list.
9. Fixed asset accounting.
10. Purchase order writing and control.
11. Audit of all fiscal records.

Human resources management

1. Personnel inventory in terms of speaking, writing, activity performance skills.

 2. Actuarial statistics.
 3. Personnel services budget requests.
 4. Established position control.
 5. Effective employee–public ratio for service.
 6. Payroll.
 7. Payroll distribution accounting.
 8. Psychological test scoring.
 9. Eligible applicants roster listing.
10. Personnel evaluating and rating records.
11. Time and leave records.

Construction of recreational facilities and places

 1. Construction cost accounting.
 2. Bid rating.
 3. Contract progress estimates and payments.
 4. Work order distribution
 5. Force account accounting.
 6. Traffic survey for traffic pattern evaluation.
 7. Origin and destination programs.
 8. Right-of-way taking line computation.
 9. Terrain handling data.
10. Earth work computation.
11. Functional space analysis, carrying capacity.

Planning for recreational spaces, areas, and facility placement

 1. Land use data and analysis.
 2. Site situation and geographical indexing.
 3. Area and percent vacant land analysis.
 4. Land use by area and number of units.
 5. Land use by geographical location.
 6. Transportation needs and studies.

Population information

 1. Population movement and trends, both internal and external.
 2. Population distribution by age, gender, race, religion, ethnic background, education, social, and economic status.
 3. Population densities.
 4. Population distribution in terms of where employed for transit projections.
 5. Recreational area and facility placement and projections in terms of population movements.
 6. Types of activities and/or programs that might be arranged in terms of popularity or expectation.

Program possibilities

1. Listing of all possible areas, facilities, or spaces where potential planned recreational activities might occur.
2. Listing all possible recreational activities in which people may participate on an organized or spontaneous basis.
3. Scheduling all available spaces in terms of activity demand.
4. Providing information as to the maximum size of instructional activities for most effective performance and participation.
5. Matching participant skill, talent, and knowledge with available activities.
6. Offering various alternative choices to participants in terms of available leisure, skills, and interests.

Recreational service managers are constantly challenged in selecting the type of computers and software programs that are compatible and able to provide the rapid processing of information, improved efficiency and effectiveness of operations, the exclusion of overlapping tasks, the minimization of costs through the more efficient use of personnel, the production of financial reports and budget statements that are accurate and timely, and the ability to generate accurate data and reports whenever needed. Finally, an interconnection between all units within the agency for easy communication and monitoring, to guarantee attention to the aims and objectives for which the organization was developed, is vital.

Computer impact on recreational service management

The chief modification to be observed from the technological confrontation between human beings and machines, particularly as it applies to the field of recreational service, is that a specialist breed of professionals must be developed to administer the various functions of the system. Automation may certainly replace the clerical workforce which is now of importance to current departmental operation. However, increasingly sophisticated machines may one day make these ancillary positions obsolete. Of course, there will always be the need for technical support staff to troubleshoot software and hardware. It is also probable that many of the so-called middle management positions will be relegated to the dust heap as well. The age of EDP should require individuals who are both technically and professionally prepared to perform decision-making functions so as to meet the increasing complexities of modern life. As society becomes more bureaucratic, technology-oriented individuals will be required who can interface with machines and use the information being rapidly produced. It may well mean that those recreationists who desire to achieve managerial responsibility will have to combine both the professional preparation of the humanist and people-oriented education (including those exposures designed to effect optimal program experiences), with a scientific and technological education.

It is understood, however, that recreationists, at the management level, should probably be generalists, for they will need the leadership qualities that are pertinent to those individuals in areas where influence by emulation is a key factor. The need for recreationists who can understand the intricacies of computer technology in all of its ramifications is undeniable. For the best possible mix, insofar as understanding the nature of computer technology, systems analysis, and operational research are concerned it is probable that recreationists will have a great deal of knowledge of management science as well as the professional preparation now offered. It is certain that, as technology becomes increasingly esoteric and intricate, it will be necessary for more administrative functionaries to have sound technical education.

The generalist will always be a part of recreational service by virtue of the nature of the field. It is a people-oriented field and cannot be divorced from that concept. Much more to the point is that recreationists will have to think more in terms of an automated environment that necessitates an understanding of the EDP concepts. To be successful as a manager, the recreationist must begin to lend him/herself to a rational mixture of philosophy and science. Despite the seeming dichotomy involving the development of such personnel, it now appears that logic and reason decree the necessity for discovering individuals who have the blend of humanism and technology to perform the complex function of management. It seems obvious that continued progress with computer technology and the imminent onset of the human–machine interface demands a combination of talent, personality, and knowledge that will permit the achievement of managerial effectiveness.

15 Public relations and management impacts

Whether in public or private recreational service agencies, public relations is one of the most important managerial functions.[1] The attention of the public must be aroused, interest in the organization-sponsored activities must be created and maintained, knowledge of agency problems must be disseminated, especially in the governmental field, and support must be enlisted.[2]

A recreational service organization cannot render the fullest service of which it is capable without the support of favorable public opinion, which is based on understanding and goodwill. Private enterprises have long recognized that favorable public relations are vital to their success and that they may be consciously planned and created.[3] For this purpose they give attention to every detail of their operations that brings them into contact with the public and often employ specialists as public relations counselors to organize a comprehensive program of public relations for the entire establishment.

It has been generally recognized that public agencies and departments have an obligation to inform the public concerning the work done and the services and benefits available through their operations.[4] The expenditure of a reasonable portion of the funds for disseminating information and for reporting has been construed as a proper use of public funds.

Although public departments do not advertise, they are employing the methods of publicity more and more. Publicity promotes goodwill and understanding. Advertising is a commodity for which a price is paid; publicity usually is associated with news and flows through free communications channels. The propriety of the use of publicity in public work has asked to be judged in relation to its purposes. Publicity, however, represents only one of many methods of public relations used by recreational service agencies.

Education and propaganda

Education is the basic instrument by which recreationists can cultivate a desire on the part of the public to conform to stated agency policies. It is, perhaps, the most tedious process and simultaneously the most effective and durable. Once an individual has learned to appreciate the objectives of recreational service and to enjoy recreational experiences, he/she more willingly supports the agency's program and contributes to its success.[5]

Education for leisure, particularly as it concerns recreational service, implies that communities should have at least a minimum of personnel to give leadership to the community's leisure. It is vital if the public is to utilize safely and profitably the abundance of free time now generally available. Education influences the attitudes and behavior of individuals and groups toward whom it is directed and reduces management problems or areas of friction. Through enlightenment of potential participants voluntary interest and performance are garnered and monetary savings that can be translated into more effective programs for continued public betterment are made.[6] In the private sector, however, whatever interest and participation is generated in activites, while these may contribute to the recipient's development, they are offered for profit.

Public recreational service should employ a more complete educational program, through home visitations by recreationists, who can establish contact with potential clientele, provide information, create incentives, organize groups, and otherwise stimulate participation and support of recreational policies and programs.[7]

In all public relations undertaken by public departments there is a mutual interest on the part of both the public and the department: the improvement of the public service. The public desire is to express their wishes, demands, and criticisms and to bring about adjustments. The department, on the other hand, desires to ascertain the public's interest and needs, and to adapt itself to the changing interests and needs insofar as it is permitted to do so consistent with its powers. The department considers as part of its public relations program measures it may take to become informed concerning the public as well as the means it adopts to interpret itself to the public and to create public goodwill toward the department.

The public relations section of the department acts as a two-way funnel by directing and channeling information to the public, interpreting the facts about the agency, and serving as a sounding board for the programs initiated by the agency. It discovers what the community has to say about recreational activities and is therefore in a position to assist in the determination of policies and to recommend immediate changes in the program offerings as interest mounts or declines.

Community organization and public relations

Good public relations are generated through activities conducted by the department and through contacts made with organizations and groups of many kinds that use department facilities on permit. The numerous volunteer leaders involved in these group activities and the many participants become agents of goodwill for the department and its services, assuming, of course, that their experience is satisfactory and that the service given them by the department merits their approbation.

Agencies with which the department is officially affiliated also mirror the esteem in which the department is held and assist in cultivating a favorable public image. Among such organizations are councils of community social services, interagency recreational councils and coordinating councils.

Levels of coordination

It is sometimes erroneously assumed that two or more agencies can be coordinated through efforts at the uppermost levels. It is not sufficient to have the executives of two or more policy-making bodies agree on a co-ordinated plan of operation. Coordination can be effected only through cooperation at various levels of management. Unless the employees in each agency understand the need for such coordination and are willing to work harmoniously with their opposite numbers from other community agencies, or even private agencies, there is little hope for actual joint effort.

Thus the factor of personality enters into the problem of coordination. In many instances, efforts at coordination have been unsuccessful because of personality clashes between key members of the council or between personnel in contributing agencies. Harmonious official relations tend to be cultivated through personal contact and joint effort. A plan of coordination can be effective only if it cultivates goodwill between the representatives and disseminates information among them of what each is doing and can do toward the common objective.

If personality factors are allowed to intervene, the goal of total recreational service for the community is obscured. Professional personnel should rise above petty bickering, minor irritations, or supposed personal slights and point the way toward purposeful activities that accrue from objective relationships.

Mutual assistance

Cooperative relations between agencies and their personnel at all levels are cultivated by mutual assistance rendered by one agency to another. For example, the municipal recreational service agency may supply a dance instructor or square dance caller to direct a Girl Scout jamboree; advise the school board on school playground equipment and placement; offer pre-packaged picnic supplies and equipment to community groups; provide instructions and plans for social events; establish leadership workshops or other professional development programs for participation by any community agency; supply skilled volunteers for instructional or leadership purposes in the program of different agencies; provide necessary officials for athletic events and contests; hold classes for instructors in various activities (dance, arts, crafts, or photography).

The recreational service agency can serve the community by establishing interagency priorities for use of recreational facilities. Such use must not conflict with or supersede activities sponsored or controlled by the agency in possession of the facility. In this way all buildings, structures, and land or water areas available for recreational purposes are utilized to a maximum degree. This necessitates a higher level of coordination and cooperation between all of the community agencies. Each agency indicates the type of facility or space that it operates and the times when these places may be used by others. Individual organizations could request specific facilities and confirm appointments for their use without concern about conflicting interests. Individual agencies may even establish fees for the use of their facilities. Such a plan would also be beneficial to neighborhoods without adequate facilities. Duplication of recreational structures and areas might thus be avoided and optimum use made of existing venues.

Coordination may also be fostered by organizing a master schedule for facilities within the community, indicating when, where, and what activities are programmed. Naturally, such a schedule would have to be prepared at least one month in advance if it is to be useful. The master schedule serves as a central communications device so that unnecessary competition for the enlistment of the same participants is avoided. Such a plan reveals where there is a dearth of recreational activity in the community and what organizations should supply service. (It is presumed, of course, that the public agency program is supplemented by other agency activities.) Better relations between agencies might result, for each agency may plan its activities for a specific group and know that it was contributing to the provision of overall community recreational service. A more harmonious climate is engendered and coordinated action for recreational development encouraged.

Coordination by conference and agreement

Various other devices to effect coordination of recreational agencies have been adopted with beneficial results. The simplest is the frequent interchange of information through conferences. Conferences are arranged between representatives of two agencies when problems of mutual concern arise. To facilitate such conferences, regular meetings are sometimes held. Occasionally a third agency or person, such as the Parent–Teacher Association, the Chamber of Commerce, or the mayor, calls representatives of both agencies together to initiate the process of coordination.

The neighborhood recreational council or committee

Neighborhood recreational councils, which may receive their impetus from the public department of recreational service or through the enthusiastic support of laymen within the community, exemplify the democratic process in the field. They are at once a laboratory, a school of instruction, and a device for the formulation of public opinion. These councils can facilitate neighborhood recreational planning and cooperative enterprise. Such un-official groups usually gain prestige from their early support of urgently needed recreational facilities, areas, or personnel. Members may be drawn from any agencies or groups located in the neighborhood. When such councils are organized by the department of recreational service, they are strictly advisory, although their functions may include raising funds for the improve-ment of neighborhood facilities, interpreting the department's recreational operations to the public, circulating recreational information throughout the neighborhood, assisting in neighborhood surveys that may lead to better recreational facilities or activities, sponsoring certain recreational activities, and implementing public inspections of local recreational centers.

The basic goals of these councils are to promote public interest in the services the public department offers, to support the department's budgetary request, and to assist in the planning of recreational activities in the neigh-borhood in conjunction with the community-wide program. The enlistment of the neighborhood residents in councils of this nature may result in a widespread demand by citizens that various public agencies pool their resources or coordinate their activities in order to promote a larger com-munity recreational service. Extra-official affiliation with other community-based organizations creates avenues for promotion of public relations.

Physical facilities and public relations

Many persons gain their impression of the organization from its facilities and their physical condition. If the office has a neat and business-like appearance, if the grounds are well laid out and carefully maintained, if the buildings are in good repair and kept in a clean and orderly manner, the esteem in which the agency is held by the public grows.

Political officials tend to quarter the public recreational service depart-ment away from the city hall, sometimes with facilities incomparably worse than those enjoyed by other departments. A standard of maintenance far below that acceptable for fire stations, police stations, and other longer established departments is sometimes tolerated. Recreational service depart-ments themselves are partly to blame for this condition, because they are so imbued with interest in the activity program and its educational implications that they are sometimes inclined to accept improvisations unacceptable to other public departments. Recreational service departments must insist that the standard of physical appointments be equal to that applied to other municipal agencies.

Employee contacts

Every employee in the agency is a public relations agent. A larger percen-tage of the employees of a recreational service department come into contact with the public than in any other municipal department. Maintenance of favorable public relations is the duty and obligation of such employees as well as their privilege. A slovenly caretaker at a neighborhood center, a disgruntled recreational director, or a discourteous office clerk can do more damage to the public relations of an agency than reams of published material can correct. Also important are telephone contacts, not only in the office but at the several centers, the courteous conduct of correspondence, and the strategic position of the information clerk or receptionist in the central office.

Newspapers[8]

The metropolitan newspapers in the largest cities and the leading dailies in other cities are undoubtedly the most important printed media in terms of publicity. The attitude of the agency toward newspapers should be friendly, cooperative, and at the same time persistent. The employee in charge of agency publicity should regard him/herself as a reporter for all newspapers and attempt to give them the kind of material suitable for their particular purpose. Different newspapers have different policies and different ways of presenting news. The publicity person must know what these are so that he/she may supply their needs. Frequent contacts with news executives are of vital importance in improving the relationship of the agency to newspapers. It is not sufficient simply to write news releases, mail them out, and hope some of them will be used. By going to the editors in person, reasons for the use or rejection of stories may be ascertained and put to good advantage in the future.

The utmost impartiality in dealing with the papers, if there is more than one, is vitally necessary. The greatest frankness must be observed in writing news releases and real news should not be withheld. Through a long period of contacts with editors, their confidence is cultivated and an atmosphere conducive to the growth of cooperation is created.

Regular news. This news includes such stories as those dealing with action of the recreational service agency, announcement of new policies, dedication of new playgrounds, adoption of budgets, summary of attendance figures, and similar items.

Features. Features offer the best opportunities for securing space in metropolitan newspapers, since they belong to the class that is known as "human interest" stories. The opportunities for developing this type of publicity are almost unlimited: boys make a new type of kite; immigrant children get together and organize a band; lifeguards getting new equipment. The metropolitan newspapers are very willing to cooperate in working up these features. A regular news event may be arranged so as to bring much greater publicity by treating it from the feature angle.

Continuous publicity. Under this heading comes publicity intended to popularize municipal camps, swimming pools, golf courses, boathouses, and similar facilities. It is the most difficult kind of publicity to get across because it is necessary to go over and over the same ground, to hammer away with news stories and pictures on these subjects without necessarily having any real news on which to hang the story. This work requires ingenuity in discovering new things to be said about these facilities. Special programs and events at playgrounds or swimming pools help in securing publicity, because they furnish an excuse for writing about them. When there are no special effects, it is up to the person in charge of publicity to "make" news about them. One way of making news about a municipal camp is to arrange what is known as a "tie-up" with an automobile dealership, or its advertising agents: the automobile dealer sends one of its cars to the camp and uses the camp as a means of publicity for its automobile. In this way it is possible to secure "motor logs" in automobile sections of newspapers, which are read by numerous persons planning vacation trips. The municipal swimming pools are always good places where feature publicity may be worked up, whether or not an occasion has arisen to provide an excuse. Special stunts may always be developed there and prove satisfactory for use as swimming pool publicity.

Use of special departments. When a playground is built, the real estate section may yield some desirable publicity. The automobile section may be used as outlined above. The sports section, of course, is always useful in chronicling tournaments and sports of all kinds. The Sunday feature section is valuable for the publication of some special items. The picture and rotogravure sections offer fertile fields for the placing of recreational publicity.

Cooperation with promotion departments. When it is desirable to get continuous publicity for some special activity, the promotion department of a newspaper may be willing to cooperate. The promotion department works to increase the circulation and advertising volume and any event or activity that will enlist the interest of any additional readers is carefully considered by this department. Model airplane tournaments, backyard playground contests, and swimming carnivals are events that have been backed by newspaper promotion departments in many cities. One paper, by publishing a series of 12 Christmas carols on the 12 days preceding Christmas, gave effective aid to a recreational service department program of carol singing on the streets.

Newspapers sometimes conduct athletic and other contests of their own as part of their promotion program. In doing so they solicit the assistance of the recreational service department to conduct or officiate at these events. If these contests are free and open to all and are not tied in with subscription campaigns, departments often render assistance. Occasionally the events are held at playgrounds. When the department lends its collaboration, excellent publicity can be obtained for as long as the events receive notice in the papers. For their own events, papers devote a quantity of space far in excess of the space they would allot them if they were conducted under other auspices. The Soap Box Derby and the Roller Skates Derby held in all large cities, with final national contests, are events that many newspapers throughout the country have conducted. Recreational service departments assist in conducting these contests and in return receive much favorable mention in the papers.

When a tie-up with one newspaper is made, other papers, as a matter of fixed policy, withhold cooperation. When the department evidences willingness to associate itself with one paper, it must, to preserve goodwill, be equally willing to join with other papers under substantially the same conditions. Nothing is more destructive of newspaper cooperation than partiality in dealing with several papers or media.

Annual editions. Newspapers put out annual editions summarizing various activities for the year. Editors are often willing to use recreational articles of the summarizing type.

Editorials. When frequent mention of recreational articles is made in metropolitan newspapers, editorials come without being sought, as an outgrowth of the goodwill of the newspaper and its interest in the subject. However, another method of securing editorials is by sending material to editorial writers, packed with food for thought, for example, the annual report of the department, statement of attendance for the year, or similar analytical material.

Printed circulars and reports

The annual report, which all recreational service departments prepare and submit to the appropriate authorities, and which most departments publish and distribute in considerable quantity, provides information helpful to the citizens in interpreting the value of the work. It is a comprehensive and consolidated statement of the purposes and accomplishments of the department during the year. Its format should be attractive and the contents readable and interesting. Even before publication portions may be extracted and released to newspapers and other media. The citizen particularly needs information as to where the facilities of the department are located, what services are offered there, and how the individual and his/her family may avail themselves of them. The annual report is too voluminous to serve this purpose well or to be published in sufficient quantity. Accordingly, departments frequently publish brief circulars containing this information. These are available throughout the year at the central office and are passed out at meetings, exhibitions, and demonstrations. Separate inexpensive circulars may be published in quantity for different types of services, such as camping, picnicking, swimming, playgrounds for children, and adult hobbies.

Printed publicity

Under this heading may be listed folders, posters, window cards, and other printed material calculated to carry the message of the department to the public. It is best to make these as attractive as possible with photographs, art work, and the like.

The recreational service department has splendid opportunities to distribute printed material. It may be posted and handed out at the neighborhood recreational places. Children attending the recreational center may be asked to take the material to their parents. Since it concerns public business and is not commercial matter, the heads of large industries and business houses are generally willing to distribute the material to their employees. Such printed material may also be displayed in local food stores, banks, drugstores, malls, and other commercial enterprises where they will be seen by many thousands of people.

Weekly and neighborhood papers

The issuance of a regular news bulletin to these papers produces much publicity. This bulletin should contain stories of general interest that are not too lengthy so that they may be used in any space a newspaper or magazine has available. When special information affecting a particular district is available, such as the dedication of a new playground or park, it is well to send a special story to the newspaper covering that neighborhood.

Magazines

In every community there are numerous publications of both general and special interest in which it is possible to place articles on recreational work, including: parent–teacher bulletins, teachers' journals, magazines of special interest to women, Chamber of Commerce publications, and others. Before writing articles for these publications it is always best to consult the editor and secure his/her version of what the magazine needs and wants.

Motion pictures

A number of the largest departments have developed motion pictures, videos, or Apps illustrating department activities and dealing with public recreational service problems. Some have presented programs at civic meetings and other occasions. It is advisable, if a good impression is to be made, that films be up-to-date and, if possible, in color with sound accompaniment. With a tremendous rise of amateur motion picture photography, the voluntary aid of competent persons can be enlisted to produce these pictures if professional assistance is prohibitive in cost. Volunteer assistance in dramatization is readily available everywhere.

Radio and television. Television is probably one of the most important media for publicizing the activities of the department. The radio too may be used as a significant means of mass communication. Television and radio stations are required by the Federal Communications Commission to devote a certain percentage of their time to affairs of civic interest and public service. Recreational activities conducted under public auspices fall in this category. Station managers often welcome opportunities to present good programs emanating from the public recreational service.

There is much competition for television and radio time so programs need to be carefully planned to meet the exacting requirements of the stations. The address is the simplest form of presentation but it is also of least value. Amateur dramatic programs are acceptable to many stations if well presented, but stations are usually more receptive to amateur musical programs than to amateur drama. Interviews and novelty programs, such as contests and presentation of awards, are effective. For projects that serve obvious public purpose, such as programs for Memorial Day, Christmas, patriotic occasions, and the like, stations frequently make a series of spot announcements or telecasts in intervals between programs or for later release on videotape. If an event is of sufficient public interest, radio or TV stations consider the practicability of installing remote control equipment on the site for broadcasting or telecasting the event.

The internet

The development of a web site with concomitant subsets can be a most effective means for providing specific information to any person who has a computer. The web page should be developed with both sound and illustrations to capture and hold the attention of the browser. Advances in computer programming technology enable the web master to create the kind of informational presentation that is easy to understand while offering complete and appropriate material about the recreational service opportunities available from the department. Any activities, facilities, or places operated by the recreational service department can be highlighted and projected with eye-catching graphics. Both public and private agencies should make excellent use of the internet and other electronic devices in bringing their message to the public.

Program demonstrations

The recreational service department has the best opportunity of all municipal departments to cultivate good public relations. The total of its individual contacts with citizens is greater than that of the other departments, the contacts are of a somewhat intimate nature, and they take place on occasions which the citizen enjoys. The mood of the citizen when he/she makes his/her contact with the department is almost always a happy, expectant, and appreciative one, which is conducive to the formation of a fine impression. If the experience of the citizen is a positive one, he/she will publicize it widely by word of mouth. The effects of work conducted on an efficient and high plane and in a manner meriting the approbation of the citizenry are far-reaching in any public relations program.

Exhibits

Exhibits are worth the effort required to put them on only when large numbers of people get to see them and when they present material of general public interest. Consequently, exhibits that are carefully arranged with a view to presenting a real message, and that are seen by an adequate number of visitors are of considerable value. Recreational service departments, when invited to participate in general exhibitions, fairs, and shows, should give serious consideration to participation and its possible benefits. If an exhibit is entered, it should be truly representative of the department's work.

The most effective exhibits are live demonstrations. Practical demonstrations of skill in archery, badminton, fly casting, sketching, horseshoe pitching, handicrafts, or any of a thousand activities are immeasurably more effective than posters or printed matter referring to them. Any recreational service department can easily find many persons among its large clientele who delight in exhibiting personal skills in activities.

Window displays

Window displays may be placed in the windows of banks, department stores, large drugstores, food markets, and similar business organizations. These should be attractive and representative of departmental activities as well as giving times, place, dates, and any cost involved.

Tie-ups[9]

In addition to tie-ups with newspapers and their special departments, tie-ups with other civic agencies in a joint program are also of great value. One department had a most effective tie-up with the local fire department in a fire-prevention and educational program. Another department had a tie-up with the Parent–Teacher Association and the department of education in a "Planned Vacation Program for Every Child," including a backyard playground contest. These associated projects resulted in favorable mention of the recreational service department in all publicity relative to these events. If the newspaper can be associated in the project, it is most generous with its space. The recreational service department must be careful that standards of competition and recreational values are left to their determination in such joint projects. It must be assured that participants will not be exploited for private or commercial advantage.

Public addresses

Public speaking affords another excellent venue through which public relations may be cultivated. The recreational service department has many interesting stories to tell about its general services, events, and activities, the philosophy of its work, and related subjects. Its representatives are welcome speakers at many community occasions. Members of the recreational service board/commission, the general manager, and the several executives in charge of features of the work may fill speaking engagements. Efforts should be made to solicit opportunities of this kind and staff should be prepared by practice and encouraged to cultivate the ability to act as spokespersons for the department at public meetings or at private organizations.

Organization of public relations[10]

Small departments of recreational service cannot afford to employ a specialist to organize and dispense publicity, but this should not deter them from considerable effort in obtaining a good hearing. Board/commission members and managers should devote much time to public relations work, more in the recreational service department than in other municipal departments because recreational activities are so closely related to the public interest. Other members of the staff can be drawn into the program is well. Each department should have a carefully worked out program in which responsibility for the publicity devices outlined above is divided among the department employees. This division of responsibility should recognize the particular abilities of each person involved.

At present, no less than a score of park and recreational service departments in large cities assign the major duties and the general management of public relations to a specialist. The specialist is a staff employee and should have access to all phases of the work of the department. He/she should be associated with the chief executive officer and should work closely with him/her and with the board/commission, if there is one, so that he/she may be aware of the policies and plans of the department. The employment of a special publicity person should not absolve other employees from public relations responsibilities, but any special publicity undertaken by other employees should be cleared through the specialist.

Development of public support[11]

Determining the needs of the community in relation to recreational needs and financial capacity is difficult because there are few, if any, standards to guide the recreationist. Recreational service, including the areas and facilities or improvements required for it and personal leadership involved, remains unstandardized. It is still an amenity, something added when the essential things have been taken care of.

Does appraising the park and recreational needs of the community begin with public demand? This is a high-minded concept: all public service depends on public demand. How is public demand appraised? Is it judged by petitions? Petitions are uncertain and inconclusive. Diligent campaigners can get any number of names signed to any petition, especially if the signer does not thereby commit him/herself immediately and directly to pay for something.

Appraising public demand

Is public demand appraised by attendance at a promotional meeting or public hearing? This is a method of public expression, but only a small percentage of the interested and affected citizenry attend such meetings, and every public officer knows that a meeting can be systematically packed with proponents or opponents, as the case may be. Is public demand appraised by letters to the editors of newspapers or by newspaper editorials? These are important indicators of public opinion but not altogether reliable or representative. But all of these, together with correspondence, telephone contacts, departmental computer web page hits, visits, casual expressions of citizens, and actions by civic organizations, are indices of public demand.

Role of leadership in formulating public demand

Public demand, however, is not always enough. Sometimes the public does not have the basic information for the intelligent expression of its demand. Sometimes leadership must promote public demand in accordance with prudent judgment. Those officially and unofficially endowed with responsibility for exercising judgment must apprehend needs, guide community opinion, and formulate expressions which come to be recognized as embodying public demand. This is one of the prime responsibilities of recreational service managers.

Mobilizing fragmented public opinion

There is strong public demand for recreational services but there are few means for implementing this demand. The difficulty is that public opinion is expressed in support of a multitude of little things. It is easy to mobilize public opinion toward effective legislative action in favor of a main highway, an airport, more schools, police and fire stations, and the like because everybody can visualize the results. The mobilization of sectional opinions favoring a multiplicity of recreational interests, each having no communication with the others, is more difficult – but it must be done. Public action must be made responsive to public opinion in the field of recreational service.

Community effort can be enlisted in support of simple concepts capable of comprehension by everyone. The public demand for separate recreational entities must be related to a whole concept – for example, the concept of parks, playgrounds, or beaches. Campaigns on behalf of tennis courts, bowling greens, a golf course, an art workshop, a bandstand, a launching ramp, or any of a multitude of things avail little unless they can be consolidated in terms of public demand for parks or some other large recreational concept which embodies them all.

Recreational service systems throughout the country appreciate the importance of public relations and the attendant responsibilities for analysis and interpretation. With effective public relations, most public recreational service departments will succeed in presenting well-rounded and suitable programs that can stimulate and sustain the enthusiasm of the public; without effective public relations, few systems can succeed – and most fail.

Part IV

Primary influences on management practices

16 Program practices

The program is the fundamental reason for any recreational service agency. By the program is meant all of the direct and indirect recreational opportunities that are or can be delivered to the agency constituency. Direct services are those planned, organized, and led by the recreational service department. Indirect services are those opportunities afforded to the general public via ethically coordinating, cooperating, or collaborating with any community institution in the furtherance of obtaining recreational experiences and/or resources for the benefit of citizens residing in the community.

It represents the basic concept of recreational service. Patrons are attracted to recreational places because they expect to be entertained, amused, satisfied, or otherwise be a part of the enjoyment, excitement, and social action that accrues to both spectator and participant. Planning is essential to programming. It is the development of many different activities into a combined schedule, integrated, supportive, and having some relationship, regardless of the distinction drawn by category or major classes of activity. It is the presentation of various activity forms, active and passive or in combination, in such a manner as to stimulate some participation. Functionally, the program is everything occurring in a recreational context at, in, or on a recreational place. The program is viewed as a dramatic interplay of events in the routine course of human affairs. Such confrontations deal with peer relations, spontaneous activity or performance, modified behaviors, adherence to pre-arranged schedules, conformity to particular codes, individual adjustment to changing conditions, and the free exercise of the individual's desire to achieve as far as such activity does not infringe on the rights of anybody else. The program then, is the coordinated effort of the recreational service system to organize, manage, guide, lead, direct, or offer resources so that people may lead more satisfying leisure lives.[1] Programming, in the strictest sense, is the arranged activities that the system or agency sponsors, organizes, or for which it provides leadership. The program, on the other hand, is all those activities that can or may occur at a recreational place. The program consists of spontaneous, organized, routine, special, recurring, or intermittent activities through which people seek recreational outlet and value.

Modern public recreational service systems generally recognize that certain types of facilities should be available for "free play" or unscheduled individual activities and for self-organized and self-directed group activities. There is also the need for a certain amount of promotion and organization to multiply the number of activities and participants in the program, and to make for greater efficiency and larger usefulness of the public facilities. The necessity for supervision of activities and the provision of leadership by recreationists so that educational, social, and cultural outcomes may be realized is also appreciated. The problem of providing recreational experience to satisfy felt needs is one of great significance to the recreationist. As the professional gains comprehension of the problems of human behavior and human motivation, he/she must attempt to find activities that provide satisfaction and stimulation to participants. The activities recreationists consider basic are those generally found to produce positive benefits. After comparing recreational experiences, the recreationists include in his/her own program those appearing to have valuable outcomes.

Activity program of a recreational service system[2]

The term *program*, as applied to public recreational service system, includes the entire range of recreational activities for all ages on public grounds, areas, parks, and schools under various sponsorships. Many activities in the program are those which public agencies organize, sponsor, and conduct, ranging from encouragement, promotion, and general oversight to face-to-face instruction. Other activities in the program are those sponsored by voluntary agencies or commercial companies desiring only the use of public facilities.

Recreational programming begins with what the people want, but it does not default on exercising enlightened leadership to influence the selection of recreational activities and to guide the behavior of people in the direction of socially acceptable goals. This calls not only for adroit leadership, but also for highly qualified and inspired professionally prepared recreationists.

Programs for children require a great deal of attention by recreationists and volunteer helpers. The older the clientele, the less personal attention is required, except that the highly organized competitive activities do not prosper without competent direction and organization. It may be necessary to make resource personnel available when instruction or other direct counseling is required so that participants gain full benefit from their performance. Teenage clientele cultivate their own leadership if permitted to do so. Among adults competent leadership can always be recruited.

That activities for teenagers are considerably in the minority is somewhat symptomatic of programs of all youth service agencies. Except for the mass activities of high schools and extracurricular participation in seasonal sports, youth drop out of agency programs in numbers that are giving concern to the long-established agencies, owing partly to the fact that many young people, perhaps a third to a quarter enter the employment market in part-time jobs. It is also due to the unprecedented mobility of this age group today. Another factor may be the intrusion of fads and various momentary interests that draw the attention of these adolescents to other places and other activities, for example, texting, computer use, and gaming.

In organizing and promoting programs in public recreational centers, it is desirable to achieve a balanced program.[3] Balance should be sought in the involvement of all age groups of both genders, and in the distribution throughout the days and hours, day and evening, of the week. More particularly, there should be balance among the types of activities so that attractions and opportunities for recreational experience are available for all, with wide variation in recreational preferences and aptitudes, and degree of competence in participation. Balance also implies that groups of people standing in special need of recreational experience and leadership are not denied them.

Important as the function of leadership of people and programs at recreational centers may be, it must be appreciated that professional leadership is sparsely supplied. Recreational programs depend largely on volunteer leadership and many activities in the program are directed by leadership provided by those using the public facilities by permit.

The balanced program

Activities permitted and conducted by the public recreational service agency are countless. However, they may be classified into large categories for easier understanding and practical grouping. The normal recreational life of children and adults includes selected activities from all these groups. Each major grouping contains an infinite variety of sub-categories, which can be profitably utilized to provide a continuing series of interesting, challenging, and new experiences to the participants. The tendency to emphasize one category to the exclusion of others is a frequent error in programming that must be avoided. The groups may be graded from simple elementary forms to complicated expert forms. The following recreational activities have usually served as the basis for a well-rounded public recreational program.

Arts and crafts. The creative activities enable individuals to express themselves freely. These self-determining activities translate ego-centered involvement outward in a healthy process of self-realization. The individual is able to forget the normal restrictions of social custom and thereby answer a felt need for originality or, in some instances, reproduction.

Dance. Dance in its many forms is popular since it deals with the universal and basic need for movement. It is a process of symbolic communication, expressing many sentiments as well as serving as a fulfillment of emotional and physical feeling. It satisfies the ambivalent desires and may be one method by which human beings satisfy hostility urges in socially acceptable ways.

Drama. Drama is a form of communication through the human voice, body, and materials.[4] As a communicative process it gives satisfaction by transmitting ideas and emotions and providing self-expression either vicariously or directly. The elements of catharsis and empathy are closely related to dramatic reproductions.

Education. All experiences are educational, whether or not the participant is conscious of learning. Some learning takes place in formal settings (school); other learning is informal (recreational activities). Although it is true that nearly all recreational activity results in some learning, there are specific educational aspects of recreational experiences. A formally organized class in baton twirling, social dancing, or fur-coat remodeling closely approximates a classroom situation. Adult classes offered by the public recreational service department are both educational and recreational. Even informal subject courses, taken during leisure, may be recreational.

Hobbies. Hobbies offer engrossing, stimulating, and sustaining interest in activity usually not connected with vocational experiences. Hobbies include almost any human activity. A hobby provides an outlet for creative self-expression, self-determination, and self-realization, and fulfills the need for gregariousness, since hobbyists come into contact with one another as they explore manifestations of their particular interest. Most hobbies are of the acquisitive or appreciative type.

Motor activities: games, sports, and exercise. The enhancement of physical vigor, improvement of physiologic functioning, and release of hostility or sublimation of socially disapproved of feelings through competitive experiences or individual acts in a social setting provides satisfaction. Although many people take part in gross motor activities for achievement and self-realization, significant behavior toward others is also developed. Activities are composed of group and individual sports and games, team sports, calisthenics, and other competitive or non-competitive forms. In some instances, extreme activity types such as mountain biking, skateboarding on enclosed ramps, arcs, and slides, and similar experiences may be included.

Music. The value of music to the individual varies from person to person. The effect that music has on the individual, either as a participant or as a listener, illustrates its unique attraction. Whether music is listened to for the pure sensual pleasure of sound, for the esthetic effect, for the rhythm produced, or whether the individual plays or sings, empathy and emotional release are apparently generated. There is hardly anyone who does not appreciate some form of music.

Nature-oriented activity. Outdoor activities of many kinds belong in a well-balanced recreational program. One of the most requested and important is camping. Camping combines many skills and satisfactions. Wilderness camping, in particular, provides the participant with the exhilaration that comes from being close to unspoiled nature. There is a need for some camping activity in every recreational program, because many people have a traditional attachment to nature and intuitively seek to refresh themselves outside the artificial environment of community living. Nature lore, nature science, and all of the subjects involved in such activity are invaluable in building satisfying knowledge in the individual.

Service. Service is concerned with all activities normally associated with altruistic or humanitarian programs. Social service activities have long been utilized by recreationists to fill leisure productively, whereas other forms of activity may not satisfy the human urge to extend sympathy or give aid. The release one obtains from whole-heartedly giving service to others, the exchange of too much self-concern for self-giving, results in a feeling of warm satisfaction. Service enables the individual to voluntarily devote him/her self to others. No other experience provides this sense of personal extension.

Social activities. Social needs are satisfied when people have to meet, mix, "get along," or adjust. Social activities of a wide scope have a place in any program in which socially approved actions and good mental health are objectives. Relationships developed through social intercourse contribute to the maturity of individuals, the development of empathy, sympathy, catharsis, personal esteem, and self-expression.

Special events. Special events are the occasions that give "spice" to the program. They attract new patrons or participants, new talents may be discovered, an incentive to practice may be provided. Such activity offers an ever-changing flavor or emphasis to the program, and creates opportunities to secure some educational outcomes not otherwise possible. The variety is endless and limited only by the imagination of the recreationist in charge and the participants who may assists in the planning.

All of these activities should be part of the balanced recreational program, for each activity contributes its part to the overall program. It is important for the public recreational service agency to offer a comprehensive and balanced program that has the potential to appeal to the full variety of people's interests and needs.

Problems of programming

The program is not an arbitrary measure imposed on people; it is planned, developed, and operated in response to their needs. In establishing a new program, it is desirable to offer a wide range of activities to discover where participant interest lies. By developing only the specific activities for which there is a distinct call, the agency avoids the risk of spreading itself too thinly. It also places its program on a firm groundwork of interested participants. Although this may be ideal for budgetary reasons, it does present a negative aspect as well: the program may become unimaginative and stagnant. Because a particular activity meets the needs of some individuals does not mean that the agency is fulfilling its full potential. There must, therefore, be constant evaluation and appraisal of the program. The department must continue to build or actually create demand by stimulating the interest of the public in new and varied activities. It must offer its constituents opportunities to grow recreationally; it must provide the means and the leadership to enable participants to find new wholesome methods of expression in leisure.

Each type of public recreational place presents its own peculiar problems in program organization and promotion. Some recreational places are established primarily for a single specialized recreational experience. The program at such places tends to become a matter of mere routine. The patrons desire only to be granted freedom to pursue their interests and enthusiasms with a minimum of interference. Programming management therefore consists primarily in arranging the physical facilities for efficient use, issuing permits for use, establishing regulations governing use, and promoting activities to ensure maximum participation. Programming management on these recreational places may be in the organization of certain competitive events, staged shows, carnivals, town barbecues, or festivals.

Factors for consideration

Some scheduled activities may require no special organization of players in advance and may be engaged in at the whim of the player. These undirected activities (or free play) tend to become routine for certain regular attendees. Other activities, particularly group and team games, class meetings for instruction, or group participation, must be planned in advance and scheduled for a given time and place, usually taking place again and again, but according to schedule. Still other activities occur only once and require preparation for days and sometimes weeks in advance, and terminate in a performance or demonstration. These are the eagerly anticipated spectacular events that build or sustain interest in the program.

Relative value of activities. The routine activities are of greatest value from the standpoint of development of the powers and skills of the individual, because they are repeated day after day and their effects are cumulative. Their developmental value increases in proportion to the frequency of their repetition. The special events are valuable chiefly because of the preparation and instruction required to make them possible, and because they sustain interest in a program that might otherwise tend to become commonplace and monotonous.

Patrons involved. Some people prefer only to "drop in" at recreational centers or other facilities and participate informally as the whim strikes them, or they prefer not to take part in any scheduled contests or meetings. Others come only to attend special events either as performers or as spectators. Still others come only by appointment to meet in a regular class, play, or scheduled game. Some parents permit their children to attend the recreational facility only when a scheduled event is to take place. At every center, playground, or other facility, a regular clientele is almost always present and ready for anything. The program should be planned to provide some attraction for all these potential patrons.

Patrons' assistance in program planning. The participant-planning technique is a process whereby interested individuals help to plan activities. The program does not develop in a vacuum; it is the product of selected ideas, directed interests, and self-stimulating experiences. Participant planning is necessary to the continuing success of the program.[5] The ideas generated from such groups are essential for the development of future activities. The ideas of patrons are important and may even be highly significant to program outcomes. When potential participants have a hand in developing the program, they will feel, and rightly so, that the activities are theirs. They develop a closer feeling for and responsibility toward the program. As a result, they derive much greater value from their efforts, they find the activities more stimulating, and they bring new ideas and views to what might become mere professional routine. Recreationists should utilize participant planning in attempting to satisfy the recreational needs of the public.

Programming

Every recreational center should have a daily, weekly, monthly, seasonal, and yearly program. The recreational center director will find it helpful to chart the program for the entire year, marking those events during the year (opening and closing of the schools, holidays, thematic projects, historic events, memorial commemorations, and seasonal emphases) that will influence the program. The program for each month or season may be worked out in more detail as the year progresses.

The program for the week should be posted in a conspicuous place so that all may see it, become interested in its activities, and be free to suggest other stimulating experiences. The daily program is the recreationist's plan of work for the day. The director plans each day's work in advance, always including something new or interesting and never depending wholly on the inspiration of the moment. He/she may also avail him/herself of a lay planning committee for additional help in formulating the program.

It is inadvisable to prescribe the same program for all the centers and playgrounds in a public recreational system, although a coordinated series of events and some special activities may be observed throughout the system. These are set forth in a master program for the entire year, announced in advance. The program of each facility should be designed for and adapted to the needs, interests, traditions, and organizations of the neighborhood, the programs of other agencies, the completeness of the facility itself, the availability of professional leadership, and the skills, talents, and prior experiences of the people residing in the neighborhood. These factors vary greatly between any two recreational centers. The director of each facility should be given freedom to establish the program for his/her center with no more control from the central office of the department than seems necessary to ensure a well-balanced and varied program.

The program is only a plan. Numerous unforeseen situations may arise, which dictate the necessity for a change in the program. To adhere blindly to prescribed or preconceived programs devitalizes the recreational facility and its activities. To arouse new interest in people, to capture their transitory and changeable focus of attention, and to involve them in newly programmed events are a real test of the recreationist's discernment, leadership, and skill.

No recreationist can have at his/her fingertips at all times of the day all the information necessary to conduct a successful program. The individual director finds it helpful to build up – for his/her facility and for his/her own personal and professional use – a library containing materials on all phases of the activities that he/she organizes and conducts. The director who refers again and again to such material generally has the most diversified program. Computerized data concerning recreational activities may prove invaluable in the development of stimulating leisure experiences.

Self-directed groups

The use of public facilities for recreational activities by private groups whose membership is exclusive is often permitted by recreational service departments if the facilities are not required by public groups. Permits usually set forth the regulations governing the use. Some departments charge for such permits, especially if the group wants to charge admission. The charge is determined by the cost of making the facilities available, the ability of the group to pay, and the purposes for which the proceeds are to be used. If the proceeds are to be used for public benefit, the charge is usually low; if the proceeds are to be used for private gain, the charge is determined on a commercial basis.

Program supplies, materials, and equipment

The successful conduct of a recreational program requires not only suitable areas and structures but also supplies, materials, and equipment. Goods consumed in the maintenance of structures or operation of the program are termed *supplies*. *Materials* consist of all wood, metal, paper, sand, clay, liquids, and other goods that are formed into objects produced in program activities. More durable items, consisting of expendable goods utilized for maintenance or in the recreational program, are termed *equipment*. Articles are classified as equipment when they are considered to have a useful life of more than one year.

Supplies and equipment required in the maintenance of properties are usually furnished at agency expense. Supplies and materials used and consumed by participants in recreational activities present a problem. It is not advisable for a public recreational service agency to be lavish in the provision of such supplies and materials. In public recreational service budgets are still too low to allow generous furnishing of all goods required in the program. Practice is not uniform among recreational departments but the following general rules may be deduced.

Supplies, materials, and equipment should be furnished:

1. For group activities when the item in question is used by the whole group or groups (basketballs, tennis nets, baseball bats).
2. Generously for children but sparingly, if at all, for adults.
3. For individual activities when failure to provide material would definitely render a highly important activity impossible to conduct (handicraft materials in very underprivileged neighborhoods).
4. For demonstration purposes in order to get an activity started but which, when under way, will be furnished by the participants (tonnettes or harmonicas to initiate interest in playing these instruments).
5. When the cost of supplying the activity is insignificant or relatively low (inexpensive handicraft materials for children).

Supplies, materials, and equipment should not be furnished as a general rule:

1. When the activity requires an item peculiarly adapted to individual use (fielder's glove, gymnasium shoes, and musical instruments).
2. When the cost is high in relation to the use derived (tennis rackets, badminton shuttlecocks, fencing foils).
3. When the item is easily stolen (hand balls, arrows, tennis balls, golf balls).
4. When tradition favors individual possession of articles (marbles, tops, roller skates).
5. When the article can easily be made by the participant (kites; model planes, cars, boats).
6. When the supplies are to be utilized elsewhere than at the public recreational place.

Inventories

The individual recreational facility, as well as the entire recreational system, must maintain an inventory of its supplies, materials, and equipment. Only with an inventory will the department be able to control the costs of issuance and replacement and be able to make cost analyses for accounting purposes and to justify budgetary requests.

A perpetual inventory is maintained at all centers in the system. If facilities are open for public use only seasonally, the inventory is taken at the beginning and end of the season. Notations of items used or delivered to the facility should be made on the appropriate forms. A certain amount of loss through damage, wear, or theft is to be expected. The facility director, however, must make every reasonable effort to account for all items in his/her custody.

Check-out

A procedure for the issuance of supplies, materials, and equipment must be developed to ensure the return of loaned articles. It is advisable to establish a list or index of all supplies, materials, and equipment on hand at the recreational facility. If patrons using the facility are not registered, they should be required to produce some identification when any item is issued. The participant's name is checked off when he/she returns the item.

Although there is less danger of loss or theft at a small playground or at a center where the recreationist is acquainted with all the patrons, there is a great likelihood of loss in a large recreational center that is heavily patronized and where the recreationist cannot know all of the participants, particularly when the center is utilized by transients.

Responsibility for supplies, equipment, and materials

Efficient operation and conduct of the program call for systematized handling of supplies, materials, and equipment. Failure to provide the needed items may cause serious delay and unnecessary inconvenience. Materials, supplies, and equipment represent substantial costs and render imperative the avoidance of waste, loss, and damage.

Central stores

Quite apart from the issuance or loan of supplies, material, and equipment to patrons are the establishment and maintenance of central stores or stocks. The following procedures are found to be efficacious:

1. A central storeroom should be established for all departmental supplies, materials, and equipment, for all areas.
2. Responsibility for the central stockroom should be lodged with one employee with complete authority to receive and issue items to the several divisions of the department.
3. Location of the stockroom should be convenient to all divisions and secure against unauthorized entry.
4. Stock must be organized to facilitate issuance. Items should be indexed by established code for easy reference and fast location.
5. Supplies should be issued only on written requisition as authorized by departmental policy. A record should be maintained that indicates all items issued and entries should be posted from a requisition file.

The record indicates the date of issuance and the division, section, or office to which it was issued.

6. Ordering dates should be established and adequate stocks, based on the rate of consumption, should be maintained.

7. Periodic inspection of supplies, materials, and equipment should be made to determine whether they are being utilized in the proper manner.

Recreational activities conducted or enabled by the public recreational service department offer countless opportunities for all those who participate in some way to experience the satisfaction of having an enjoyable time. Coupled with learning a new skill or exhibiting a highly thought of technical performance, recreational activities provide an atmosphere of compelling attention. Those engaged in the program benefit from the sense of achievement or personal fulfillment they receive. This leads to individual feelings of well-being and promotes the social fabric.

17 Resources for a recreational service system

With the legal establishment of the agency and a confluence of authority to carry out the duties and responsibilities for which it was inaugurated, the stage is set for the development of a system that will encompass all of the identifiable recreational resources within the community. Whether in the public, quasi-public, or private domains, the process of coordination between these agencies must be implemented so that the greatest scope of recreational opportunities will be available to potential participants.

What constitutes a total recreational service system in modern cities? At the outset it must be recognized that a variety of public entities contribute to an array of recreational possibilities in any given community. Added to this is an agglomeration of private concerns, including companies, consultants, teachers of various skills, and for-profit organizations that cater to the gamut of needs, wants, or desires of people with leisure. Of course, voluntary, non-profit organizations must also be included in this listing of resources because they serve a broad segment of the population recreationally as well. Quasi-public agencies tend to satisfy some recreational needs of specific populations. All of these have an impact on the direct delivery of recreational opportunities to the people in the community.

Development of the park function

Parks have been established in cities through the centuries to serve several purposes, including those arising unpredictably as population proliferates and social problems (which must be solved) emerge in a turbulent society. Among these purposes has been the need to provide places for organized and self-directed active recreational pursuits; and to give guidance and direction for them when suitable.[1] This modern function of parks derives from the expanding role of leisure and the recognition of the importance of recreational service in contemporary society.[2]

Historically, parks have been used as places for public assembly, public markets, and refuges in times of disaster. They have served as mobilization centers for common defense against an aggressor. As cities have become heavily populated, parks have tended to relieve the effects of congestion.

Always, they are favored as places of beauty and repose, and as sites for civic and recreational buildings.[3] Today their use as places of active recreational experience, passive reflection, appreciation, as places for children's play, and the competitive sports of youth and adults is widely recognized.[4] Depending on population congestion or dispersion, permanent recreational installations may be augmented by mobile[5] and/or portable[6] recreational facilities.

A modern park system contains neighborhood parks[7] – comparatively small areas supplementing neighborhood schools; community parks – larger areas providing special facilities for all age groups; regional parks, frequently within or near large metropolitan complexes; reservations and wilderness areas, wherever nature has placed them; special areas of extraordinary beauty; and places for active recreational pursuits, such as large sports areas, lakes, trails, golf courses,[8] conservatories, arboretums, zoological gardens, museums, and so forth. These large areas and highly specialized facilities are within the category or component of regional parks. The larger a city becomes in area and population, the greater its need and inclination to provide regional recreational places.

The park-school concept

Park-school is a term applied to a situation in which a school and park are in juxtaposition. It should not be confused with school-park, which is used to describe a complex of school units (elementary, secondary, and others) and certain special social service facilities in a park-like development. The positioning is sometimes planned deliberately to afford the school more outdoor space than would otherwise be practicable and at the same time to provide a park. On the other hand, it may be a fortuitous situation resulting from land being available for acquisition which is suitable for either purpose but which is too large to be afforded by either agency alone. The park is then used by the school for its program of outdoor education and for more recreational activities than would be possible under other circumstances. If the park is provided with facilities used in a park-administered program that are not found in a standard school-ground development, the combined facilities permit a broader and larger program. The park-school may become a single operable unit offering amenities and opportunities for recreational experiences that could not be attained by other means.

The park-school concept has gained great favor, especially when planning new communities. It is difficult to apply to the redevelopment of communities where the schools are surrounded by other buildings rendering the acquisition cost of additional land prohibitive. In the long view, the principle may well be applied, but not to the exclusion of other properties removed from schools where the need for a park might transcend the need to add park improvements to a school property.

Under the park-school plan it becomes incumbent on the two independent administrations, municipal recreational service or parks and schools, to affect harmonious cooperation in coordination of day-to-day operations. The school system is not set up to administer park services, nor can the city recreational service administration assume the functions of the school. The ideal is that programs emanating from the two independent agencies appear, for practical purposes, to be programs of a single agency.

Physical components of a local public system

The management of a recreational service system requires understanding of the various necessary components designed to provide significant opportunities to the department's constituency.[9] This means that neighborhood and community recreational centers must be emplaced to serve the diverse needs of the people residing in the local legal subdivision. A neighborhood is the area served by an elementary school, a residential area approximately half a mile in diameter, or an area in which local service facilities are accessible within walking distance for use on a day-to-day basis. Neighborhood recreational centers may be at a school, in a public park, or in a combined park-school complex, equipped primarily for the recreational needs of children and, within limits, for others in the neighborhood.[10]

A community is a natural grouping of districts containing many neighborhoods with a common civic life and historic identity. Community recreational centers must be larger than neighborhood centers and contain facilities that are required by teenagers, adults, and family groups. Their facilities require more space (preferably 10 acres or more in already developed communities and in communities being planned in totality) than is found in neighborhood centers, and their location is often determined by fortuitous circumstances, such as availability of land for park use, rather than by precise planning according to the general standards employed.

Standards for spaces and facilities

The quest for authoritative standards has been a preoccupation of recreationists from the beginning of the recreational service movement. A number of provisions of space for outdoor recreational activities and cities have been a consideration since the late 1920s. Although several authorities in the field agreed with the concept that 100 persons per acre was a reasonable provision, there has never been a well-founded research attempt to determine the precise spatial needs of people for recreational purposes. The rule of thumb has simply become an accepted substitute for hard facts. The 1 acre per 100 persons is typically defined as including recreational and park areas lying within or immediately adjacent to the city; areas desired for neighborhood and community use, as well as areas serving a regional park for conservation purposes.

Any study of recreational needs insofar as spaces and facilities are concerned immediately reduces the probability of stated minimum space requirements for the various types of open areas because of the widely divergent aspects comprising local conditions. Even more importantly, minimum standards may erroneously be thought of as suggesting completely adequate provision. It is probably true to state that there is no excessive provision for recreational purposes except in terms of economic capability. Therefore, each recreational service system can only establish space set-asides based upon what the local population considers adequate and is willing to finance. Despite praiseworthy efforts to devise standards based upon population density, land availability, particular facilities, and financial capability, great disparity exists between the creation of reliable standards and the data being produced by current research to determine user patterns, carrying capacity, resources, and recreational needs of potential participants.[11]

In fact, there is no agreement on the amount of space that is necessary and desirable for regional parks. Incorporating large spaces in the public domain for conservation of open spaces, wildlife conservation, and regionally oriented recreational activity is still to be realized as a goal.

Standard determination

There are two main approaches that might be taken in the establishment of recreational space and facilities standards: (1) criteria expressed in terms of ratio of population to space (acres) and to essential facilities; and (2) criteria based on the habits, dispositions, and characteristics of the public (users or consumers). The former is a logistic computation to determine comparative supply or adequacy. The latter is a strategic determination based on value judgments of the activities deemed to serve the objectives of the responsible administrative system and to meet the public's demand.

These judgments take into account demographic facts, the variable and changing recreational culture, prevailing fads and fashions, the leisure time the public has available, the disposition of the people involved in public, quasi-public, or privately sponsored programs, mobility, transportation to recreational places, and the like. Standards for land space should begin with a consideration of open areas required for environmental beautification and conservation, the space required to relieve the effects of congestion and proliferation of population in the urban setting, and the space needed for the installation of facilities and the organization of activities for the public. Of course, the urban area itself may become a useful recreational resource.[12]

Strategy dictates the need for specific areas, structures, and facilities situated so that the recreational needs and interests of the constituency will best be served. This can occur when public management gains the fullest cooperation from and coordination of any and all community-based agencies that have a primary or secondary interest in the delivery of recreational services. In any case, the several components of the system must be enumerated and recognized for eventual application.

Facilities for a neighborhood recreational center

The activities in a neighborhood recreational center require both indoor and outdoor facilities. Indoor facilities should probably include a large all-purpose room for meetings, entertainments, all kinds of dancing, table games,[13] parties, and limited fitness activities (aerobics and/or calisthenics). There should be some food service capability and storage space for chairs, game tables, and other supplies, equipment, or materials. A craft room or shop permitting elementary crafts requiring work tables and hand tools is always beneficial. Finally, clubrooms for small clubs or group meetings provide a sound investment.

Outdoor facilities necessitate softball or junior baseball diamonds adaptable to the official rules of Little League baseball. Junior diamonds are smaller replicas of official diamonds and should be of turf. Paved surfaces, not normally in the best interests of the users, are most frequently found in elementary school yards because the foot traffic is too heavy to permit the maintenance of turf. Paving and asphalt surfaces are typically used when maintenance considerations are more important than user safety.

Children's playground apparatus for vigorous activity needs to be installed with a view to safe use with soft landing surfaces.[14] An outdoor gymnasium equipped with apparatus offering graduated challenges to teenagers and others can be a useful facility.[15] Equipment should be at hand for "pickup" games and the area should be night-lighted for extended use. Game areas and courts should be placed close to the outdoor gymnasium to allow better safety-surface installation, better supervision and economy in lighting during the evening hours. Court dimensions should be adjusted to the maturity of the users.

Facilities for a community recreational center[16]

The community recreational center requires all of the elements proposed for the neighborhood center plus elements to accommodate persons of all age groups who come to the center from several districts in larger numbers than those attending a district or neighborhood center and who participate in a greater variety of activities. The additional facility elements should include indoor facilities with a gymnasium large enough for a standard basketball court.[17] The ceiling should have no beam or other obstruction lower than 20 feet from the floor. Spectator accommodations are desirable and dressing rooms with shower facilities are necessary. Obviously the gymnasium may be used for sports other than basketball, that is, gymnastics, wrestling, tai chi chuan, martial arts activities, etc. An auditorium with a stage, separate and apart from the gymnasium, designed for lectures, dramatic presentations, exhibits, and musical concerts should be included in the design. It is always preferable to have a swimming pool installed to be used for instruction and recreational purposes.[18] Senior high schools often have indoor pools to meet the requirements of a compulsory physical education program. Park pools are almost always of the outdoor type. Whether indoor or outdoor, pools are not yet accepted as a standard facility for neighborhood parks, nor for neighborhood elementary schools; therefore they are specified among the essential facilities for community recreational centers. Tennis, volleyball, handball, racket ball, and other courts should be available in the community center design where space permits. These areas allow organization of tournament play as well as class instruction.

Auxiliary parks or centers[19]

Auxiliary parks and centers are not required in all neighborhoods or in all communities of a city. They may be desired in some neighborhoods, or in one or more communities, or in a location apart from other parks. The auxiliary parks may be park triangles, park circles, park strips, sitting areas, tot lots, and parklets, or vest-pocket parks.

Park triangles and circles. When cities and subdivisions were laid out, it was considered good practice to provide park circles about 50 feet in diameter at the intersection of two major streets. The areas were intended to be planted to provide an interesting landscape as they were approached from any direction, a sitting area and a place for statues or fountains or unusual planting. The traffic circled the area to the right; persons on foot could cross the streets at any point in comparative safely and linger on the circle. This plan does not fit the conditions of today as traffic moves too fast to make access safe. Traffic signals are usually installed, the view is obstructed, and traffic is delayed. The circles typically remain, but are no longer planned in new developments.

Park triangles at intersections were improvised when two streets did not intersect each other at right angles, sometimes when a new development joined an older one. They were intended to perform the same function as the circles. Both are difficult to maintain in a manner satisfactory to the owners of nearby property. Maintenance of the property houseward from the curb, including the sidewalk, belongs to the property owner; maintenance of circles and triangles is the responsibility of the city and uniform maintenance is difficult to achieve.

Park strips. When a wide street was planned, a strip of land in the center of the street extending for any distance was provided. They were planted in a manner similar to the circles and triangles. Often they were intended as rights of way for interurban transportation. Sometimes the strips were owned or held as easements by whoever owned the transportation company, especially if the lines preceded the adjoining area in development. When the rights of way were abandoned or taken over by the city, with or without compensation, the strips became parks or were used to widen the street on either side. In congested areas they are still a much-appreciated amenity and perform a very useful park purpose. In re-planning business areas, decorative malls have been laid out in the center strip of the street, the traffic has been made to detour into other streets, and a whole area has been improved to provide an attractive locale for shopping. Sidewalks and building fronts have been dressed up. Parking has been accommodated, when it can be, at the rear of commercial buildings.

Sitting areas. In places of impacted population, as in the downtown areas of older cities, places to sit and pass the time of day become very important. It is good planning, appreciated by the business interests, the shoppers, and the people residing in the area, to take advantage of any odd land to provide sitting areas with attractive landscaping.

Vest-pocket parks. The origin of this term is not known but it came into common use in New York City and Philadelphia in the 1950s. It was first used to denote a vacant piece of property, privately or publicly owned, on which a playground was improvised for children or youth, in the absence of any other play areas serving the block or neighborhood. Frequently they were inadequately improved and had non-durable apparatus and they tended to fall into disuse or were deliberately misused and vandalized. Municipal park or recreational departments were loath to take them over because of planning constraints, the necessity of re-planning and reconstruction. Funds were not budgeted to do the required work or to provide the supervision that was deemed necessary for the protection of the neighbors to obtain proper behavior for recreational activity. However, some have proved themselves. Above all they have demonstrated the desirability of auxiliary park facilities in areas of great need.

Tot lots. The term *tot lot* has long been used to denote a small area within the residential block for children of preschool or early school age. It is an equipped area within a residential block available to mothers and small children who reside there, without street exposure, fronting on the street or, perhaps, at a corner, thus being available to the mothers and children of several blocks. It must be regarded as an auxiliary park planned for neighborhoods where there is a special need and not as one to be provided throughout the city. There are two conditions that indicate the need for tot lots. One is the percentage of women (particularly mothers) in the labor market, and the other is the average family income of the neighborhood. A third condition might well be the density of population of the neighborhood.

Teenage recreational centers. Modern experience in the conduct of recreational activities for youth makes it very plain that the conventional programs conducted by most agencies leave a void insofar as participation of some of the youth is concerned. Many of the youths from age 15 to 19 are dropouts from the established programs. They appear to be waiting for some opportunity to socialize with their peers and to pursue a variety of opportunities for recreational experience. It is not unusual to see teenagers congregating in shopping malls, in electronic arcades, or at seasonal facilities where they can mix and mingle. If the recreational center is going to attract this age group, it must offer inducements that will draw their attention and engagement. The teenage recreational center should be an integral unit, preferably part of a community park, which can be described best as a "drop-in" center at which there are a variety of incentives to participate freely in many activities known to be pleasing to older teenagers. The center is presided over by specially prepared and dedicated youth leaders who cultivate the involvement of the youth in self-directed and self-managed activities. Preferably it should be an outdoor and indoor facility, operated the year-round, day and evening. In short, it should be a place that teenagers regard as their own. It must still be considered as an optional facility in the public recreational service system and should be introduced where experience and investigation reveal an unmet need. A large community park, if otherwise well located, is the appropriate place for the center.

Senior citizens' recreational center. This facility is accepted and recognized as more of a necessity than the teenage recreational center, owing to the rapid growth of the elderly segment of society.[20] Special indoor and outdoor facilities, somewhat removed from the areas used by children in a public park, are in great demand. Organized programs, conducted in large measure by the older adults themselves, are indicated, with some professional oversight.

Optional elements. The facilities listed as essential elements in several categories are minimal with respect to the number of each and to the inclusion of other components. Every recreational service system should seek to have at least one outstanding park development to give the city distinction and recognition.[21] The locale of the city, such as beside an ocean, or with a lake or other geographic, geological, climatic, or historic situation, frequently causes a city to exploit its uniqueness by an addition to its inventory of park facilities and advantages.[22] Unique facilities cannot be considered as standard components found in every neighborhood, district, or community. By their nature they are extraordinary features. They may be outstanding by virtue of their completeness, as in the case of a railroad exhibition, a world-class zoo, botanical garden, art museum, planetarium, or aquarium.

Public conveniences in the park and recreational system. Not mentioned in the catalog of elements for a recreational service system are sanitary conveniences for people. Often it is desirable to have separate conveniences for children and adults, and for persons participating in indoor activities and those using the outdoor facilities. They may be in the same building with a wall dividing them, for when an admission is charged for indoor activities or when a group must be supervised, such as for a teenage dance, exit through the lavatories to the out-of-doors is not desirable.

Parking. Early plans for neighborhood and community parks included no space or arrangements for parking the automobiles of clientele. Parking areas are now considered to be an essential facility in community parks and sometimes in neighborhood parks as well. These may be constructed as underground spaces or as freestanding parking garages. In well-organized cities of considerable size, building and construction regulations applicable to building permits require certain numbers of parking spaces related to the attendance capacities of the facilities.

Night-lighting. To add utility to a neighborhood and community park night-lighting of play areas is very important. Except for children, there is more recreational activity for people in the evening hours than at any other time. The recreational service system must be developed to provide for activities during the evening hours. Portions of large parks through which people must pass to reach the activity areas require illumination as well.

Landscaping. Landscaping of parks, playgrounds, and recreational centers might well have been mentioned as an absolute imperative in the development of a park and recreational system. Traditionally, this was the initial improvement to be made of an area acquired and developed for park purposes. Parks were places for the enjoyment of the beauty of the landscape. Recreational facilities gradually intruded on the landscape, and park planners sometimes opposed this seeming intrusion. Some believed that the two functions – parks and recreational service – were mutually exclusive. Gradually, the view changed and it has come to be accepted that a park, especially in local neighborhoods and communities, should be a place of beauty with an equitable share of the area devoted to landscape developments, and that a playground or recreational center should be efficiently and functionally developed for active recreational experiences with ample attention to landscape. The two functions are not incompatible even in small areas. Grassed areas for certain play places should be provided, because some activities require softer and safer surfaces than asphalt or cement.

Minimal standards for the physical plant

The table of minimal standards may be developed and used for comparing the adequacy of recreational spaces and facilities in one community with that of another within the same city, or between two or more cities. Utilization of the device requires four steps: (1) identification of census tracts within the several community boundaries and computation of the total population of each; (2) inventory of the physical resources for recreational purposes according to the categories in the devised table of standards; (3) computation of the percent of adequacy within each category; and (4) summation of the separate percentages for each community and determination of the average adequacy for each.

The use of this instrument is, of course, less than perfect. Its validity depends on the degree of standardization of specifications of the facilities and the accuracy of the inventory. Another inaccuracy in the use of the device derives from the fact that all elements are not of equal importance. Moreover, totaling of averages is not a precise statistical technique. Nevertheless, the instrument can be beneficially applied to indicate guidelines for achieving parity in spaces and facilities among communities in the same city. It will forcefully reveal past errors in planning and development, and it provides a sound basis for determining priorities in the current and future allocation of funds.

Inventory of a system

Any system composed of finite entities requires an inventory of its parts in order to measure and appraise it. A well-organized recreational service system should have inventories of real estate and of permanent structures and equipment to assist in providing equitable allocation or distribution of the properties, in terms of need, among the neighborhoods, districts, and communities. Inventories of movable equipment and supplies are used for several purposes, including accountability for its care and replacement. Compiling an inventory in a form that makes its data available for study can become an involved procedure; to relate its data to other available data, such as demographic studies obtained from the decennial United States Census, complicates the procedure. Fortunately, technology has provided computers to expedite the process and permit countless comparative displays, summaries, and rankings.

An acceptable principle guiding the selection of facilities to be placed on neighborhood and community recreational sites is that the facilities permit a satisfactory program of day-to-day and seasonal activities suited to the needs and demands of people generally, and arranged for the most efficient and economical use of the available land and buildings. Of course, the need for the physical plant is obvious. Without the areas set aside to provide recreational opportunities there could be no delivery of service. To this must be added the organizational component of any system. This means the need for human resource development, fiscal management, coordination, record keeping, programming, public relations, leadership, and evaluation. All of these efforts combine to make up the structure and arrangement of the comprehensive recreational service system.

18 Liability and recreational service management

Every person requires a perception of security, in the abstract or concrete, as a condition of life. People need to feel safe in their person and property. Security is fundamental to the stability of society. A person should sense that appropriate behavior will be reciprocated by others. Unfortunately, reality is quite different from the ideal. By deliberate or inadvertent action people may be injured or their property damaged through willful misconduct, ignorance, or neglect. That is the reason for law. Law is a compilation of rules of behavior derived from common practice and codified by some recognized authority that legally forces adherence.[1]

Law is dynamic, constantly in flux, and developing in the context of changing conditions and situations. Simultaneously, laws maintain stability, accountability, expectability, and protection. In other words, law comprises the entire range of rules, values, and ideals that govern the course of human events. To this may also be added the necessary enforcement of government or individuals in the courts when the rights of people are infringed.

The standard of care owed to all those who participate in organized or sponsored recreational activities under the control of some agency must be consistent with legislative intent and judicial interpretation. In order to fulfill their mandate to see to the safety of participants, those involved in supplying or delivering recreational service need to know the requirements for reasonable and prudent operations.

There is really only one sure way to escape the pressures, bad publicity, and possible monetary loss which lawsuits against recreational service organizations reflect – prevent them. Allegations of negligence can be successfully prevented through a focus on the simple but central ideas of safety and education.

To be sure, this is in an era where litigation is brought against any organization or individual for real or imagined injuries.[2] Even when there are no grounds for a suit, litigants will attempt to intimidate the alleged defendant by bringing suits. There is any number of reasons for these actions. The plaintiff was actually injured or had property damaged and seeks redress. The plaintiff believes that the organization was responsible for a mishap, despite his/her own negligence, and seeks redress. The plaintiff is merely being a nuisance and hopes to obtain some monetary reward despite the fact that there has been no injury or damage suffered. In the latter instance, there is no basis for a suit, but the plaintiff hopes that some out-of-court settlement in his/her favor will ensue or that the insurance carrier will be directed to pay off to forestall any unpleasant publicity. People are perfectly willing to bring suits at any time they feel that they have been imposed upon. This is particularly true if the agency is somewhat vulnerable to such litigation by virtue of weak or questionable standards of the care which the agency owes to its patrons. Today, much litigation is initiated against agencies and individuals for injuries suffered that would never have been brought to court if the plaintiff was unaware that the defendant was covered by insurance.

This material is designed to relieve all those who work in any aspect of the field of recreational service from the costs which accompany lost litigation. It has been produced to make recreationists, and others associated with the provision of recreational service, cognizant of the complexities of fulfilling legal obligations they have to those whom they serve. Furthermore, although information is presented about tort law as it applies to the provisions of recreational services, it is more important to make recreationists recognize their legal responsibility for patrons' safety. Protection of the health and safety of patrons and seeing to their welfare should be the standard operating procedure of all those concerned with the provision of recreational service. Such standardized practices and responsible approaches, which must be ingrained in the work habits of all employees, will become the shield that protects recreationists and those to whom they deliver recreational services.

Recreationists, and most particularly managers, need to apply themselves to an understanding of what reasonable and prudent behavior is for a professional. However, when actions that herald the likelihood of litigation against the department occur, legal counsel must be sought and technical advice obtained from appropriate professionals. The topics discussed in this section are of a generalized nature and may not be valid in every situation.

A more liberalized view of the accountability owed to patrons of recreational places by the courts has, in part, been one factor in the rising incidents of litigation. Legislative enactments, which permit the basis for bringing tort claims against public jurisdictions, have also assisted in the public's desire to sue for damages or injuries incurred in publicly sponsored/ operated places. Of course, the plaintiff must fully prove that the defendant was negligent in the administration of the area, facility, equipment, or degree of supervision available.

Several variables inevitably impact on any understanding of liability and the court actions that may be undertaken by private citizens against recreational operators. This chapter supplies some information concerning the various aspects of tort claims and offers defenses against alleged claims of negligence.

Planning against litigation

It is imperative that managers of recreational service agencies have a protective plan of action to ensure the safe operation of all recreational areas under their control. More to the point, however, diffident or haphazard and complacent attitudes, or casual toleration of potentially dangerous situations, can only lead to the waste of tax monies or private capital. It really means that recreational service departments/organizations are laying themselves open to litigation against which they have no defense. When there is neither a comprehensive patron safety policy, nor one for employees, nor logical plans for the implementation of safety practices, and operational routines which will ensure that behaviors are reasonable and prudent actions have been taken to avoid placing patrons in jeopardy, successful suits follow. In effect, then, recreational service providers must recognize that they are responsible for the health, safety, and welfare of their patrons. Minimization of this responsibility is tantamount to being called culpably negligent and irresponsible.

Risk

This by no means suggests that public recreational organizations should eliminate activities that are risky. Rather, it recommends that recreational service agencies refrain from acting in ways that are calculated to bring about property damage or personal injury. There is little doubt that almost all recreational activities have some element of risk for the participant. Perhaps this is one of the reasons that individuals become involved with such recreational activities. If these experiences were abolished or curtailed, people would certainly find ways to accomplish the same objectives in less safe environments. One need only observe the current fad for extreme sports and games, such as bungee jumping, hang gliding, vertical skiing, and all-terrain vehicle racing. Therefore, recreational service agencies of all types have a three-fold task: (1) they must offer stimulating and perhaps adventurous activities; (2) they must supervise those activities in such a manner that the consequences are neither perilous to the individual nor catastrophic to the agency; and (3) they must protect the individual from committing foolish acts or behaving in a reckless manner. All of the foregoing requires consummate ability, vigilance, and knowledge of what constitutes the appropriate conduct of a recreational service system or operation.

Legal knowledge

The recreationist, despite being professional in his/her chosen field, is a layman in the field of law. For this reason recreationists should be given the same consideration usually offered to layman to whom knowledge of the civil law is not attributed. However, the experienced recreationist/manager knows that, frequently, a requirement to understand the civil law attaches forcibly, almost destructively, to all of those who attempt to provide recreational services to the public. Lack of such knowledge could adversely affect the department, the community at large, as well as the professional person; thus, ignorance is no excuse.

Not having the benefit of formal legal education, what can the recreationist do to reduce the potential for litigation? The only practical response, at best partial and subject to real limitations, is for the practitioner to become conversant, insofar as is possible, with the legal problems that have ensnared other members of his/her profession. Such knowledge will enable the recreationist to try to avoid repeating the errors committed by others through deficiency of understanding of technical facets of the law.

Managers must be increasingly knowledgeable about questions of equity and the standards of protection prescribed by law. Two factors are involved in any question of equity: (1) the implicit language of the law, and (2) the judicial interpretation of the law. Who or what was damaged? Who is responsible? Can negligence be shown? Did the individual who suffered injuries to person or damaged property act in such a way as to bring the injuries on him/herself? Was the injured individual or the one who committed the damaging act a minor? What was the proximate cause of the injury or the damaged property? Questions of legal responsibility and of immunity from litigation brought against the municipal corporation for damage are vital to those who seek redress.

All employees of recreational service systems or organizations must accept the risk of personal damage suits instigated against them if an individual is injured while under their supervision and if negligence is proved against them. This risk is related to the doctrine that all persons are responsible for their own acts. Injuries may occur anywhere, at any time, on playgrounds or athletic fields, in swimming pools, locker rooms, craft or shop rooms, and in recreational structures of all types. It is only human to seek a cause of the accident other than one's own negligence; hence negligence of another is frequently alleged. Often a suit against the city will name an employee as co-defendant. The counsel for the city usually defends him/her. Only in a few cases have judgments been made against employees. Personal liability insurance is available at the employee's cost. The municipality may also carry insurance protection against litigation. Actually, the only adequate protection is prudent and correct action on the part of the recreationist under all circumstances. Laxity, at any point, invites disaster.

Governmental and proprietary functions and immunity[3]

When a new municipal function is established, local officials become apprehensive about the community's financial posture or exposure in liability cases in which injuries to persons or damage to property is sustained. The functions that government performs are either governmental or proprietary in character. Governmental functions are those functions performed by the state acting in its sovereign capacity or by a subdivision acting for the state that is essential for the protection of the state and for the general welfare. Proprietary functions, on the other hand, are defined as those that municipal corporations perform in their separate corporate capacities. They are not performed for the people of the state generally but optionally for the corporation itself and its people. Liability accrues with proprietary functions, but immunity is attached to governmental functions.[4]

Immunity

The theory by which municipalities are held to be free of tort liability when operating in a governmental capacity is that liability would place a deterrent on their performance of an essential governmental duty. Taxes are assessed and raised for definite governmental objectives and to channel them to the payment of damage claims arising out of necessary governmental duties would tend to restrain municipalities in the performance of those duties.[5]

Although there is no firm definition, it has been generally agreed that public education, indigent care, law enforcement, fire protection, and public health regulation are governmental functions. The construction and maintenance of streets, bridges, and sewers; the collection of garbage and refuse; and the operation of water, gas, electric, and other public utilities are generally held to be proprietary functions. The distinction between the two functions originated in the courts, yet, in its application to particular cases, there is wide division of judicial opinion. Whether recreational service is a governmental or proprietary function when performed by a governmental entity is a moot point. There have been many decisions on both sides by courts. Those leaning toward the proprietary interpretation take the general view that in the particular case the municipality was not acting for the state or the people at large but, on the contrary, was acting in an optional manner for its own benefit. Decisions interpreting the service as governmental have generally pointed out that the benefits of recreational service have value far beyond the corporate boundaries of the municipality and as such are not restricted to the inhabitants of the city in question.

Almost all the decisions in the public sector have been based on two specific factors: the purpose of and the source of authority for the function in question. Five primary purposes are cited: public welfare, health, education, specific benefit, and monetary considerations. Authority for the performance of a function derives from expressed or implied power of either a mandatory or a permissive nature.

Fees and charges and public liability

The effect of charging fees for recreational services has had some influence on court decisions concerning liability. If the fees were of an incidental nature and were not established for the purpose of conducting the activity at a profit to the municipality, the function retained its governmental character. But if charges consistently produced a profit, the function usually has been deemed proprietary.

The nature of the municipality's responsibility for performance of public recreational service devolves on whether such services are mandatory for the general welfare of the people. If they are, the doctrine of governmental function applies. But the mere fact of permissiveness does not preclude immunity; there are jurisdictions where permissive right is immune to liability. Whether the function is expressed in the charter or granted in state legislation is held to be immaterial.

The wide divergence of legal opinion with regard to the subject makes generalization almost impossible. Because the law is not static but reflects both the growing knowledge of the jurists and the shifting of public opinion, court interpretations, regardless of decisions, can and do change. The operation of parks and other recreational places may very well be considered a governmental function, but a particular activity may be interpreted as a proprietary function. For example, a department may operate an amusement park, a swimming pool, or other facilities that consistently produce a profit and that could be shown to be not wholly limited to public agencies, but also typical of private endeavor. In some cases courts have held that cities conducting profit-making activities were of a governmental character.

Negligence

Years ago, the courts recognized the fact that certain hazards accrue from recreational activities, but they felt that if reasonable care was exercised the benefits derived from such experiences would greatly outweigh the possible results of injury. However, the immunity doctrine is being carefully considered as a matter of equity in terms of what is in the best interest of the public welfare. Negligence and hazards that occur because of stupidity are no longer questions of morality; they have assumed the aspect of legal responsibility. Accidents ensuing because of the negligence of those individuals responsible for such recreational service activities have caused a change in the attitude of the courts. The courts are now returning decisions that uphold the plaintiff when negligence can be proved.[6] Conservatives who maintain that payment for injury and damage constitutes a misapplication of public funds seem to be fighting a rearguard and losing battle. More and more, liberal court interpretations hold that no individual should bear the cost of personal injury or damage to property when negligence can be shown. Equity and justice will be served only when the cost of injury and/or damage to individuals and property is shared by all. No person should have to bear the burden of personal injury or property damage when the proximate cause has been negligence. All persons have a basic right to be free of the wrongful behavior of others.[7]

In view of the current situation and the continued liberal opinion of the courts, it is imperative that recreationists maintain close contact with legislative enactments and those court decisions that are pertinent to the provision of recreational services. Regardless of whether recreational service is viewed as a governmental or proprietary function, the recreationist should understand what his/her position is as an agent of the city.

Fundamental concepts of liability

Liability is that condition for which an individual or corporation is answerable and out of which arises a responsibility to perform in specific ways, which obligation is enforceable by court action; hence, a legal responsibility. When an individual is injured or property is damaged through proved negligence on the part of any agent of a recreational service system or enterprise, that agent and/or the department may be sued in order to obtain redress. Even though ordinarily protected from liability by reason of the nature of the function performed, the municipality, its agents, and its employees can be held liable in the event of negligence.

Courts have consistently held that reasonable diligence by members of governing boards or commissions in assigning duties is sufficient to absolve them of personal liability. Commission members act in a corporate capacity and not for themselves. They cannot be held personally liable for the acts of their agents or the doctrine of *respondeat superior* (let the master answer). With respect to existence of an attractive nuisance, it must be shown that they had prior notice of the condition before liability could be imputed to members of governing commissions for the existence and continuance of the attractive nuisance.

Torts

Tort is a civil rather than a criminal wrong, not involving a breach of contract, which infringes on the rights of another and entitles the injured party to sue for redress.[8] A tortious act is construed as the legal wrong resulting in some form of injury to another individual or damaged property. Thus, torts may accrue as a result of malfeasance, misfeasance, or nonfeasance. For recreationists, the law of torts involves participant injuries, substandard practice, and defamation of character. There are several kinds of torts; for those who are practitioners in the field of recreational services, however, there is really only one category of tort suit that is a vital concern and that is negligence.

Negligence

Negligence is the failure to exercise reasonable and prudent care in relation to a situation. The duties and obligations that are imposed on the managing authority of any public or private facility concern the exercise of reasonable or ordinary care in its operation. Four components are immediately discernible in acts of negligence. These are: (a) standard of care, (b) immoderate risk, (c) proximate cause, and (d) injury suffered.

Standard of care. The courts have held that recreationists have the responsibility for providing a suitable standard or level of care for those who participate within the activities organized or sponsored by their agency of employment. Criteria dealing with the care of those involved with recreational activities are expected to be of a higher degree than would ordinarily have been required of the average person concerned with responsibility for others. Recreationists who are charged with working with the very young and very old, or who instruct them in activities that are considered to be inherently dangerous, that is, gymnastics, football, soccer, some craft or shop work, scuba diving, etc., therefore must maintain a higher standard than the others.

The standard of care is directly associated with supervision. The higher the degree of care necessary (based upon type of activity), the more close and continuous must be the act of supervision. The typical recreationist exercises what has been termed indirect or general supervision. He/she is expected to practice a broad and moderate standard of care over participants. However, recreationists working with the very young or the very old, or in high-risk activities, are responsible for maintaining a higher degree of care. These recreationists are expected to offer a much more direct and constant level of supervision over those for whom they are responsible than the indirect supervision provided by recreationists in areas of low risk.

Immoderate risk. The second factor of negligence is immoderate or inappropriate risk. The courts have held that recreationists have the duty to prevent exposure of participants to an unreasonable risk. Recreationists should not place their constituents in situations that lead to an unnecessary risk. Thus, recreationists who are charged with instructing shop activities, physical activities, or other high-risk activities, must provide those who are participating with the best possible instruction and provide appropriate supplies, materials, or equipment utilized in such activities in suitable condition. Anything less than optimum instruction and safe equipment and the risk level becomes unacceptable.

Proximate cause. The third factor of negligence is proximate cause. Proximate cause is defined as the attendant development of the sequence of action between the recreationist's negligent behavior and injury to the participant or spectator. The recreationist's conduct does not have to be the immediate cause of injury or even the indirect cause. It must, however, be the proximate cause – the sequential steps must be closely connected insofar as, time, space, or arrangement is concerned. Proximate causes are usually associated with improper conduct or failure of supervision. The major question, under these circumstances, is whether or not the injury or accident could have occurred or been prevented if the worker had been performing supervisory duties properly.

Real injury. The final factor in negligence is actual harm or real and evident injury. In tort law, there is little question about injuries that are of minor degree and that heal quickly without lasting effect. Real injury, of a substantial nature, is the kind that leaves the injured party with permanent damage, impairment, or disability. For negligence to have occurred, all of these factors must be present.

Degrees of negligence

Negligence is a matter of degree. Those who deliver recreational services in whatever capacity they perform, whether in the public or private sector, must recognize that negligence allegations are not clearly delineated cases. There are conditions or grades of negligence, which need to be considered. Negligence may be defined as slight, ordinary, and gross depending upon how state laws are written.

Slight negligence means that the practitioner failed to exercise the degree of necessary care. This definition states that a higher standard of care existed and was necessary, given the conditions of the situation, and the recreationist failed to supply it. Those workers who normally perform their functions in activities or with age groups that require a high or higher standard of care than is typically necessary in most recreational activities, could be held to be slightly negligent if they did not provide that additional measure of care that the standard requires of them.

Ordinary negligence indicates failure to exercise ordinary care. The degree of care necessary in the operation of a public facility is sometimes referred to as the "highest degree of care," such as is associated with the handling of high tension lines, and "ordinary care," such as is concerned with the usual and customary activities of daily living. Ordinary and reasonable care is the degree of care that would be exercised by a reasonably prudent professional person under similar circumstances. The question of whether such care has been exercised must be determined by a jury.

Gross negligence is the failure to provide even slight care. To be guilty of gross negligence, a recreationist's performance must be found to be of lower quality than that of an indifferent person. Essentially, gross negligence carries with it the implication of willful misconduct, recklessness, or an apparent intent to cause harm.

Negligence is the fundamental factor to be proved before liability is assessed for injury or damage. In negligence, the law attaches great significance to foreseeability of hazard. *Foreseeability* is a term applied to an event or action that could or should have been anticipated and prevented by reasonable and prudent action. It is a significant factor in liability cases because it relates to whether a not a defendant, as a reasonably skilled and prudent person, should have been able to foresee and thus avoid the possibility of the plaintiff's injury. Negligence, in terms of foreseeability, must be based on factual evidence. Recreationists should specifically strive to anticipate all possible risks in any given situation and make every effort to prevent, alleviate, or curtail them.

The issue of foreseeability is the crucial point upon which any negligence suit hangs. All the aspects of reasonableness really come down to focus upon this basic determination.

As with all cases of negligence, there are certain acts of commission, omission, or non-performance that are used to determine the presence of negligence and the degree of negligence that can then be applied to the particular situation. Among the actions taken, which fall below the standard required, are those of malfeasance, misfeasance, or nonfeasance.

Responsibilities to participants, patrons, or clients

The courts have consistently held that recreationists, or persons acting in the capacity of recreationists, have several duties to perform with regard to those who are nominally placed in their care of charge. The first requirement is to provide adequate supervision. The second requirement is to provide appropriate instruction, and the third requirement concerns properly maintained buildings, grounds, and equipment so that accidents can be avoided. These are parts of the degree of care essential to avert unnecessary risk and avoid the eventuality of injury that so often accompanies careless or haphazard direction.

In loco parentis means acting in the place of a parent, that is, assuming a guardian's responsibility for a minor. When a child is injured in a recreational situation through some aspect of negligence, it is assumed that the degree of care owed to the child by the individual acting in the guardian's role was not maintained in a reasonable manner. In such a situation, the guardian has a recognized obligation to use a high degree of care to prevent exposing the minor to risk.

Adequate supervision is closely associated with the standard of care required in terms of the age of participants, activities engaged in, and circumstances surrounding the activities that put them at low or high risk. In the case of children between the ages of 5 and 17, who are invited to participate within the scheduled program of activities ranging from residential camps and playgrounds to competitive athletic teams and shop work, the courts have held that counselors, instructors, and other agency supervisory personnel stand *in loco parentis*.[9] When children are attending some recreational activity sponsored or directly supervised by some recreational agency, recreationists or other agents of the organization are expected to exercise the same standard of care that a parent would exercise. For the most part, however, adequate supervision refers to indirect or general supervision.

Supervision. For those recreationists who control activities that fall into a high standard of care category, adequate supervision becomes something much more special and consistent. In the former instance, the recreationist conducting a glee club or chorus would exercise an ordinary or customary standard of care. Adequate supervision for this person would merely require his/her presence in the session and the use of prudence in dealing with participants. For recreationists who direct high-risk activities, adequate supervision is considerably more intense, close, and constant. The recreationist should never absent him/herself from the place of activity, should always be alert to dangerous circumstances within the activity environment, and should closely supervise each participant as they take part in the activity.

Instruction. Appropriate instruction is the second basis that forms the support required of recreationists in carrying out their responsibilities to those placed in their charge. The most typical kind of negligence suit involves improper instruction.[10] Instruction is a vital element in situations where participants are learning a new skill to handle potentially dangerous materials or equipment. Acquisition of information that is necessary to perform satisfactorily in some activity must be appropriate. When the participants are injured in shop/crafts, physical activity, on playgrounds, in boating, fishing, shooting incidents, or other such activity forms, the essential questions that will be asked are: What specific kinds of instruction were given as opposed to what was actually needed? Was the participant properly instructed as to the use of the kinds of power saws, drill presses, or belt sanders and their protective guards in the shop or crafts room? Was the participant appropriately instructed as to the procedure for rappelling down a cliff face? The idea of appropriate instructions can cover almost any piece of equipment or material used in a given activity. If the individual is injured while using such equipment, can it be proved that he/she received appropriate instruction as to how to perform the activity or utilize the materials necessary for accomplishing the activity?

Maintenance. The third leg of responsibility concerns the place of activity and the maintenance of equipment used. To avoid potential injury and reduce the element of risk, recreationists are obliged to perform environmental inspections so that unnecessary hazards are removed or eliminated and proper warnings are in place. This may mean the filling of potholes in the outfield baseball diamond, the erection of a barrier to prevent some person from walking onto the field, or posting of prohibitory signs indicating obvious or hidden dangers. Of equal importance is the necessity for recreationists to be responsible for the proper maintenance of all equipment under their control. Thus, sport and game activities, crafts, playground experiences, diving, sliding, and recreational activities that use various pieces of apparatus and equipment should have routine maintenance. Recreationists or other agency employees should check for unsafe electrical connections, cables, and cords; broken light fixtures; broken windows; and similar physical defects of the plant.

The courts hold recreationists liable if a participant is injured because equipment and other aspects of the physical plant are not properly maintained. This means that the department should develop a preventive maintenance schedule for inspecting both the equipment used in the various activities, and the lands, buildings, and facilities being managed by them. It has frequently been suggested that inspections should be carried out at least four times each year insofar as the physical plant is concerned. Equipment inspections should be carried out more frequently. The more the equipment is used the greater the danger of breakage. It may be that playground apparatus and devices have to be inspected on a daily basis in order to ensure safety of participants. There are no instances when participants should be permitted to use equipment that is defective and, therefore, probably dangerous.

Age and negligence. Children up to the age of 7 years are held to be not negligent when, in fact, they are the direct causes of injuries to others. Young children may not be held legally responsible for the commission of acts, regardless of how vicious their conduct may be. The child younger than 7 years is not legally responsible for stabbing another or throwing an object that can blind, disfigure, or cripple another despite intent or previous history of such actions. That is why agency personnel who are charged with the responsibility for the behavior of children under 7 years of age have a higher standard of care to maintain then do other personnel dealing with older participants. Moreover, the law presumes that children between the ages of 8 and 14 are not negligent. Children of these ages are thought not to know better when they engage in activities that lead to the injury of others or the damage of property. This presumption may be argued, but the burden of proof lies with the recreationist to show that the child actually knew better than to behave in the manner that resulted in injury to him/herself or others. Between the ages of 15 and 18 children are held to be possibly negligent. This means that the burden no longer rests with the recreationist, but is upon the youthful offender. Older children are held to a higher standard of conduct than are younger children, but not as high as the standards that apply to an adult.

Defenses to negligence action

One method for dealing with the risk of liability is by eliminating or reducing the factors or conditions that may cause injury or damage.[11] The recreationist who acts competently, thereby fulfilling his/her functions in a reasonable and prudent manner, can expect to escape the burdens of litigation for alleged tortious acts. There are defenses, however, that may be used in cases in which the defendant has acted reasonably, the incident could not have been prevented by any known means, or the plaintiff brought the injury on him/herself. These defenses are the primary means to avoid false assertions of impropriety insofar as adequate supervision, instruction, or prudent behavior is concerned.[12] Among the defenses are: (a) contributory negligence, (b) comparative negligence, (c) assumption of the risk, (d) *Vis Major*, (e) immunity, (f) trespassing, and (g) waivers.

Contributory negligence. Personal negligence of one's own safety occurs when the injured party acted in a manner that is clearly substandard toward what is required. When an individual fails to perform properly or foolishly exposes him/herself to danger and thereby contributes to the sustained injury, contributory negligence may be claimed. However, children below the age of 7 cannot be found negligent in this way. Children between the ages of 8 and 14 must be proved to have acted in such a way as to bring about their own injury. Of course, children can be shown to have been guilty of contributory negligence, but the courts are unwilling to find youths, even those over age 15, to be culpable of conduct on a lower level than is required for the activity.

Comparative negligence. The second possible defense concerns the negligence of more than one person involved in the injury sustained by the participant. Comparative negligence permits the plaintiff to recover for injuries received in an accident if the degree of negligence is less than or equal to the negligence of others named as defendants in the action. Thus, an individual who actually contributed to his/her own injury might still be able to allege that the defendant's negligence also contributed to the injury that was sustained. Where this can be proved, the courts apportion the damages among the negligent parties. If the recreationist is found to be guilty of a certain percentage of negligence, then that is the percentage that is assessed. To the extent that other defendants may also be involved, the proportion of negligence charged against them will have to be paid to redress the person injured. Under such circumstances, the amount to be awarded to the plaintiff (if comparative negligence is proved) may not be 100 percent of the amount determined, but will be allotted among the several parties who have been found guilty of negligence. This is a defense because it lessens the amount that any one guilty party has to pay.

Assumption of the risk. This defense is associated with the idea of reasonable and unreasonable risk. Where an individual voluntarily engages in a situation with the understanding that there is some chance of injury during the course of the activity, it is said that that person may assume a reasonable risk. Thus, individuals who participate in body contact sports and games or use or come into contact with hazardous materials or dangerous equipment knowingly assume a certain risk of injury. However, courts presume that participants have received appropriate instruction, if they are playing in leagues, tournaments, or are involved in learning skills sponsored by the recreational service agency. Additionally, such participants are expected to have used the best possible equipment if it is supplied by the agency. It may be that individual participants must supply their own protective equipment. Where this is true, the recreational agency cannot be held responsible if individuals played with inferior equipment. In the case of school-operated activities or where the sponsor supplies uniforms and equipment, the equipment must be of the best possible type. Failure to conform to this requirement or to the provision of adequate instruction when instruction is a primary prerequisite for performance will negate the assumption of risk defense. When children are participating, the courts have held that the participants cannot assume risks unless they are aware of the risk. This means that those who conduct the activities must inform participants of the possibility of being injured regardless of whether they use the best possible equipment or receive sufficient instruction. For all practical intents and purposes, it will serve the interests of all concerned if written notification is presented to those taking part with a copy signed by participants (or their guardians) indicating that they recognize the potential risks involved.

The last clear chance. Even if contributory negligence can be proved, the plaintiff may be able to recover damages if he/she can show that the last clear chance doctrine was an operational factor at the time of the incident. The last clear chance doctrine assumes that both parties to the injury or property damage were negligent, and the negligence was a contributory cause to the accident. However, if it can be shown that the recreationist defendant had the last clear chance to avoid the accident and did not take advantage of this opportunity to prevent the injury or damage, he/she may be held liable despite any contributory negligence on the part of plaintiff.

Vis major. An act of God or an uncontrollable natural force, therefore completely unforeseeable, is another defense against negligence. It is regarded as an accidental occurrence caused by some superior and unpredictable force beyond human control and one that could not have been prevented even with reasonable and prudent care. For example, the proverbial bolt from the blue strikes and kills a player. It is an act of God. Nothing could have been done to prevent it. However, if the lifeguard on duty had seen a squall forming and did not order all swimmers from the pool, the lightning death would be held to be negligence, because the probability of such an occurrence could have been foreseen.

Immunity. Where governmental immunity attaches to the recreational service function, injuries sustained by participants in publicly organized and sponsored activities may not be pursued. Under the circumstances the doctrine of *respondeat superior* is evoked. If the state holds itself immune from liability, it will not permit itself to be sued in its own courts. While the situation is rapidly giving way to abrogations by the courts or enactments of state legislatures, where the doctrine exists it may still be possible to sue individuals who were involved rather than the commission or department

Trespassing. A trespasser is one who is in a given location without invitation or right to be present at that time. Trespass is a clear violation of the right of protection from interference with one's person or infringement on one's property through unauthorized presence.

An exception to the rule of nonliability to the trespasser is the *attractive nuisance* doctrine and it generally applies to children. The attractive nuisance doctrine applies to children whose immaturity prevents them from exercising ordinary good judgment. Since the courts are not disposed to hold children guilty of contributory negligence, the fact that the child was a trespasser will not serve as a defense. Furthermore, the doctrine of attractive nuisance in such cases stipulates that the unsafe condition actually drew the child onto the property and was, therefore, the proximate cause of injury.

Among the conditions that create liability involving attractive nuisances are: (a) probability of trespass by children or youth; (b) the trespasser will be unaware of any danger due to immaturity; (c) the attractive nuisance must be clearly and closely associated with its potential for harm; and (d) the individual responsible for the area knows of the risk that such a condition has for any trespassing child. Recent court decisions indicate that public authorities owe more to the trespassing child than just refraining from willful injury. The authority must use reasonable care to prevent exposing the child to unreasonable risk or injury.

Negligence is not proximate cause of damage. When a minor was struck on the head by a baseball thrown on a playground by another minor to a third player who ducked the pitch, proximate cause of injury was the unforeseen action of the child who threw the ball. The absence of the recreationist, who was handing out craft supplies from a nearby supply room, was not the proximate cause of the injury and therefore there was no liability for damage on the part of the recreational service department.

Denial of negligence. The denial of negligence on the part of the defendant would require a court proceeding thereby presenting a factual situation on which the court or the jury must decide. The defendant would have to prove that he/she acted in accordance with standard operating procedures universally accepted or known, that his/her actions were those of a reasonable and prudent person under similar circumstances, or other evidence that will absolve him/her from liability.

Waiver. A waiver is an instrument wherein an individual, usually a performer, agrees not to seek redress in the event of injury sustained while participating. It is a contractual form that may be required by the sponsor, organizer, or operator of a facility, agency, or place that conducts the events in which the performer participates. Generally, waiver is the voluntary and intentional relinquishment of a known right, benefit, or advantage. If the waiver is freely entered into by an adult or competent person, who has presumably read the stipulations of the agreement, the courts will hold that it is binding. Thus, the person who disposes of his/her rights to sue another party can do so under contract law. And this can be done despite the fact that such disposal of rights may protect the sponsor even though the injuries to the participant are the result of the sponsor's negligence. The only time that such exculpatory agreements will not be upheld is when there is evidence of force, fraud, or deceit. Enforcement of the contract will be permitted when the person who waives understands the terms of the release, was aware of the waiver because of its prominence and appearance, entered into the transaction freely and openly, and where the stated terms are appropriate to the specific improper behavior of the party whose latent responsibility is waived.

Informed consent. Informed consent agreement is a contract that limits the liability of the provider for the risks involved in a program to which the assignor is subjected. The agreement provides full disclosure to the individual concerning both the known risks and the anticipated outcome or benefits of the activity. The participant is thereby enabled to make an informed decision regarding acceptance of the risk. While the assignor agrees to assume whatever inherent risks he/she was informed about, the assignor does not agree to relieve the activity organizer from liability for injury in consequence of negligent acts of the organization or its employees.

Professional responsibility

Injuries that are profound, permanent, or fatal can and do happen at publicly and privately operated recreational areas. These tragic incidents can be caused by the substandard behavior of participants, incompetence of employees of the organization, negligence by operators, or combination of these inappropriate acts.

Questions of competence, professional knowledge and skill, degree of care, elements of risk, negligence, and incautious behavior all derive from a poor understanding of safety practices that are essential to the protection of patrons as well as for those who manage recreational functions. Until a well-established pattern of safety education is combined with a system for safeguarding the patron, either from ignorant action or environmental hazards, conditions of jeopardy will prevail. Such jeopardy is unnecessary, and the accompanying deviant or substandard behavior on the part of agents of the organization in question must be eliminated at all costs. Surely, there are behaviors of the individual who has been injured that may have contributed to his/her situation, but an inclusive safety program together with wide distribution of information dealing with hazardous conditions can probably reduce both the injury rate and likelihood of suits being successfully brought against those delivering recreational services.

19 Infrastructure and management

The physical maintenance of recreational properties and equipment is one of the major concerns of any recreational service operation.[1] In the public sector this function is not always performed by personnel of the system.[2] In many cities the public recreational service system is responsible only for the activity program; maintenance is done by a separate department. The coordination of recreational activities with maintenance is difficult even when both functions are performed by a single department. The difficulty is increased sharply when coordination must be effected between two departments. The maintenance of all buildings, grounds, and facilities is subordinate to the activities program from the standpoint of the fundamental purposes of the system. The requirements of the program should dictate the kinds of facilities to be provided and, to some extent, the manner in which they are to be maintained. The recreational program is too often subordinated to details of maintenance with disastrous results. A recreational service system that does not control its own maintenance work is usually subjected to severe handicaps in bringing about the proper relationship between maintenance and program functions. No matter how a city is organized, however, the problem of detailed management of infrastructure and maintenance is fundamentally the same.

A department responsible for the maintenance of the system of recreational areas, structures, and other facilities located in different parts of the city views the problem of management as having both local and general aspects. If only one recreational place is to be maintained, all duties of maintenance may be localized. In an extensive system certain maintenance duties may be economically and efficiently decentralized. In this chapter, routine maintenance refers to that performed by the staff of a recreational center or place, and general maintenance refers to that performed by a staff organized to serve all units of the system.

Routine maintenance of infrastructure

Routine maintenance consists of all indoor and outdoor janitorial and inspection duties. Indoor responsibilities include the opening and closing of buildings and their rooms; sweeping, cleaning, scrubbing, and waxing; heating and ventilating; minor repairing and painting; and arranging furniture and equipment for indoor activities. Outdoor duties consist of collection and disposal of refuse; arranging equipment for outdoor activity programs; watering and marking fields and courts; minor grading of grounds; repair of walls, pipelines, and water fixtures; irrigating, cultivating, mowing, pruning, and fertilizing; and inspection of recreational equipment for wear or for hazards to users.

Care of grounds

The objective of every recreational service system is to create an environment conducive to recreational experiences or activities. To achieve this objective, the smallest details of maintenance must be attended to because each step has a cumulative effect on the successful operation of the recreational program.

Since playgrounds and parks are looked upon as havens of safety for children and adults, it is the responsibility of all departmental personnel to ascertain that no condition jeopardizing the health, safety, or welfare of participants or visitors exists. Any condition that might lead to injury of persons or damage to equipment or property should be remedied at the earliest possible time.

The department must supply the safest apparatus and equipment available, but such devices are not immune to wear or breakage, and require periodic inspection and, when necessary, servicing or replacement or repair. Children's play areas should be inspected daily and the grounds should be level and free of objects that could result in injury. If immediate repairs cannot be made to faulty apparatus, the apparatus should be moved or closed to use.

Some of the hazards on playgrounds or other recreational places are dirty or unsanitary buildings and facilities; broken benches, windows, and park furniture; overflowing garbage and trash receptacles; cracked or damaged drinking fountains; and unsafe wading pools. These conditions may be remedied and, in most cases, prevented by systematically cleaning in a prescribed maintenance program and by repairing when necessary.

Insects can be controlled by judicious use of pesticides. Rodents can be treated with poisons, traps, and the elimination of conditions favorable for their breeding and existence. Toxic plants can be controlled by defoliants in amounts that destroy the noxious plants without endangering other growing things. Such herbicides must be used carefully to avoid ecological problems and to make certain that such materials are kept away from human beings and their pets.

Maintenance of infrastructure

A number of places in every recreational service system receive constant use and require routine upkeep if they are to serve the public.[3]

Work on recreational areas should be scheduled on a routine basis. Schedules vary with different grounds and types of activities so flexibility and practicality are fundamental guides in devising them. A list of maintenance duties is posted on a work board by the director of the facility the day before the work is to be performed. When large grounds have to be covered, it is advantageous to organize the crew to work sections, thus, all areas are allocated to particular individuals with concomitant responsibility for completion of tasks. When the center contains buildings and grounds, it is necessary to assign indoor and outdoor crews. Every member of the maintenance crew should be able to carry out any job on the grounds and provide assistance to his/her fellow workers when needed.

Time schedule of infrastructure maintenance workers

The daily cleaning of a recreational center is done most efficiently when it can be scheduled during the hours that the facility is not in use. Many systems require their infrastructure workers to report early in the day so that their work may be completed before the afternoon crowds arrive. Beach cleaning crews, for example, who sometimes report for work at 4 or 5 a.m. and complete their work before noon, work six and sometimes seven days per week during the summer season. Auditoriums are often cleaned at night. Some incidental cleaning and other work must often be done while activities are under way in the afternoon and evening, calling for varied schedules of the hours for some workers. Each type of recreational facility has its own problems in this regard, and, for this reason, standardization of hours and duties for local infrastructure workers throughout the system is inadvisable.

Truck use

Trucking plays an important part in infrastructure upkeep and, unless some thought is given to it, much time can be wasted. Routing a truck properly cuts down on unnecessary mileage. Trucks should drive around playing fields rather than across them. Speed in a park or on a playground should be as slow as possible, because no amount of time saved can justify injury to a patron or damage to structures or equipment. The condition of the truck is the sole responsibility of the driver. Preventive maintenance should be practiced continually so that the truck is kept in a state of good repair and able to perform the work for which it was purchased.

Inspections of infrastructure

Preventive maintenance requires a uniform inspection procedure to bring about the highest standards of recreational facility operation through the continual upgrading of physical plant by the use of appraisal methods. It is the responsibility of managers at all levels to conduct regular inspections to ascertain the level of efficiency of the system of recreational facilities, structures, and grounds. The responsible personnel should conduct regular field inspections as part of their supervisory responsibilities and make corrections as required. All inspections made by personnel other than those of the specific recreational park, center, or other facility should be held by central office personnel. Managerial officers are responsible for the organization of formal inspections and for overseeing the establishment of routine inspection procedures.

Follow-up inspection is made by central office supervisors approximately 21 days after the formal inspection to determine the progress made by the facility manager in correcting discrepancies, if any, noted in the inspection report.

Informal inspections may be carried out by any supervisor without notice. When inspections are being conducted, the inspector should report to the office of the facility director and inform him/her of his/her presence and be accompanied on the tour of inspection by the director or an appropriate designee, if practical.

A formal inspection is conducted at each active recreational area or facility within the system at least once every three months. The central office is responsible for setting up the schedule, and notification to each facility and area director should be provided at least ten days in advance of the inspection. Each quarterly inspection places special emphasis on a particular aspect of a park or other recreational facility operation. Major import is given to selected areas to be designated by the central office at the commencement of the inspection quarter, including accountability and maintenance; cleanliness; legibility and placement of signs; traffic patterns; emergency and safety equipment; and the like.

An inspecting team, including representatives of the various divisions of the department, is assembled by the responsible manager. The manager is the inspection team leader and is responsible not only for assembling the team, but also for team briefings and for developing the required reports. If at all possible without interfering with public recreational service, inspections should be carried out during the peak days and hours of operation.

Formal facility inspections are guided by written policy enacted by the department. Major areas for inspection are listed with sub-headings also provided. As particular items are inspected, they are checked off. Check-offs should not constitute the entire on-site inspection. During the course of the inspection, the inspector should make appropriate comments about items on the checklist. Any discrepancies should be identified by name, number, or other specific designation. All facilities should undergo inspection whether in operation or not, to determine proper security, cleanliness, and storage of equipment.

A formal inspection report should be forwarded to the facility director no later than one week after the facility has undergone inspection. It should detail whatever deficiencies are noted and any remedial activity to be taken. The report consists of a memorandum containing the inspector's comments. If the discrepancy is a repeat from a previous quarterly inspection within the same calendar year, the notation must indicate this. Comments may be made on any checklist item, but unsatisfactory or superior ratings are explained in the memorandum on the inspection report.

Replies to facility inspections reports should be returned to the appropriate managerial office within seven days of the receipt of the report and all corrective actions taken should be explained therein. Responses to inspection discrepancies should indicate what action was taken and the date of completion. If the facility director disagrees with the inspection report, a justification is submitted by a memorandum attached to the inspection report when returned. All reasons for the exception are noted.

When the next administrative staff meeting is held after the quarterly inspection, and when the various reports have been filed, there is a review of all unsatisfactory and/or superior ratings. Additional comments on the strengths or weaknesses of the facility operation are noted and maintained in the central files.

General infrastructure maintenance

Every recreational center requires repair work, from time to time, that is beyond the ability or facilities of the maintenance staff. Either this work has to be let out to tradesmen and contractors, or it must be done by department mechanics other than those regularly assigned to the center. Most departments choose to have such work performed by traveling department repairmen who are equipped with a light truck in which they carry the tools and supplies most likely to be required. They usually have a regular route bringing them to every center at least once each week. From the director of the center or from local maintenance workers, they ascertain what ordinary repairs are required and, if they have the necessary materials and tools, they proceed with the work. Extraordinary repairs or alterations are referred to the central office where they are given proper consideration. Each repairman is required to keep a record of visits, the time spent at each job, and the work done. Costs of labor and materials are computed from the repairperson's original record and are charged against the proper centers and budgetary accounts.

Infrastructure support

When it is necessary to secure infrastructure support beyond the personnel or equipment of the recreational department, or when specialized projects call for special shop facilities, a central office record form is available so that the director of the recreational facility can initiate a work order. The several copies of the work order are forwarded to the proper review authorities for approval or reappraisal of the situation.

The project requiring specialized assistance should be described in concise terms, but in sufficient detail to enable all parties to understand and execute their respective roles. Diagrams may be utilized and attached to the official report form. The individual who originated the request or who is directly concerned with and familiar with the project should be indicated as the person to contact for details. When special requests are initiated, it is necessary to be aware that there is considerable time required to complete the work order. This period of delay is reflected in such variables as other priorities and the complexity of the request, as well as available personnel, materials, and/or other resources needed to complete the project.

Every effort must be made to anticipate specialized work projects that necessitate extraordinary maintenance support and they should be submitted at the end of the season for accomplishment prior to the opening of the facility or program the following season. If extensive materials or unusual supplies or equipment are needed for construction of the project, it may be necessary for these projects to be initiated as much as 18 months in advance so that consideration may be made in the budgetary process to secure the necessary materials.

On the satisfactory completion of a work order, the facility director forwards the original copy of the request for maintenance to the administrative section involved within 24 hours. Maintenance personnel check with the facility director or his/her designated representative at the completion of the project to inform him/her of the completion.

The section manager charged with the responsibility for maintaining a control system reports the status of the work order requests on a bi-weekly basis. This report is published and circulated to the concerned supervisory personnel. It is the responsibility of the facility director to inform the managerial tracking section in every instance when an uncompleted work order could affect the opening of a facility, activities, or operations in an ongoing program, so that appropriate expediting actions may be undertaken.

Infrastructure support procedures should be followed for extraordinary situations except when an emergency arises. An emergency will be considered to be any condition that poses a hazard to persons or property, causes great embarrassment, or threatens security. In such an event, the director of the facility involved or his/her appointed representative should call the responsible managerial unit advising of the situation. The necessary arrangements are undertaken immediately for the initiation of emergency actions concerning maintenance operations.

The central shop

The central shop is a necessity in every system of recreational service large enough to support one. It is the headquarters for the supervisor of infrastructure maintenance and for all centralized mechanical services. It is the place where materials required for upkeep are classified, stored, and prepared for delivery to the various recreational facilities and places. It is the site where seasonal equipment is put in order for the next use; and it is the place where tools and mechanical equipment are serviced.

Even a small department requires such a shop, unless the community has a shop in a general maintenance department providing services to all operating agencies of the community. Large departments must have elaborate central shop facilities and may have several shops consolidated at one location, including a millwork and carpentry shop; a painting shop; a forge and machine shop; an electrical shop; a repair shop for keys, canvas goods, nets, play supplies; and a garage and automobile service shop. The garage is important, even though automobiles and power equipment may be repaired by outsiders on contract. The storage, oiling, greasing, and routine servicing of department automotive equipment at the central shop contribute to the long life of the equipment, economical operation, and effective control.

Central warehouse

Any department large enough to have a central shop also needs a central warehouse and storeroom for recreational supplies, materials, and equipment. Supplies are purchased in large quantities to obtain the advantage of lower prices from bulk or volume buying, and are then parceled out to centers on requisition. The dispensing of supplies from the storehouse requires careful control and accounting to keep proper cost records and prevent unauthorized use. The management of the storehouse is not ordinarily an infrastructure upkeep function but is more properly related to the accounting division. The storeroom, however, is usually situated at or adjacent to the central shop, because it dispenses maintenance and construction supplies and is then accessible to transportation equipment used in delivery.

Costume storage. Many departments assemble and manufacture numerous costumes for use in dramatic programs, which must be renovated, repaired, remade, and repacked. For convenience, the central costume storage and repair facilities should be situated at the central shop.

Horticultural nursery

Still another central feature in a large department is the horticultural nursery. Many departments find it practicable to propagate their own shrubs and trees. In determining a suitable location for the nursery, consideration must be given to soil conditions, wind exposure, temperature, and sunlight.

Construction

The public recreational service department is concerned with the following types of construction:

1. Grading and paving of recreational and landscaped areas, roads, paths, and sidewalks.
2. Installation of pipelines, water systems, sprinkler systems, sewer lines, septic tanks, and storm drains.
3. Bridges in recreational areas.
4. Installation of electrical illuminating systems for outdoor recreational areas.
5. Manufacture and installation of fences, backstops, bleachers, and playground or other recreational area apparatus.
6. Reinforced concrete swimming pools, wading pools, tennis courts, and similar structures.
7. Frame, brick, and reinforced concrete buildings.
8. Landscaping on the areas.
9. Manufacture of various types of equipment, apparatus, furniture, and fixtures.
10. Maintenance and installation of piers, jetties, marina docks, and other marine facilities.
11. Manufacture and installation of special facilities: shooting ranges for skeet, rifle, pistol, archery; picnic shelters, fireplaces, and lodges.

Contract work versus force account

In public work the question frequently arises as to whether the designing and construction shall be done by force account, that is, by persons already employed by the public department, or by private architects and contractors. Private organizations may also consider the same arrangements. Minor design and construction are almost always done by regular employees of the public department. In major construction, however, there is no uniform practice. Sometimes the structures are designed by personnel of the public departments and let out to contract; sometimes architects and engineers are engaged to make the design which is then executed by the public departments' personnel. So many variables influence the situation that a decision should be made only after deliberate consideration of all factors and with reference to each phase of the construction plan.

Electrical work and street illumination are handled on contract as are the construction of concrete walks and curbs and the dredging of lakes. Plumbing work, grading, painting, and landscaping, on the contrary, are done under force account. The procedure in each case is determined by whether the department has a continuously sufficient amount of work in any field to justify, develop, and maintain an efficient crew of workers of the type required. Even if a crew can be maintained, the wages of public employment and prevailing wages in private employment, the condition of the construction industry, the relative efficiency of public and private employees in various crafts, the size of the project, the labor union situation and its effect on both public and private work, the time factor (emergency or routine situation), and similar matters must be considered.

Minor construction

The recreational service department's staff of mechanics is also used for minor construction. Several of the larger recreational service system staffs do all of their own designing and construction except on the largest projects, such as building a stadium, public auditorium, or similar structure.

Contract jobs are handled on a cost-plus basis or on a stipulated total bid.

Designers

Every recreational service department that maintains its own facilities and does any construction can use the services of competent architectural draftsmen, topographic draftsmen, structural engineers, and landscape designers. Expertness in all these lines is rarely found in one person. The department with sufficient work to employ four draftsmen would do well to select them so that all of these special fields are represented.

Frequently the recreational service department calls on the city engineering or other departments for expert assistance in designing and supervising construction if not also in the actual construction work.

Coordination of design and operation

One of the most difficult problems in construction is the coordination of design with operation. Designers are not usually familiar with the operational aspects of the agency and those skilled in operation are not adept in interpreting their needs to the designers. Regardless of whether designing is done on force account or on contract, every opportunity must be taken to allow the designers to become cognizant of the operating problems in relation to their design. Obviously, if the designing is done by the departmental staff, there is ample opportunity for the designers to become familiar with the operating requirements.

Manufacture of equipment

Personnel of the construction and maintenance shop with equipment for repair may manufacture much of the equipment required in public recreational places. It is quite common practice for department infrastructure workers to fabricate equipment such as bleachers, benches, desks, game tables, banquet tables, drinking fountains, shower mixing valves, filters, chlorinators, ladders, playground apparatus, tennis nets, marina docks, and similar structures or equipment. But mass-produced equipment can usually be bought more cheaply than it can be made by department mechanics. However, innovative equipment of the non-traditional, maintenance-oriented type usually found on most playgrounds may best be fabricated by force account. Until such time as playground equipment specifically and recreational equipment generally are developed to meet the increasingly sophisticated demands of users, creative designers will be in demand and should be utilized as part of the force.

Infrastructure is vital to the upkeep of the entire organization and its most essential function – the recreational program. Without the dedicated efforts of many ancillary workers and their managers, property would fall into disrepair, the facilities might become prey to vandals, and the foundation of the department would be permanently undermined.

20 Office and records management

A public recreational service system must routinely plan to satisfy present and future needs by recognizing what is to be done, when certain steps must be undertaken, where such action should be performed, and by arranging priorities for the completion of the work. Planning is essential if future outcomes are to be anticipated, thereby avoiding difficulties. It includes the identification of techniques necessary for efficient performance and an understanding of the logical steps that will produce optimized results for the department. The necessity for establishing an operating structure through which the department may be coordinated and made to serve the community requires development of a central office to facilitate the work of the system.

A central office permits the establishment of the base of operations so that specific assignments can be apportioned among the various units and divisions of the system.[1] It is in the central office that primary decisions typically affecting the total system are made. All office work is a service or facilitating function – the main medium through which the widespread efforts of the public recreational system are coordinated. All administrative functions depend on the convenience-producing assets of the office.[2] A tremendous volume of factual data is required for intelligently planning and coordinating the recreational service program, personnel, infrastructure, equipment, and financial resources. Such information involves report writing, record keeping, and filing procedures for retrieval purposes, which in turn necessitate office work. Even with today's computer technology available, hard copy materials still require filing and eventual retrieval. Whether a department is large or small, the need for a central office to channel requests, disseminate information, and maintain the records so vital in terms of public accountability remains.[3] Additionally, management requires appraisal and evaluation practices so that a determination may be made as to how closely predetermined objectives have been approximated. Furthermore, the technical function of each division within the department is implemented, integrated, and kept informed by communication processes necessitating office work.

Office management and control

Office work facilitates the operation of the system, and it is performed chiefly to promote the efforts of the divisions of the system. It is a staff function because it assists the personnel of other units to carry out their jobs more effectively, economically, and efficiently by removing many of the routine and time-consuming tasks normally associated with recording, filing, making reports, transcribing statistics, and supplying whatever information is required to various divisions for their use. Office work is essentially handling and managing paper. Paperwork is produced in volumes through the receipt of applications, permits, insurance forms, legal documents, reports, plans, blueprints, and other written materials.

Although it constitutes a large portion of the work performed in public agencies, by reason of legal requirements, the work of the office is not directly concerned with the line function of the department; rather, it contributes indirectly to the overall success of the operation by servicing the components with records, statistics, files, and internal communication.

Office work should be judged by the consequences of the tasks it carries out. It is not an end in itself but is a medium by which the recreational services, generated by the system, may be expedited and offered to the public. Office work may be analyzed and appraised readily. It may be divided into several segments for easier examination and determination as to whether it is accomplishing the purposes that it was originally intended to perform. The whole concept of management – organizing, coordinating, controlling, planning and directing – thus may be imposed on the work of the office.

The functions of office management may be outlined best as:

1. Establishment of a useful office organization

    (a) Functions determined and proper personnel deployed
    (b) Specified lines of hierarchical relationships
    (c) Delegation of authority and responsibility for execution of work
    (d) Definite assignment of responsibility among workers.

2. Maintenance of infrastructure and design of the office

    (a) Physical layout and arrangement of space, supplies, equipment, and furniture
    (b) Environmental planning: heating, light, ventilation, control of noise,[4] and appropriate interior decoration.

3. Identification of needed furnishings, material, supplies, and equipment.
4. Purchase of specified office equipment, material, and furnishings.
5. Development and maintenance of appropriate information services

    (a) Report writing, record keeping, and filing
    (b) Correspondence
    (c) Reception or information functions
    (d) Public relations center.

6. Management of office personnel
   (a) Position analysis and job description
   (b) Selection, orientation, and assignment
   (c) In-service education and development, supervision, and promotion
   (d) Discipline
   (e) Salary and/or wage administration
   (f) Safety practices.

7. Technical improvement of office practices
   (a) Work simplification
   (b) Criteria for performance
   (c) Analysis of time and motion studies for better efficiency.

8. Control of office output
   (a) Planning organizing, and scheduling of assignments
   (b) Development of standardized work procedures and manuals of practice
   (c) Analysis of costs, control of expenditures, and budget making.

Not all of these office management functions are carried out in every recreational service system. The ramifications of office work and its management depend on the size of the department, how extensive the area and work of the system is, the number of personnel employed in the system, and the need for coordinating diverse and far-flung units of the department. In one-man departments the chief executive considers him/herself fortunate if he/she can obtain the service of a full-time secretary. He/she must usually content him/herself with a part-time assistant. Therefore, the manager must spend a considerable portion of his/her time handling routine paperwork that a clerk would be better able to perform. Small departments often have insufficient money to employ specialists who can perform the tasks that are typically involved in office management. The executive must be prepared to function accordingly. As a result, necessary office management functions are typically curtailed or, at the very least, are not used in the most efficient manner. In larger departments, the employment of a director of the central office may be necessary if an entire cycle of office activity is carried out by a variety of office personnel whose work is essential to the successful accomplishment of the system's purpose. In the largest departments, there is a tendency to appoint a specialist who is responsible for the management of all office work. He/she may combine a variety of functions including that of controller, business director, or personnel manager, but he/she has the responsibility for managing the work of the central office.

Office divisions

For purposes of clarification, it is necessary to indicate the major units that make up the activities of the central office. As previously indicated, the individual responsible for the central office is the administrative head of one of the divisions of the department or system. For this discussion, a large recreational service department will be depicted in order to illustrate the functions and activities that comprise the division. A chart shows the relationship and organization of the three major divisions of the department – planning and its ramifications, programming and its ramifications, and management with its component features. Figure 20.1 indicates the major divisions into which the department is divided. Figure 20.2 shows the ramifications of the office and business administration division. This division is composed of a manager or director and three sections composing the division: office management and clerical section, public relations and information section, and the finance and purchasing section. Subsections of the office management and clerical section are composed of personnel services, main office, and district office. The latter indicates the influence of decentralized practices within the system.

The subsection of the finance and purchasing section indicates the nature of activities conducted by this component, in this case Stores and Accounting.

Generally, all public departments, whether large or small, require some office practice. If such practices are not undertaken, only confusion and misadventure result. As systems grow larger and are more widely distributed

Figure 20.1 Major divisions of a recreational service department.

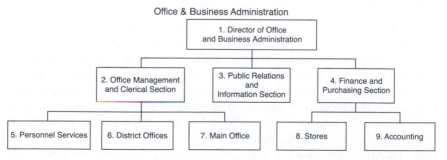

Figure 20.2 Sections and subsections of office and business administration divisions of a recreational service department.

within a metropolitan region, the necessity for implementing good office management and control activities is even more striking. Often overlooked in the establishment of the office management division is, perhaps, the essential reason for its existence – control. Control is the method by which the work of the office is expedited and, in fact, is the influence that sees to the actual performance of the functions of the office.

The effective output of any office is regulated by the methods and procedures developed for the operating efficiency of the division and the system as a whole. It is the central office manager, for example, working in coordination with other divisional managers, who develops the standardized forms on which records and reports of the system are maintained. The central office is responsible for the working up of whatever manuals are required for the most effective personnel performance throughout the system. Additionally, standard operating procedures are researched and implemented to accomplish office-related work. The management of paperwork, the sequential steps or stops that any routine or extraordinary record, report, or correspondence must pass prior to taking action, is reviewed for time-saving and work-saving simplification. Whatever intermediate steps can be omitted, consolidated, or improved are acted upon.[5]

Constant thought and consideration must be focused on departmental organization so that the most effective structure can be designed to accomplish the purpose of the system. Although the organization of the central offices does not conform to any preconceived model because of the different needs of local departments, there are universally recognized principles which may be applied. In general, office management and business administration rely on certain principles that, when followed, tend to produce effective, efficient, and economical operations. Good office management practices are basic to a logically developed organization. Depending on local conditions and requirements, effective office organization assists in the maximized achievement of goals determined to be fundamental to the existence of the recreational service system.

Office situation

The utilization of technologically advanced machinery and equipment has contributed in no little magnitude to the increased capacity of the central office of public recreational systems to fulfill their responsibilities.[6] Adequate consideration must therefore be given to the types of equipment available, their respective costs, the maintenance costs, and the actual work processes that will profit most by being adapted to automatic, or at least machine, attachment. The decision to use a piece of equipment should be based on the individual requirements necessitating its adoption. Not all office functions require mechanization. Only when there is constant repetitive work will such obvious necessity make partial or complete automation desirable. The question as to whether a certain type, size, or unit of machine should be purchased must be evaluated on the basis of need, number required, speed of production, accuracy obtainable, cost, and other factors.

A final consideration is the effect that office machinery, equipment, and furniture, as well as office layout and decor, have on the personnel and their requirements.[7] In some cases, the installation of new furnishings, equipment, and physical arrangement may modify the requirements for the number of personnel and their respective skill levels. Wherever machines can be employed to replace time-consuming, repetitive, and monotonous work – they should be. A workforce that does not have to perform boring assignments is more productive in the tasks for which they have responsibility and some discretion.

Space requirements and utilization of available space are two of the chief conditioning factors in the physical development of an office. The amount of space desired or needed and the arrangement of the interior so that maximized functional usage is obtained can be considered as critical items. Essentially, the layout of the office deals with available space and the practical placement of furnishings and equipment. Layout involves such diverse conditions as traffic patterns into and out of the office, work flow, and functional use of space without waste. Generally the physical arrangement of any office may be designed on the basis of:

1. A chart or blueprint of the office area.
2. An understanding of the kinds of work to be performed in the office.
3. Analysis of work flow.
4. Identification of traffic patterns in relation to entrances, exits, waiting rooms and the like.
5. Identification of the different work groups using the office.
6. Determination of the number, size, and type of physical units to be placed.
7. Formulation of functional design on the basis of scale models or the use of templates with identifying types clearly marked.
8. Arrangement of the office through model manipulation until the most effective and functional use of space is reached.
9. Ascertaining that traffic patterns conform to appropriate areas so that visitors' movements do not conflict with the continual movements of office employees. Conversely, employee traffic should not restrict visitor movement.
10. Reevaluation of the entire design to ascertain whether or not all office functions and traffic flow are suitably taken care of by the physical arrangement.

Careful treatment should be given to space requirements for the types of furnishings, equipment, and office space necessary for the comfort, convenience, and functional utility of the workforce within reasonable cost. The need for segregated office space for executive and managerial personnel should also be accounted for in the layout. General office workers may have access to the largest space available in one room or in partitioned spaces. The layout of the office must reflect a design that will assist in gaining the greatest output from the office staff thereby minimizing per capita costs. Features such as window space, power outlets, entrances and exits, support columns, railings, or individual offices must be considered in the physical development of the central office of the system.

Office procedures

To achieve effective operation of the public recreational service department, executives and their subordinates must have factual records to serve as a basis for planning future work, to appraise current performance, and to evaluate the system as a whole. Efficient management of the system is founded on written records of situations and occurrences. Valid information must be obtained, examined, disseminated, and deposited for reference when necessary. Of course, computers may be used for just this purpose. However, when records and reports are not faithfully compiled and correctly filed for retrieval, they may not be conveniently available for their many uses. The filing procedure, proper record and report forms, written data, and available pertinent information are essential for the orderly and effective management and administration of the department and the system that it represents.

Records are the factual bases on which an accounting of the work done is made to higher authority and to the public. They are invaluable as reference material for managers and office employees to use in performing their respective duties; in fact, they are the basis of managerial action. The recorded information is used as reference material in planning facilities and programs and evaluating personnel performance.

Although the form of some records is regulated by law or by higher authority, the form of most reports and records of the recreational service system is left to the discretion of the department itself. It is impossible to set forth the form of all written materials kept by recreational service departments because of the wide variation in plans of organization and the size and function of the departments. However, a sampling of the kinds of forms that may be utilized is provided as well as the information that should be logged on any given record.

Records

Records have several significant purposes for the management and general program of recreational activities:

1. *To provide valid evidence.* Proper records deal with the actual happenings and outcomes that occur in the daily operation of the department. Mere opinion or approximation need not be relied on for records present the facts.

2. *To indicate the status of the department.* Records make it possible to understand why the department was established, what authority it has, what its structure is, what position it holds within the municipal organization (or other governmental or private auspices), whether it is developing, maintaining status quo, or is inadequate. Levels of achievement may be ascertained and indications of various aspects of the operation may be evaluated or determined.

3. *To detect inefficiency, duplication of other agency services, and errors.* Records assist in the determination of efficient and effective service. They provide the tools whereby measurement may be made between standard and substandard performance. They help to evaluate the department in terms of goals set and actual attainment.

4. *To afford a basis for compliance with legal regulations.* Records are valid evidence of the current operation of the department. They provide the required written information pertaining to custodianship and an accounting for public funds and property. They may be utilized in litigation cases in which accidents, fraud, misfeasance, malfeasance, or nonfeasance may be a central issue. They may be the instruments whereby tax assessments are made, insurance benefits paid, and gifts, bequests or awards donated.

5. *To effect comparisons.* The consequences of operating the department and providing a program of recreational activities may be appreciated and evaluated more readily by comparison with other departments. Certain standards have been established as a basis for such measurement. The service performed by the recreational system can be evaluated by comparing these criteria with what has actually been produced and noting any deviation from good practice. In this way, too, contemporary practices in comprehensive and balanced programming can be appraised. Both the quality and quantity of opportunities may thus be brought under scrutiny.

6. *To provide a basis for policy formulation and orientation.* Examination of the records by recreationists offers a better understanding of why certain activities succeed and others fail. Analysis tends to reveal the strengths and weaknesses of the program and the current operation of the system. From this analysis comes the origin for many policy decisions, modifications in programs, and better service to the public.

Reports and their purposes[8]

A report is a synthesis of many records on the same subject which have been summarized for cogent analysis. Reports are vital to management.

The somewhat specialized and therefore decentralized functions necessary in the daily operation of a recreational service department make it increasingly necessary for the chief executive and other managerial staff to receive concise data so that they may keep in touch with all phases of the agency.

Coordination, direction, and management are significantly aided by the use of reports. Reports supply the required factual data from which policy decisions are rendered, program and departmental planning is accomplished, and public information is disseminated.

Reports are expository and present concisely the facts about a specific subject. The main purpose of the report is to define the object under consideration and specify the problems – if any – which were encountered, the method of collecting the information, the conclusions drawn on the basis of known facts, and any recommendations if further action is necessary.

Routine administrative reports. It is good management practice for the head of a department to require periodic reports from the chief managing employee of each division of the department, whether the division is concerned with the administration of a group of separate facilities, or places of recreational service, or with the administration of programs of special activities. Division heads usually require periodic reports from the directors of separate recreational places. These reports, which may be daily, weekly, or monthly, enable a cumulative record of the work to be assembled and summarized, and assist the managers in keeping abreast of the progress and trends of the work. Those required to render reports are encouraged to think in terms of factual material related to their work and to analyze measured accomplishment in relation to expended effort. The contents of such reports vary according to the nature of the work.

Annual department reports. Heads of governmental departments are usually required, by the city charter or other legal enactment, to render an official annual report of the work of their departments. These reports must be submitted to the mayor, the city council, or the city manager. The reports of all departments are then synthesized, consolidated, and published for the information of the general public. The department reports are sometimes published separately by the departments and sent to interested persons and to public and institutional libraries. They are always available at the central office at the request of any interested citizen. Most voting and taxpaying citizens are conspicuously uninterested in the reams of published government statistics and accounts and are inept at analyzing and understanding them. This is not wholly the fault of citizens, for the material has been published in a form that is not easily comprehensible. In fact, it has frequently been charged that some public officials publish their reports in highly complex and technical form for the specific purpose of confounding the inquiring citizen. In recent years there has been a distinct effort on the part of progressive public officials to encourage public interest by publishing reports in more attractive and understandable form. Some have carried this to such an extreme that it is difficult to distinguish the official report from advertising matter. The printing of attractive and comprehensible circulars and other material to cultivate public interest and to inform the citizen has an important place in the work of public relations of any department, but it should not replace the annual report, which is a comprehensive outline of the state of the department and its accomplishments. The annual report can be improved by art work, charts, photographs, and popular narrative form, but the essential information that distinguishes it as a report should not be omitted.

Contents of the annual report. The report should contain such material as will enable the reader to obtain a better understanding of the work of the department, to appraise the accomplishments of the department for the period to which the report refers, and to learn about the department's plans for the future or the important needs of the city with respect to the matters for which the department is responsible. It should be as brief as is consistent with its purpose and should not be an encyclopedic compendium of information about recreational services or about the department. It should include the following information:

1. *Functions.* A clear statement of the functions of the department and the legal authority by which they are undertaken will assist in interpreting the rest of the material. The division of these functions into sub-functions, upon the basis of which the department is organized, may also be included.
2. *Organization.* A description of the manner in which the department is organized, internal relationships, and relationships to other agencies. A chart is often valuable in making these relationships clear. Any changes in organization should be reported.
3. *Properties.* The number of properties on which the department operates and the improved facilities located thereon indicate to a degree the extent of the department services. Since one of the most important problems of the city is to obtain a sufficient number of areas, buildings, and other structures to enable its services to cover the entire city, tabulation of such additions year by year is an important index of growth. Noteworthy new acquisitions and alterations should be mentioned and stressed according to their relative importance.
4. *Program.* Although the program of activities is perhaps the most important item in the report, it is not necessary to describe each event in detail. It should rather be the object to summarize the program to indicate the underlying purposes in conducting certain types of activity and the extent to which such purposes were accomplished.

Yearly summaries of attendance of participants, non-participants, or spectators, classified according to types of places (i.e. playgrounds, swimming pools, indoor recreational centers, or golf courses) are almost inevitably quoted. These are often unduly emphasized. In connection with some activities they are at best inaccurate estimates, albeit the only quantitative measure of public response. Their imperfections should be acknowledged and interpretations, perhaps, provided. The familiar bar, pie, and curve charts are valuable for interpretive purposes.

Special problems for which specific programs have been devised should be discussed briefly. For example, if evening activities have been stressed to attract older youth from unwholesome pursuits, or if the department has inaugurated winter sports for the first time, these features might be discussed. Such incidents create opportunities to emphasize qualitative considerations that cannot be treated statistically.

5. *Human resources.* The organization of personnel, number of employees, seasons employed, changes in staff, and similar information might well be included. Measures taken to select competent employees and to provide in-service education might be used to emphasize qualitative aspects. The names of all employees need not be included, but it is customary to publish the names of members of the commission and secretary, if any, and the chief executive and divisional heads.

6. *Finance.* A report is not complete without certain financial statements. An essential one is the report of financial operations giving sources of revenue (taxes, fees, gifts, or other) and details of expenditures classified by principal objects for which they are made. Both revenues and expenditures should be further classified according to the functions to which they apply (e.g. playgrounds, indoor community centers, swimming pools, or golf courses). Unit costs of rendering various services may also be included, but with interpretations, for they can be easily misunderstood.

   A capital statement, showing the book value of lands, buildings, and equipment, and any important additions or losses during the year, is often valuable in an annual report. If the department controls its own funds entirely, it is advisable to include a balance sheet with classified assets and liabilities (including bonds unredeemed).

7. *Needs.* The needs of the city with regard to public recreational service as viewed by the department are an important part of the annual report. If these needs can be based on valid surveys rather than on opinion, they are all the more valuable. It is, of course, the duty of the department not only to operate the facilities it has as efficiently as possible but also to inform the general city officials and the public concerning problems that are unsolved and needs that are unprovided for. The annual report is a proper instrument through which to emphasize such points.

8. *Recommendations.* A list of specific recommendations, made logically, follow the factual record.

Files and filing procedures

The file is a repository for current as well as long-term operational documents related to the management and control of the recreational service department. It is merely a physical container for records and reports which, by law or policy, must be maintained in proper form for a given period of time. The file also serves as a convenient receptacle for a variety of written material, both current and historical, that is continuously utilized for reference purposes.

Filing has a very important place in the control of personnel, program, and finances. Sooner or later most of the paperwork that flows through the department finds its way to some part of the filing system of the agency. It is through this procedure that intradepartmental communication is made. A competent filing system facilitates the smooth coordination of department operations. Filing does not merely indicate placement and retention of documents, it also concerns the selection of specific materials at any time for the pertinent information they contain.

Filing serves one other important purpose: it provides the necessary repository wherein physical evidence of a legal nature may be kept until disposal or exposure is required. The law states that certain papers must be maintained for definite periods of time. Thus tax records, insurance policies, land and property records, and other legal instruments are safeguarded until such time as they are needed for examination.

Filing of records, reports, and miscellaneous information in a manner that admits of convenient reference presents a problem in all public executive offices, although to a lesser extent in the private commercial world. Few departments, however, encounter greater difficulty than the recreational service department. The recreational service department is not concerned with a single activity but with many diversified activities. The recreational service office must have available not only the official records of business transactions, but also a great quantity of reference material concerning these countless activities. Such material is of great assistance to the staff as a source of information in planning programs and in answering the public's questions about all sorts of recreational activities. Moreover, the department program is not static or routine but constantly changing and developing.

The filing of material according to subject and the logical relation of the subject matter to the organization of the department's functions is the most efficient method in recreational service departments. This procedure results in the accumulation of material of similar nature in one location. It also renders indexing and cross-indexing unnecessary and helps those who consult the files, since they must continually think in terms of organization and interrelation of the several functions of the department rather than in terms only of a particular subject.

A filing system appropriate for a recreational service executive office is one that assigns all materials to three separate files: one having to do with administration of business transactions, facilities, and programs; another with miscellaneous information concerning activities; a third with information concerning the field of work, or the community.

All, or most, of the paperwork that comes into the department may eventually be computerized and saved in one of the various software programs available commercially.

21 Evaluation of recreational service

Evaluation concerns the collection of factual information about any experience, concept, process, or thing.[1] The information is then presented so that some judgment can be made. The judgment assumes that standards or criteria exist by which a factor may be measured. Thus, the value of one aspect, such as an experience, may be determined on some known basis – for example, its promise of social contact or lack of interpersonal relationship. The value of each of several possible experiences may be assessed by comparison. In one instance, the intensity of relationship or social contact made possible, in another by the relative superficiality, denial, or rejection of the individual in question. How effective an experience is can be judged on the basis of information received dealing with what the individual obtained from participation. The value of any experience may be gained from its impact upon the participant – that is, by the extent to which it, in itself or in comparison with other potential experiences, concludes in specifically desired changes in those having the experience.

Evaluation as a process

Recreational activity, while not a complex process insofar as the individual is concerned, is, as a social institution, among the more complex procedures attempted within any sector of society. Recreational service becomes a complex process dealing with the selection of concepts, objectives, delivery systems, administration, and all of the ramified functions which have come to be identified with the provision of recreational service. Choices have to be made in the design and implementation of a recreational service program, and the effectiveness of the program must be carefully scrutinized. The process of evaluation is a constant function to which all facets of departmental system, organization, operation, and services must be submitted for study so that assessments can be made.[2]

Evaluation is a continuous process of improving any enterprise by the application of information so that the deliberate selection of alternatives can be made. By *process* is meant a specific and consistent activity comprising a variety of techniques and concerning several procedures. Evaluation is an ongoing process and should not be perceived only as a finalized comparison between some objective and actual performance. The sole reason for evaluating anything is its improvement.[3] Whatever information is generated is utilized with the immediate end of making the recreational service better. This betterment may come in terms of program, managerial practices, human resource performance, facility planning, design, construction, or operation, and any other condition, situation, or factor involving the provision of recreational service. Unless improvement is the net result of evaluation, evaluation has not been performed realistically.

The application of intelligence is conceived not only in terms of intellectual command, but also as the gathering, analysis, and utility of information designed to identify the possible alternatives before any decision can be reached. In this sense, intelligence is viewed as perspicacity as well as a means for diminishing ambiguity in achieving a correct choice of the alternatives which present themselves. Deliberate selection has to do with intentional choice directed toward monitoring operations so that their enhancement is forthcoming. Deliberate selection is based upon differentiated alternatives which accrue in response to information collected about the action that might be taken concerning some enterprise.

Alternatives are two or more diverse measures that could be performed in reaction to some condition needing modification. Enterprise improvement takes place only when current behaviors, activities, or operations are changed. There are at least three situations which might require desirable altered action; if there is evidence that (1) some unsatisfied need exists, (2) a problem exists, or (3) a favorable condition exists which should be exploited. Where there are limited resources, as is so often true of public recreational service agencies, priorities must be assigned and decisions made on the basis of available means. The focus of evaluation is to come to some decision about a number of alternatives based upon assessed values and benefits determined by careful analysis.

The determination of objectives

The process of evaluation is based upon information which permits a comparison between any entity being scrutinized and its proximity to the objective or objectives which had been predetermined as achievable. The objectives of recreational service, regardless of their derivation and kind, can be shown to have a number of sources. As an instrument for the benefit of society, recreational service is responsive to the needs or demands of the society from which it originates. Whether recreationists seek out these needs and initiate programs to satisfy constituent requests or actually propagandize the potential clientele, thereby creating demand when none existed previously, as would commercial operators, recreational service has responded both as a mirror of the culture and as an advocate for new and expanded horizons, as well as producing monetary return for services rendered.

Societal needs

The inexorable weight of society has required the establishment of the field of recreational service – at least in the public sector – to fulfill certain functions that otherwise would not or could not have been accomplished by other sector enterprises. Now that the public sector agencies have demonstrated the feasibility of providing specific recreational activities for which there is a steady demand, private entrepreneurs have moved into the provision of services for commercial gain. There would have been little in the way of private racket clubs, ski resorts, camping facilities, sports clubs, aquatic clubs, and other private-sector delivery services unless the public sector departments had not first shown the popularity of specific recreational activities.

Individual needs

The need of individuals comprises a second source for objectives. The extent to which recreational service can supply experiences, places, leadership, and instruction in order to meet the common needs of all people, or the variants of these for individuals, who constitute the potential participants of each agency, must be faced by each department sooner or later. The law plays a significant role in the determination of objectives. Although some legislation is broad and generally calls upon public agencies to perform in certain ways so that minimum services of a recreational nature are provided, other statutes or codes may itemize and specifically demand that public or other agencies offer particular recreational services of a certain type and other relatively regulated conditions. The ability of social sector agencies to live up to demands placed upon them by law offers a real source by which objectives may be selected.

Authoritative statements

Another source of objectives is found in the scholarly statements issued by a number of recognized authorities, professional associations, conferences, institutes, or commissions. The objective of the field, whether broadly or narrowly construed, may be developed by scholars in the discipline and these writings, almost by default, may become the authority from which objectives for the field are defined.

From these very resources, a number of objectives may be formulated which will serve as the goals achievable by the means available. Investigation of needs and decisions on those for which recreational service should provide involve both systematic research and value judgments. Among the many possibilities some choice must be made, essentially by the assessment of the rationale and logic supporting the divergent alternatives. Study of the consequences of pertinent information and of its relevance to recreational service planning is a form of evaluation. Philosophical orientations, by their very nature, concern and compel consideration of values. If all of these factors are not involved in choosing objectives, the ones which have been omitted may nullify efforts at achieving the objectives. As with any objectives, there may be freedom of choice, but the accomplishment of goals will be determined by the ability to perform and the availability of resources to ensure success.

Establishment of objectives

Establishment of the ongoing process of evaluation requires the development of well-defined objectives. Initially, consideration must be given to the items through which evaluation of the agency may be made. Additionally, objectives should be signified which set forth what the agency is attempting to accomplish and what its constituent personnel should achieve. Agency objectives will best be understood and accepted when there is cooperative effort on the part of all professional personnel at every level of the agency hierarchy. Neither the executive alone, nor supervisors alone, should set objectives to be reached. Objectives should be broadly stated.[4] However, the wide latitude of objectives must be susceptible to singular means for enactment. Other objectives will inevitably grow out of an appraisal of participant performance. Evaluation can never be looked upon as something apart from the performance of professional services to people. It is an integral factor of what the recreationist does to make his/her function more effective. Evaluation of performance is as significant as performance itself.

In establishing objectives, a distinct set of responsibilities is readily apparent. These facets of the organization can be grouped in general as agency organization, jurisdiction, finance, management, human resources, planning, programming, infrastructure, land, public relations, coordination, participation, and policy-making. Thus, 14 separate areas emerge as having need for evaluation.[5] These may be stated as:

1. The implementation of recreational service having to do with the initiation and development of the agency.
2. Jurisdictional control, comprising the sphere of service within which the agency operates as well as the authority to organize and operate the agency.
3. Adequate financial support from whatever resources are available to the agency.
4. Operational aspects for the management of the agency.
5. Personnel standards, professional development, and management practices.
6. Planning for recreational services.
7. Programming recreational activities.

8. The development and maintenance of the physical plant including all structures and facilities.
9. The acquisition and preparation of land for inclusion within the recreational system which the agency operates.
10. The development of an ongoing program of public relations.
11. The development of coordination between agencies for comprehensive and effective services.
12. The appraisal of the quality of participation and the number of users which the agency has.
13. The institution of policy to guide substantive behaviors and operations so that the most efficient and effective services will be provided to the agency's constituency.
14. Patron perceptions of recreational service.

Continual procedures designed to determine the value of the recreational service agency in the community are essential if the department is to realize its objectives in the provision of a comprehensive and balanced program of activities to meet the recreational needs of people.[6] The idea of evaluating recreational agencies is not new. Everyone who has ever been to a recreational agency intuitively knows the good and bad aspects of the service received. Almost every layperson fancies him/herself an expert on the subject of recreational service. After all, "Isn't recreational activity a subjective and personal matter?" Because evaluation continues uninterruptedly, it is absolutely necessary that its standards, devices, and techniques be understood. Methods must be developed for gathering facts so that judgments can be made as to how closely the recreational agency approximates its goals.[7] Evaluation must be based upon reliable information and the sources of these facts need to be identified.[8] Therefore, instruments or measuring devices that are accurate, consistently applicable to the areas undergoing evaluation, and easily administered by competent professionals are required.

Program evaluation

One example concerns the recreational program. Efficient management must not only facilitate the formulation and conduct of a satisfactory recreational program, but must constantly evaluate this program qualitatively and quantitatively. Qualitative evaluation is rarely possible in terms of objective measurements, but depends on appreciation of values, sense of fitness, awareness of clearly defined purposes, and subjective appraisal of performance and outcomes. Except in terms of personal interviews with a random sampling of the patrons who attend and participate in the program of activities, there is little that can be done to measure the program qualitatively. Qualitative evaluation of programs requires frequent visitation by supervisors to recreational facilities where observation may be made of the program in operation. Observations and evaluations by executives and program specialists should be the basis for counseling the program recreationists and for the issuance of written program material and instructions.

Quantitative evaluation can be more accurate. The "productivity" of a recreational center may be evaluated constantly by the inauguration of a reporting system of such factors as attendance of participants and observers, group activities, financial receipts, special events, and so forth. The total attendance of participants in the recreational program and other spectators is used to compare the work of separate facilities of the department. Departments also compile attendance statistics to study recreational trends, to measure their progress year by year, and to use in public relations. The use of statistics as a means of program control and evaluation has possibilities that have not yet been fully realized. More effective use of statistics for such purposes requires greater refinement of methods of recording and reporting than has so far been achieved by most recreational service departments.

Municipal recreational service systems with various kinds of facilities should be able to devise methods for recording and reporting attendance that are applicable to the several types and allow for adaptations to local conditions. For example, the director of a neighborhood playground with an attendance of not more than 100 in any half-day session can estimate quite accurately at the end of each session the number present. Directors of large neighborhood and district playgrounds, where attendance is dispersed over a large area must be content with gross estimates.

The gross attendance at recreational facilities is of little value in program evaluation, but the attendance – particularly of the participants – at scheduled activities and special events has immense value. Such attendance is directly related to the efficiency of recreationists in planning and conducting the activities and events. For this reason the system of reporting should provide for accurate statistics concerning events where attendance reflects planning, organization, and leadership. Among the activities at playgrounds and indoor recreational centers for which fairly accurate statistics may be reported are the recurrent scheduled activities, such as classes under leadership; club meetings; team, dual, and individual competitions; musical and dramatics performances or rehearsals; tournaments; meets; excursions; and shows. The number of participants in special events may be reliably reported, but the number of spectators usually can only be estimated unless the events are held indoors or admission tickets are issued or sold.

The forms used by a department to report activities should be carefully designed to provide for accurate reporting of those units of activity that lend themselves to more or less exact treatment. They should be consolidated for study by supervisors and by the top manager, and used as a basis for counseling recreationists, reformulating activities, and making administrative adjustments. Instructions should provide that records be made daily or at the conclusion of each activity. At the same time care must be taken that superfluous information is not requested and the task of recording information does not become a burden to the program recreationists and keep them from other essential duties.

Evaluation of the recreational program indicates whether the program has achieved its stated objectives. The recreational program has a great deal to commend it in terms of the positive aims inherent in the comprehensive experiences offered by the department. A list of its positive objectives includes social acceptability, enjoyment, health, skill development, participation, challenges, and opportunity. These significant outcomes that result from well-planned, well-directed, and inspired recreational programs may be appraised and demonstrated.

By questioning program meaning, some indication of worth may be ascertained. Thus, the following and other questions may be raised, the answers to which assist in the evaluative process:

1. Is there carry-over for participants in the program?
2. Does the individual secure a sense of achievement through his/her participation?
3. Does the individual experience a sense of social acceptability and responsibility through his/her participation in program activities?
4. Are individual differences in skill, maturity, aptitude, and intellect taken into consideration in formulating the program?
5. Is there opportunity for creative self-expression?
6. Does the activity promote public goodwill?
7. Does the activity discover and develop the qualities of leadership?

Evaluation and integration

Evaluation is or can be closely associated with every phase of the planning and operational elements of any recreational service agency; whether in the public or private sector. Because of this fact, it is desirable that the process should become a cohesive force which assures that all activities fulfill and contribute to the goals of recreational service as a field. Evaluation is both the end-in-view and a practice. As practice it includes studies and procedures designed to sustain or improve the quality of participation, methods of program presentation, professional personnel performance, and every aspect of agency operation. It is a process which discloses evidence of inadequacy, evidence of progress, and evidence of proximity to any ideal which has been selected as the agency's goal.

To the extent that evaluation is also an end, it is improvement which more nearly exemplifies its meaning.[9] Evaluation includes both ends and means, for it permits a judgment that is reached concerning some person, place, or thing and it may also be described as a process for reaching judgments. How such judgments are reached and what ends they may serve is a proper study for any recreationist who is concerned with evaluation procedures. It must be understood from the outset that evaluation is a process of determining information about the degree to which recreational service objectives are achieved by the department or organization. It should never be thought of as a mere collection of techniques, the total of which equal the process. Among the principles of evaluation which can effectively guide the evaluation process are those which deal with:

1. Identification and understanding of what has to be evaluated. No method of evaluation can be chosen or initiated until the objectives of evaluation have been clearly determined. The effectiveness of the evaluative process relies as much upon what is to be evaluated as it does upon the validity, reliability, and technical stability of the instruments employed.
2. Prior consideration should be given to the appropriateness of the evaluative technique chosen in terms of the aims to be served. Every evaluative technique has plus or minus factors in regard to gaining an understanding of what is being evaluated. Whichever technique is best fitted for the situation under examination should be utilized. It is not a question of which procedure to use, but which best meets the needs insofar as appropriateness is concerned.
3. An inclusive program of evaluation requires diverse techniques and instrumentalities if it is to be effective and valuable. No one evaluation technique is adequate for determining all the significant products of recreational service. A variety of devices, including objective, subjective, and observational methods are required to evaluate the host of possibilities which are included in the outcome of any recreational program. A variety of techniques may be fruitful, particularly when any single instrument is relatively limited in scope. By combining several or many procedures there is a greater likelihood that a more accurate and adequate judgment will be able to be made.[10]
4. Appropriate use of evaluation techniques requires complete understanding of both strengths and weaknesses of the procedures. Evaluation techniques can vary from quite precise instruments (e.g. quantitatively-based statistics dealing with participant use of departmental facilities) to highly subjective narrative reports. Of course there is always the possibility of incorrect analysis of evaluation results. Sometimes accuracy is attributed to instruments which are not precise enough. There should be recognition on the part of evaluators that most techniques are limited and should not be credited with qualities not possessed.
5. Evaluation is a process that has justification only to the extent to which the results are put to appropriate use. If evaluation were to be considered an exercise rather than a means for delivering better services, it would be better left undone. When evaluation is seen as a process for obtaining information upon which substantive decisions can be based for improved services in every phase of departmental operation, then the process has served its purpose. Implied in this rule is the concept that

objectives are clearly defined prior to the initiation of the process; that the techniques utilized are appropriate for the purposes identified; that decisions will be guided in light of what the evaluation process elicits; and that the varied evaluative techniques employed are chosen on the basis of their value to improved departmental offerings, organization, and management.

Among the identified areas that evaluation is designed to improve are human resource competence at the program, supervisory, and managerial levels; needs of potential patrons; determination of accountability for services provided; comparison of defined objectives with the actuality of system operation; and the recognition that problems can be solved if properly understood in terms of information collection and analysis, and the production of alternatives that are suitable for resolving existing problems and exploiting opportunities.

Notes

1 Strategic management in recreational service

1 Bryson, J.M.: *Strategic Planning for Public Nonprofit Organizations: A Guide to Strengthening and Sustaining Organizational Achievement*, 3rd ed. (San Francisco, CA: Jossey-Bass, 2004).
2 Gryskiewicz, S.S.: *Positive Turbulence: Developing Climates for Creativity, Innovation, and Renewal* (San Francisco, CA: Jossey-Bass, 1999), pp. 16–17.
3 Schmitt, B.H.: *Big Think Strategy: How to Leverage Bold Ideas and Leave Small Thinking Behind* (Boston, MA: Harvard Business School Press, 2007), pp. 3–6.
4 Machiavelli, N.: *The Prince*, trans. L. Ricci (New York: Mentor Books, 1957), p. 55.
5 Zenger, J. and J. Folkman: *The Extraordinary Leader* (New York: McGraw-Hill, 2002).
6 Allison, M. and J. Kaye: *Strategic Planning for Non-profit Organizations: A Practical Guide and Workbook* (New York: John Wiley, 2005).
7 Drucker, P.F. *et al.*: *Managing the Nonprofit Organization: Practices and Principles* (New York: Collins Business, 2005).
8 Austin, M. and K. Hopkins (eds.): *Supervision as Collaboration in the Human Services: Building a Learning Culture* (Thousand Oaks, CA: SAGE, 2005).
9 Wheatley, M.J.: *Leadership and the New Science*, 3rd ed. (San Francisco, CA: Berrett-Koehler Publishers, 2006), pp. 148–55.
10 Bryant, A.: "O.K. Newbies, Bring Out the Hula Hoops," *The New York Times* (June 13, 2010), p. 2 Bu. See also Meyerson, D.: "'Normal' Ambiguity? A Glimpse of an Occupational Culture," pp. 131–44 in P. Frost *et al.* (eds.) *Reframing Organizational Culture* (Newbury Park, CA: SAGE, 1992).
11 Bass, B.M.: *The Bass Handbook of Leadership: Theory, Research, and Managerial Applications*, 4th ed. (New York: Free Press, 2008), p. 753.

2 Planning for strategic management

1 Quinn, J.B. *et al.*: *The Strategy Process: Concepts, Contexts, and Cases* (Englewood Cliffs, NJ: Prentice Hall, 1988), pp. 85–104.
2 Hyde, A.C.: *Government Budgeting Theory, Process, and Politics*, 3rd ed. (Toronto, Ont.: Thomson Learning, 2002), pp. 512–17. See also Brody, R.: *Effectively Managing Human Service Organizations* (Thousand Oaks, CA: SAGE, 2004).
3 Capelli, P.: *Talent on Demand: Managing Talent in an Age of Uncertainty* (Boston, MA: Harvard Business Press, 2008), pp. 5–7.
4 Nassau County, Long Island, New York.
5 Golden, R. and R. Gavin: "Fiscal Crisis Forces States to Endure Painful Choices," *The Wall Street Journal* (October 7, 2002), pp. A1, A14.

6 Letters to the Editor, "Terminology," *Recreation* (Vol. LIV, No. 8, October, 1961) National Recreation Association, p. 394. See also Simpson, J. (ed.): *Oxford English Dictionary*, 3rd ed., Vol. 13 (Oxford: Oxford University Press, 2011), p. 373. See also *Oxford English Dictionary Online*, "Recreationist" 2010.

7 Cowan, A.L.: "Experts See a Tough Road for Schools Chief Nominee," *The New York Times* (November 29, 2010), p. CT 11. See also Saunders, Z.: "Black Lash," *The New Republic* (December 30, 2010), p. 1.

8 Oterman, S.: "Incoming Chancellor Seeks Calmer Debate," *The New York Times* (April 17, 2011), p. 21.

9 Cooper, M. and M. Williams Walsh: "Mounting Debts by States Stoke Fears of Crisis," *The New York Times* (December 5, 2010), pp. 1, 28. See also Baker, A.: "Planned Fire Dept. Fees for Motorists Criticized," *The New York Times* (December 12, 2010), p. 30.

10 Nagourney, A.: "Tax Cuts from '70s Confront Brown Again in California," *The New York Times* (January 9, 2011), p. 21.

11 Barash, D.P.: *The Survival Game: How Game Theory Explains the Biology of Cooperation and Competition* (New York: Henry Holt, 2003), pp. 1–3.

12 McGreevy, P.: "No California State Parks Will Close Governor Schwarzenegger Announces," *The Los Angeles Times* (September 25, 2009), p. L.A. Now. See also personal message to Joseph W. Halper from California State Senator Fran Pavley, September 25, 2009.

13 Scott, W.R. and G.F. Davis: *Organizations and Organizing: Rational, Natural, and Open Systems Perspectives* (Upper Saddle River, NJ: Pearson/Prentice Hall, 2007).

14 Choo, C.W. and N. Bontis (eds.): *The Strategic Management of Intellectual Capital and Organizational Knowledge* (New York: Oxford University Press, 2002), pp. 256–7, 259. See also Pershing, J.A. (ed.): *Handbook of Human Performance Technology*, 3rd ed. (San Francisco, CA: Pfeiffer, a Wiley imprint, 2006), pp. 1089–106.

15 *Ibid.*, pp. 954–6.

16 Kim, W.C. and R. Mauborgne: *Blue Ocean Strategy* (New York: INSEAD, 2010).

17 Gowdy, E. and E. Freeman: "Program Supervision: Facilitating Staff Participation in Program Analysis, Planning, and Change," *Administration in Social Work* (Vol. 17, No. 3, 1993), pp. 59–79.

18 Kettner, P.M., R.M. Moroney and L.L. Martin: *Designing and Managing Programs: An Effectiveness Based Approach*, 2nd ed. (Thousand Oaks, CA: SAGE, 2003).

19 Lohr, S.: "When There's No Such Thing as Too Much Information," *The New York Times* (April 24, 2011), p. 3 Bu.

20 Pynes, J.: *Human Resource Management for Public and Nonprofit Organizations* (San Francisco, CA: Jossey-Bass, 2004). See also Simpson, J.L. and P. Shockley-Zalabak (eds.): *Engaging Communication, Transforming Organizations: Scholarship of Engagement in Action* (Cresskill, NJ: Hampton Press, 2005).

3 From strategic planning to organizational design

1 Stanley, D.J., J.P. Meyer, and L. Topolnysky: "Employee Cynicism and Resistance to Organizational Change," *Journal of Business and Psychology* (Vol. 19, 2005), pp. 429–59.

2 Holman, P. *et al.* (eds.): *The Change Handbook: The Definitive Resource of Today's Best Methods for Engaging Whole Systems* (San Francisco, CA: Berrett-Koehler Publishers, 2007). See also Hargadon, A.: *How Breakthroughs Happen* (Boston, MA: Harvard Business School Press, 2003), pp. 10, 57–64.

3 Galbraith, J.R.: *Competing with Flexible Lateral Organizations*, 2nd ed. (Reading, MA: Addison-Wesley, 2003), pp. 8–11, 35–40, 52–4, 62–6. See also Skidmore, R.A.: *Social Work Administration*, 2nd ed. (Englewood Cliffs, NJ: Prentice Hall, 1990), p. 98; Groth, L.: *Future Organizational Design: The Scope for the IT-based Enterprise* (New York: John Wiley & Sons, 1999), pp. 42–4.

4 Feldman, M. and B. Pentland: "Reconceptualizing Organizational Routines as a Source of Flexibility and Change," *Administrative Science Quarterly* (Vol. 48, 2003), pp. 94–118.

5 Bryant, A.: "Defensive? It Leads to Destructive," *The New York Times* (November 28, 2010), p. 2 Bu.

6 Kilman, R.H. *et al.*: *The Management of Organizational Design: Vol. I Strategies and Implementation* (New York: North-Holland, 1976), pp. 105–6, 177.

7 McLean, D.M. *et al.*: *Leisure Resources: Its Comprehensive Planning*, 2nd ed. (Champaign, IL: Sagamore Publishing, 1999), pp. 111–45.

8 Holman, P. *et al.* (eds.): *The Change Handbook: The Definitive Resource on Today's Best Methods for Engaging Whole Systems* (San Francisco, CA: Berrett-Koehler, 2007), pp. 316–17. See also Bryant, A.: "Don't Lose that Start-up State of Mind," *The New York Times* (October 17, 2010), p. 2 Bu.

9 Kilman, *op. cit.*, pp. 107–8.

10 *Ibid.*, p. 45–6.

11 Keidel, R.W.: *Seeing Organizational Patterns: A New Theory and Language of Organizational Design* (San Francisco, CA: Berrett-Koehler, 1995), pp. 83–4. See also Nirenberg, J.: *The Living Organization Transforming Teams into Workplace Communities* (Homewood, IL: Business One Irwin, 1993), p. 58.

12 Bryant, A.: "Re-recruit Your Team Every Day," *The New York Times* (July 4, 2010), p. 2 Bu.

13 Driver, M.J. *et al.*: *The Dynamic Decision Maker: Five Decision Styles for Executive and Business Success* (New York: Harper & Row, 1990), pp. 212–27.

14 Simons, G.F., C. Vazquez, and P.R. Harris: *Transcultural Leadership Empowering the Diverse Workforce* (Houston, TX.: Gulf Publishing Company, 1993), pp. 186–204.

15 Stellin, S.: "Inside the New Flight Rules," *The New York Times*, Travel Section (May 16, 2010), p. 3.

4 Strategic decisions for policy-making

1 Frank, R.H.: "The Impact of the Irrelevant," *The New York Times* (May 30, 2010), p. 5.

2 Clemen, R.T. and T. Reilly: *Making Hard Decisions with Decision Tools* (Pacific Grove, CA: Duxbury, 2001), pp. 21–36.

3 Barzini, L.: *The Italians* (New York: Anthenium, 1970), p. 177.

5 Leadership: the basis for strategic management

1 Zimmerman, E.: "A Modern Mentor Is a Listener, Too," *The New York Times* (June 6, 2010), p. 9.

2 Rowe, A.J. *et al.*: *Strategic Management: A Methodological Approach*, 4th ed. (Reading, MA: Addison-Wesley, 1994), pp. 460, 462–8.

3 Bryant, A.: "Remember to Thank Your Star Players," *The New York Times* (July 11, 2010), p. 2 Bu.

4 Newcombe, T.M., R.H. Turner, and P.E. Converse: *Social Psychology: The Study of Human Interaction* (New York: Holt, Rinehart, & Winston, 1965), p. 184.

5 Wagner, R. and J.K. Harter: *12 Elements of Great Managing* (New York: Gallup Press, 2006), pp. xi–xii, 31.

6 Bryant, A.: "If Plan B Fails, Go Through the Alphabet," *The New York Times* (May 16, 2010), p. 2 Bu. See also Bryant, A., "No Need to Hit the Send Key, Just Talk to Me," *The New York Times* (August 29, 2010), p. 2 Bu.

7 Gofee, R. and G. Jones: *Clever: Leading Your Smartest, Most Creative People* (Boston, MA: Harvard Business Press, 2009).

8 Shivers, J.S.: *Leadership and Groups in Recreational Service* (Cranberry, NJ: Fairleigh Dickinson University Press, 2001), p. 104.

9 Bass, B.M.: *The Bass Handbook of Leadership: Theory, Research, and Managerial Applications* (New York: Free Press, 2008), p. 23.

10 Northouse, P.G.: *Leadership: Theory and Practice*, 4th ed. (Thousand Oaks, CA: SAGE, 2007), pp. 2–11.

11 Hesselbein, F. and R. Johnston (eds.): *On Mission and Leadership* (San Francisco, CA: Jossey-Bass, 2002), pp. 82–7.

12 Bryant, A.: "It's the Culture that Drives the Numbers," *The New York Times* (May 30, 2010), p. 2 Bu.

13 Bryant, A.: "The X Factor When Hiring? Call it Presence," *The New York Times* (June 27, 2010), p. 2 Bu.

14 Oshinsky, D.M.: *A Conspiracy so Immense: The World of Joe McCarthy* (New York: Oxford University Press, 2005), p. 259.

15 Bryant, A.: "I'm Prepared for Adversity. I Waited Tables," *The New York Times* (June 6, 2010), p. 2 Bu. See also Bryant, A.: "Distilling the Wisdom of the C.E.O.s," *The New York Times* (April 17, 2011), pp. 1, 6 Bu.

16 Bryant, A.: "Want the Job? Tell Him the Meaning of Life," *The New York Times* (June 20, 2010), p. 2 Bu.

17 Boyatzis, R. and A. McKee: *Resonant Leadership* (Boston, MA: Harvard Business School Press, 2005), pp. 2–3, 20–2, 24–6.

18 Bryant, A.: "The Quest to Build a Better Boss," *The New York Times* (March 13, 2011), pp. 1, 7 Bu.

19 Bryant, A.: "Always Keep a Few Tricks Up Your Sleeve," *The New York Times* (July 25, 2010), p. 2 Bu.

20 Bryant, A.: "Note to Staff: We're a Team Not a Family," *The New York Times* (May 15, 2011), p. 2 Bu.

21 Zimmerman, Z.: "Are You Cut Out for Management?" *The New York Times* January 16, 2011), p. 8 Bu.

22 Levinson, H.: "Management by Whose Objectives?" *Harvard Business Review* (July–August, 1970), p. 129.

23 Likert, R.: "Measuring Organizational Performance," in B.L. Hinton and H.J. Reitz (eds), *Groups and Organizations: Integrating Readings in the Analysis of Social Behavior* (Belmont, CA: Wadsworth, 1971), p. 556.

24 Heilbroner, R.L.: *An Inquiry into the Human Prospect* (New York: Norton, 1975), p. 164.

25 Tannenbaum, R. and W.H. Schmidt, "How to Choose a Leadership Pattern," *Harvard Business Review* (Vol. 36, 1958), p. 301.

26 Shivers, J.S.: *Leadership and Groups in Recreational Service* (Cranberry, NJ: Fairleigh Dickinson University Press, 2001), p. 197.

6 Development of recreational service

1 Schultz Jr, W.F.: *Conservation Law and Administration* (New York: The Ronald Press Company, 1953), p. 3.

2 Peterson, J.A.: *Risk Management for Park, Recreation, and Leisure Services* (Champaign, IL: Management Learning Laboratories, 1987), p. 24.

3 Greenberg, K.J.: "Homegrown: The Rise of American Jihad," *The New Republic* (Vol. 241, No. 4884, June 10, 2010), pp. 6–9. See also Perlez, J.: "Pakistani

Taliban Carried Out Mosque Attacks, Police Say," *The New York Times* (May 30, 2010), p. 12. See also "The Week in Review: 'Terror's Tentacles'" (*The New York Times*, July 4, 2010), p. 2 and Robbins, L. and Wyatt, E.: "Bomb Plot Foiled at Holiday Event in Portland, Ore." *The New York Times* (November 28, 2010), pp. 1, 30.

4 Breasted, M.: "Police Added after Rampage by Turnaways at Rock Concert," (*The New York Times* October 12, 1977), p. A22.

5 Vigdor, B.: "Laying Down the Law: Greenwich Reduces Capacity on Island Beach, Stamford, Ct.," *The Advocate* (July 18, 2010), p. A6.

6 Kilgannon, C. "Chronicle of a Changing City: Shut," *The New York Times* (August 1, 2010), p. 2. See also Firestone, M.: " Increase in Vandalism Concerns Area Officials," *The Chronicle* (December 11–12, 2010), pp. 1, 4.

7 Organizing recreational services

1 March, J.G. and H.A. Simon: *Organizations*, 2nd ed. (Cambridge, MA: Blackwell, 1993), p. 21.

2 Mollenkopf, J., "City Planning," in C. Brecher and R.D. Horton (eds.), *Setting Municipal Priorities, 1990* (New York: New York University Press, 1989), pp. 141–68.

8 The manager and the commission

1 Gibelman, M.: "On Boards and Board Membership," *Administration in Social Work* (Vol. 28, No. 2, 2004), pp. 49–62.

2 Warner, J.: "Egghead Alert," *The New York Times Magazine* (July 11, 2010), pp. 11–12.

9 Recreational service department structure

1 March, J.G. and H.A. Simon: *Organizations*, 2nd ed. (Cambridge, MA: Blackwell, 1993), pp. 190–2.

2 Rosenthal, A.: "The Unemployed Held Hostage, Again," *The New York Times* (November 28, 2010), p. WK 7.

10 Human resources management for recreational service

1 Rothwell, W.J.: *Beyond Training and Development: State-of-the-art Strategies for Enhancing Human Performance* (New York: American Management Association, 1996), pp. 29–50. See also Pershing, J.A. (ed.): *Handbook of Human Performance Technology*, 3rd ed. (San Francisco, CA: John Wiley & Sons), 2006.

2 Bittel, L.R. *et al.*: (eds.): *Handbook for Professional Managers* (New York: McGraw-Hill, 1985), pp. 262–3.

3 Del Po, A. and L. Guerin: *Dealing with Problem Employees: A Legal Guide* (Berkeley, CA: Nolo Press), 2005.

4 Del Po, A.: *The Performance Appraisal Handbook* (Berkeley, CA: Nolo Press), 2007.

5 Sawyer, T. and O. Smith: *The Management of Clubs, Recreation, and Sport: Concepts and Applications* (Champaign, IL: Sagamore Publishing, 1999), pp. 3–18, 23–5. See also Mathis, R.L. and J.H. Jackson: *Human Resource Management*, 11th ed. (Mason, OH: Thomson South-Western), 2006.

6 Whetzel, D.L. and G.R. Wheaton (eds.): *Applied Measurement: Industrial Psychology in Human Resources Management* (Mahwah, NJ: Lawrence Erlbaum Associates, 2007), pp. 13–26, 57–73, 97–108, 161–76, 181–97, 293–313, 320–45.

7 Brannick, M.T., E.L. Levine, and F.P. Morgeson: *Job and Work Analysis*, 2nd ed. (Thousand Oaks, CA: SAGE, 2007), pp. 3–18, 33–43, 83–89, 257–81.
8 Dutton, J.E. and B.R. Ragins (eds.): *Exploring Positive Relationships at Work* (New York: Lawrence Erlbaum Associates, 2007), pp. 159–74.
9 Kennedy, G.: *Essential Negotiation: An A–Z Guide*, 2nd ed. (New York: Bloomberg Press), 2009.
10 McIntyre, R.P.: *Are Worker Rights Human Rights?* (Ann Arbor, MI: University of Michigan Press, 2008), pp. 103–32.
11 Letter from Joseph Halper, Acting Director, Recreational Service Department, Los Angeles County (September 21, 1976).

11 Financial management for recreational service

1 Mayers, R.S.: *Financial Management for Nonprofit Human Service Agencies,* 2nd ed. (Springfield, IL: C.C. Thomas), 2004.
2 Coltman, M.M. and M.G. Jagels: *Hospitality Management Accounting*, 7th ed. (New York: John Wiley, 2001), pp. 552–3, 558–66.
3 Zeitlow, J., J.A. Hankin, and A. Seidner: *Financial Management for Nonprofit Organizations: Policies and Procedures* (Hoboken, NJ: John Wiley, 2007).
4 Romney, M.B. and P.J. Steinbart: *Accounting Information Systems*, 8th ed. (Upper Saddle River, NJ: Prentice Hall, 1999), pp. 39–49.
5 Lafferty, G.W.: "Influence of Law on the Independent Auditor in the Examination of Local Government Accounts," *Journal of Accountancy* (Vol. 90, No. 2, August, 1950), p. 122.
6 McMillan, E.J.: *Preventing Fraud in Nonprofit Organizations* (Hoboken, NJ: John Wiley, 2006).
7 Hay, L.E.: *Accounting for Governmental and Nonprofit Entities*, 7th ed. (Homewood, IL: Richard D. Irwin, 1985), pp. 710–32.
8 Pickett, K.H.S. and J.M. Pickett: *Internal Control: A Manager's Journey* (New York: John Wiley, 2001).

12 Budget management

1 Mumble, J.: "Pr. George's Criticized for Relying on Park Funds," *The Washington Post* (May 3, 2010), pp. B1, B4.
2 Rubin, I.S.: *The Politics of Public Budgeting: Getting and Spending, Borrowing and Balancing*, 6th ed. (Washington, DC: CQ Press, 2010), pp. 1–8.
3 Buck, A.E.: *Budget Making* (Charleston, SC: Bibliolife, 2008).
4 Merchant, K.A.: *Modern Management Control Systems* (Upper Saddle River, NJ: Prentice Hall, 1998), pp. 332–40.
5 Marshall, A.H.: *Financial Management in Local Government* (London: George Allen & Unwin, 1974), pp. 49–72.
6 Gosling, J.J.: *Budgetary Politics in American Government*, 5th ed. (New York: Routledge, 2009), pp. 1, 5, 27–44.
7 Roehl-Anderson, J.M. and S.M. Bragg: *The Controller's Function: The Work of the Managerial Accountant* (New York: John Wiley & Sons, 1996), pp. 15–38, 215–33.
8 Sands, J.: *Accounting for Business* (Buffalo, NY: Arena Books, 2001), pp. 282–91.
9 Kay, R.S. and D.G. Searfoss: *Handbook of Accounting and Auditing*, 2nd ed. (Boston, MA: Warren, Gorham & Lamont, 1989), section 31, pp. 13, 32.
10 Frank, H.A.: *Budgetary Forecasting in Local Government: New Tools and Techniques* (Westport, CT: Quorum Books, 1993), p. 6.

13 Budget types and formats

1 Hyde, A.C.: *Government Budgeting: Theory, Process, and Politics*, 3rd ed. (Toronto, Ont.: Thomson Learning, 2002), pp. 52–62.
2 Compton, J.L.: *Financing and Acquiring Park and Recreation Resources* (Champaign, IL: Human Kinetics, 1999), pp. 56–74.
3 Brayley, R.E. and D.D. McLean: *Managing Financial Resources in Sport and Leisure Service Organizations* (Champaign, IL: Sagamore Publishing, 1999), pp. 203–9.
4 Bittel, L.R. *et al.* (eds.): *Handbook for Professional Managers* (New York: McGraw-Hill Book Company, 1985), pp. 949–51.
5 *Ibid.*, pp. 601–4.
6 Knezevich, S.J.: *Program Budgeting (PPBS): A Resource Allocation Decision System for Education* (Richmond, CA: McCutchan, 1973). See also Freeman, R.J. and C.D. Shoulders: *Governmental and Nonprofit Accounting Theory and Practice*, 4th ed. (Englewood Cliffs, NJ: Prentice Hall, 1993), pp. 88–103.
7 Lampone, S.: "Successful and Effective Contracting of Maintenance Services," in M.E. Havitz (ed.): *Models of Change in Municipal Parks and Recreation: A Book of Innovative Case Studies* (State College, PA: Venture Publishing, 1995), pp. 37–47.
8 Kelly, J.M. and W.C. Rivenback: *Performance Budgeting for State and Local Government* (Armonk, NY: M.E. Sharpe, 2003). See also Hyde, A.C.: *Government Budgeting: Theory, Process, and Politics*, 3rd ed. (Toronto, Ont.: Thomson Learning, 2002), pp. 52–62.
9 Wacht, R.F.: *A New Approach to Capital Budgeting for City and County Governments*, 2nd ed., Research Monograph No. 87 (Atlanta, GA: Georgia State University Business Publishing Division, 1987), pp. 1–11.

14 Information technology diffusion in recreational service

1 Rowe, A.J. *et al.*: *Strategic Management: A Methodological Approach*, 4th ed. (Reading, MA: Addison-Wesley, 1994), pp. 549–52, 556–66.
2 Choo, C.W. and N. Bontis (eds.): *The Strategic Management of Intellectual Capital and Organizational Knowledge* (New York: Oxford University Press, 2002), pp. 52–60.
3 Kochan, T.A. and R.L. Schmalensee (eds.): *Management: Inventing and Delivering Its Future* (Cambridge, MA: MIT Press, 2003), pp. 261–2, 266–70.
4 Rapp, W.V.: *Information Technology Strategies* (New York: Oxford University Press, 2002), pp. 3–18, 21–37, 41–6.
5 Ante, S.E.: "IBM Buys Software Unit from AT&T," *The Wall Street Journal* (May 25, 2010), p. B2.
6 Shneiderman, B.: *Leonardo's Laptop: Human Needs and the New Computing Technologies* (Cambridge, MA: MIT Press, 2002), pp. 187, 190.
7 Cash Jr., J.I. *et al.*: *Building the Information Age Organization: Structure, Control, and Information Technologies* (Homewood, IL: Richard D. Irwin, 1994).
8 Hudson, M.: *Managing at the Leading Edge: New Challenges in Managing Nonprofit Organizations* (San Francisco, CA: Jossey-Bass, 2005).
9 Lohr, S.: "In a New Web World, No Application Is an Island," *The New York Times* (March 27, 2011), p. 3 Bu. See also Brustein, J.: "The Smartphone as Tour Guide for Central Park," *The New York Times* (May 29, 2011), p. CT 5.
10 Feng, D.D. *et al.*: *Multimedia Information Retrieval and Management: Technological Fundamentals and Applications* (Berlin: Springer, 2003).
11 Hartmanis, J. and H. Lin (eds.): *Computing the Future: A Broader Agenda for Computer Science and Engineering* (Washington, DC: National Academy Press, 1992).

12 Gomess, L.: "Quantum Computing May Seem Too Far Out, But Don't Count On It," *The Wall Street Journal* (April 25, 2005), p. B1.
13 Hutchinson, S. and S.C. Sawyer: *Computers, Communications, and Information: A User's Introduction* (Boston, MA: Irwin McGraw-Hill, 2000), pp. 1.6–11.19.
14 Guth, R.A.: "Microsoft Puts Early Spotlight on Next Windows Version," *The Wall Street Journal* (April 25, 2005), pp. B1, B6.
15 Edmunds, R.A.: *The Prentice Hall Encyclopedia of Information Technology* (Englewood Cliffs, NJ: Prentice Hall, 1987), pp. 110–20.
16 Daintith, J. (ed.): *A Dictionary of Computing* (Oxford: Oxford University Press, 2004), p. 392.
17 Bittel, L.R. and J.E. Ramsey: *Handbook for Professional Managers* (New York: McGraw-Hill, 1985), pp. 599–600.

15 Public relations and management impacts

1 Hou, W.C.: *Practical Marketing: An Asian Perspective* (Reading, MA: Addison-Wesley, 1997), pp. 271, 273, 274–7, 281, 284–6.
2 Kotler, P. and G. Armstrong: *Principles of Marketing*, 12th ed. (Upper Saddle River, NJ: Pearson Prentice Hall, 2008), pp. 441–3, 445–6.
3 Britt, S.H. and N.F. Guess (eds.): *The Dartnell Marketing Manager's Handbook* (Chicago, IL: Dartnell, 1984), pp. 1111–19.
4 Shivers, J.S.: *Introduction to Recreational Service Administration* (Philadelphia, PA: Lea & Febiger, 1987), pp. 299–318.
5 Silk, A.: *What Is Marketing?* (Boston, MA: Harvard Business School Press, 2006), pp. 49–81.
6 Kotler, P. and A.R. Andreasen: *Strategic Marketing for Nonprofit Organizations*, 3rd ed. (Englewood Cliffs, NJ: Prentice Hall, 1987), pp. 505–12, 573–90.
7 Weitz, B. and R. Wensley (eds.): *Handbook of Marketing* (Thousand Oaks, CA: SAGE, 2002), pp. 282–300.
8 Kotler, P. *et al.*, *Marketing Places* (New York: The Free Press, 1993), pp. 169–82.
9 Rosenberg, J.M.: *Dictionary of Marketing and Advertising* (New York: John Wiley, 1995), pp. 342–3.
10 Bennett, A.G. (ed.): *The Big Book of Marketing* (New York: McGraw-Hill, 2010), pp. 210–23.
11 Ottman, J.A.: *Green Marketing: Opportunity for Innovation* (Chicago, IL: NTC Business Books), 1997.

16 Program practices

1 Edginton, C.R., D.G. DeGraaf, R.B. Dieser, and S.R. Edginton: *Leisure and Life Satisfaction: Foundational Perspectives*, 4th ed. (Boston, MA: McGraw-Hill Higher Education, 2006), pp. 207–9.
2 Wellner, A.S.: *Americans at Play* (Ithaca, NY: New Strategies Publications, 1997).
3 *Ibid.*
4 Karme, T.: "Ballard's Puppets Put UConn on the Map," *The Chronicle* (June 10, 2010), p. 5.
5 McLean, D.D. *et al.*: *Kraus' Recreation and Leisure in Modern Society*, 8th ed. (Sudbury, MA: Jones and Bertlett, 2008), p. 355.

17 Resources for a recreational service system

1 Williams, S.: *Outdoor Recreation and the Urban Environment* (London: Routledge, 1995).

2 Heckscher, A.: *Open Spaces: The Life of American Cities* (New York: Harper & Row, 1979), pp. 161–91. See also Rasenburger, J. and E. Giddens: "Metropolitan Park vs. Park," *The New York Times* (July 11, 2010), pp. 1, 6.

3 Finn, R.: "At City Parks, Just Add Water," *The New York Times* (July 19, 2010), p. Ct 9.

4 Dineen, A.M.: "Mansfield Feted for Open Space Commitment," *The Chronicle* (June 10, 2010), p. 2. See also Goldhagen, S.W.: "Park Here," *The New Republic* (September 2, 2010), pp. 20–5. See also Kilgannon, C.: "Wide World of Sports in Queens Park," *The New York Times* (September 12, 2010), p. 4 Ct.

5 Shivers, J.S. and G. Hjelte: *Planning Recreational Places* (Cranbury, NJ: Fairleigh Dickinson University Press, 1971), pp. 282, 284, 290–2.

6 Rockville, D.: "Unpacking Imagination," *The New York Times* (September 26, 2010), p. 14.

7 Mooney, J.: "Grit, Glam, and Green, in One Vibrant Package," *The New York Times* (November 21, 2010), p. RE 7.

8 Johns, R.: *Turfgrass Installation: Management and Maintenance* (New York: McGraw-Hill, 2004), pp. 243–324.

9 Howard, D.R. and J.L. Crompton: *Financing, Managing and Marketing Recreation and Park Resources* (Dubuque, IO: Wm. C. Brown Company, 1980), pp. 360–74.

10 Mead, R.: "State of Play," *The New Yorker* (July 5, 2010), pp. 32–7. See also Rendon, J.: "Williamsburg, Toddlertown," *The New York Times* (January 23, 2011), pp. RE 1, 8.

11 Manning, R.E.: *Parks and Carrying Capacity: Commons Without Tragedy* (Washington, DC: Island Press, 2009), pp. 33–55, 253–73.

12 Steinhauer, J.: "The Most Popular Gym Is the City Itself," *The New York Times* (June 6, 2010), p. 23. See also Williams, S.: *Outdoor Recreation and the Urban Environment* (London: Routledge, 1995). See also Copage, E.V.: "Busy Tonight? I Know a Nice Subway Ride … " *The New York Times* (February 11, 2011), p. C30.

13 Kaminer, A.: "The Joys of Ping-Pong in the Open," *The New York Times* (March 27, 2011), pp. 1, 12 Ct.

14 Brett, A. *et al.*: *The Complete Playground Handbook* (Syracuse, NY: Syracuse University Press, 1993), pp. 11–14, 44–51.

15 Helmiich, N.: "Opportunity for Fitness is Part of the New Plan," *USA Today* (May 3, 2010), p. 9D.

16 Flynn, R.B. (ed.), *Facility Planning for Physical Education, Recreation, and Athletics* (Reston, VA: American Alliance for Health, Physical Education, Recreation, and Dance, 1993), pp. 64–173.

17 Sulzberger, A.G.: "Handmade Hoops Put the Clang into New York Courts," *The New York Times* (May 30, 2010), pp. 1, 4.

18 Farmer, P.J. *et al.*, *Sport Facility Planning and Management* (Morgantown, WV: Fitness Information Technology, Inc., 1996), pp. 231–3. See also Gabrielsen, M.A. (ed.): *Swimming Pools: A Guide to their Planning, Design, and Operations*, 4th ed. (Champaign, IL: Human Kinetics, 1987).

19 Mooney, J.: "Breathing Room," *The New York Times Real Estate* (October 17, 2010), pp. 1, 8.

20 Fishman, T.C.: *Shock of Gray: The Aging of the World's Population and How It Pits Young Against Old, Child Against Parent, Worker Against Boss, Company Against Rival, and Nation Against Nation* (New York: Scribner, 2010). See also Grierson, B.: "The Incredible Flying Nonagenarian," *The New York Times Magainze* (November 28, 2010), pp. 73–7. See also Butler, R.N.: *The Longevity Revolution: The Benefits and Challenges of Living a Long Life* (New York: Public Affairs, 2008).

21 Rybezynski, W.: "Bringing the High Line Back to Earth," *The New York Times* (May 15, 2011), p. WK 9. See also Pogrebin, R.: "High Line: The Sequel," *The New York Times* (May 29, 2011), pp. CT 1, 7.
22 Harmon, L.: "Urban Beaches – The Tide Has Turned," *The Boston Globe* (June 13, 2010), p. K9.

18 Liability and recreational service management

1 Agnes, M. (Ed.-in-chief): *Webster's New World College Dictionary*, 4th ed. (Foster City, CA: IDG Books Worldwide, Inc., 2001), p. 812.
2 Engle, D.M. and M. McCann (eds.): *Fault Lines: Tort Law as Cultural Practice* (Stanford, CA: Stanford University Press, 2009), pp. 4–5.
3 Schuck, P.: *Suing Government: Citizen Remedies for Official Wrongs* (New Haven, CT: Yale University Press, 1983), pp. 206–7.
4 *City of Trenton* v. *State of New Jersey*, 262 U.S. 182 (1923).
5 *O'Connel* v. *Merchants and Police District Telephone Company* (Ky.) 1890 S.W. 845, L.B.A. (1915), p. 508. See also Hart, J.E. and R.J. Ritson: *Liability and Safety in Physical Education and Sport* (Reston, VA: AAHPERD, 1983), pp. 11–14.
6 White, G.E.: *Tort Law in America: An Intellectual History* (New York: Oxford University Press, 2003), pp. 248–51.
7 Litan, R.E. and C. Winston: *Liability Perspectives and Policy* (Washington, DC: The Brookings Institute, 1988), p. 6.
8 Parisi, F.: *Liability for Negligence and Judicial Discretion* (Berkeley, CA: University of California International and Area Studies, 1992), p. 1.
9 Wong, G.M.: *Essentials of Amateur Sports Law* (Dover, MA: Auburn House, 1988), pp. 342–6.
10 Punke, H.H.: *The Teacher and the Courts* (Danville, IL: The Interstate Printers & Publishers, 1971), p. 529.
11 Jones, L.G.: *Preventing Lawsuits: The Role of Institutional Research* (San Francisco, CA: Jossey Bass, 1997), pp. 72–6, 81–2.
12 Appenzeller, H. and T. Appenzeller: *Sports and the Courts* (Charlottesville, VA: The Michie Company, 1980), pp. 15–20.

19 Infrastructure management

1 Oversight Hearing before the Subcommittee on Parks, Recreation, and Public Lands: "Fiscal Year 2005 Budget for the National Park Service and Bureau of Land Management and Ongoing Efforts to Reduce Maintenance Backlogs," Serial No. 108–86 (Washington, DC: U.S. Government Printing Office, 2004).
2 Lampone, S.: "Successful and Effective Contracting of Maintenance Services," in M.E. Havitz (ed.): *Models of Change in Municipal Parks and Recreation* (State College, PA: Venture Publishing, Inc. 1995), pp. 37–47.
3 Mittlestaedt Jr, A.H. "Safety Recommendations in the Design of Athletic and Sports Fields," in R.C. Schmidt *et al.* (eds.): *Natural and Artificial Playing Fields: Characteristics and Safety* (Philadelphia, PA: ASTM, 1990), pp. 6–9.

20 Office and records management

1 Johnson, H.W. and W.G. Savage: *Administrative Office Management* (Reading, MA: Addison-Wesley, 1968).
2 Becker, F.D.: *Workplace by Design* (San Francisco, CA: Jossey Bass, 1995), pp. 3–100.

3 Center Jr., C.E.: *Records Management* (Washington, DC: Association of Research Libraries, 2008), pp. 13–17.
4 Croome, D.J. (ed.): *Noise and the Design of Buildings and Services* (Essex, UK: Construction Press, 1982), pp. 1–62, 77–84, 87–99.
5 Johnson, M.M. and N.F. Kallaus: *Records Management*, 3rd ed. (Cincinnati, OH: South-Western Publishing Co., 1982).
6 Kaithoff, R.J. and L.S. Lee: *Productivity and Records Automation* (Englewood Cliffs, NJ: Prentice Hall, 1981), pp. 79–190.
7 Baettz, M.L.: *The Human Imperative: Planning for People in the Electronic Office* (Homewood, IL: Dow Jones-Irwin, 1985), pp. 119–26.
8 Sussams, J.E.: *How to Write Effective Reports*, 3rd ed. (Hampshire, UK: Gower Publishing, 1998).

21 Evaluation of recreational service

1 Rutman, L.: *Evaluation Research Methods: A Basic Course*, 2nd ed. (Beverly Hills, CA: SAGE, 1984), pp. 30–62.
2 Mathison, S. (ed.): *Encyclopedia of Evaluation* (Thousand Oaks, CA: SAGE, 2005), p. 327.
3 Chelimsky, E. and W.R. Shadish (eds.): *Evaluation for the 21st Century: A Handbook* (Thousand Oaks, CA: SAGE, 1997), pp. 124–32.
4 Chen, H.-T: *Practical Program Evaluation* (Thousand Oaks, CA: SAGE, 2005), pp. 83–5.
5 Davidson, E.J.: *Evaluation Methodology Basics* (Thousand Oaks, CA: SAGE, 2005).
6 Chen, H.-T.: *Theory Driven Evaluations* (Newbury Park, CA: SAGE, 1990), pp. 58–65.
7 Weiss, C.H.: *Evaluating Action Programs* (Boston, MA: Allyn & Bacon, 1972), pp. 6–11, 54–81.
8 Morris L.L. *et al.*: *How to Communicate Evaluation Findings* (Thousand Oaks, CA: SAGE, 1987).
9 Crano, W.D. and M.B. Brewer: *Principles and Methods of Social Research*, 2nd ed. (Mahwah, NJ: Lawrence Erlbaum Associates, 2002), pp. 148–9.
10 Denzin, N.K. and Y.S. Lincoln (eds.): *Collecting and Interpreting Qualitative Materials*, 2nd ed. (Thousand Oaks, CA: SAGE, 2003), pp. 47–145, 593–602.

Bibliography

Aaron, H.J., T.E. Mann, and T. Taylor: *Values and Public Policy* (Washington, DC: The Brookings Institution, 1994).

Allison, M. and J. Kaye: *Strategic Planning for Nonprofit Organizations*, 2nd ed. (New York: John Wiley, 2005).

Alred, G.J., C.T. Brusaw, and W.E. Oliu: *The Business Writer's Handbook* (New York: St. Martin's Press, 2006).

Alvintzi, P. and E. Hannes: *Crisis Management* (New York: Nova Science Publishers, 2010).

Anderson, D.L., Cunningham, C.E., Woodward, C.A., Shannon, H.S., MacIntosh, J., Lendrum, B. and P. Rosenblum: *Organization Development: The Process of Leading Organizational Change* (Thousand Oaks, CA: SAGE, 2009).

Andrade, L., Gabor, P.A. and A. Yvonne *Evaluation in the Human Services*, 6th ed. (Florence, KY: Wadsworth Publishing, 2001).

Anthony, W.P., Perrewe, P.L. and K.M. Kacmar *Human Resource Management: A Strategic Approach* (Mason, OH: South-Western, 2001).

Appenzeller, H.: *Risk Management in Sport: Issues and Strategies* (Durham, NC: Carolina Academic Press, 2005).

Appleton, I.: *Building for the Performing Arts: A Design and Development Guide* (Philadelphia, PA.: Elsevier, 2008).

Ashe, C. and C. Nealy: *Records Management: Effective Information Systems* (Tappan, NJ: Prentice Hall PTR, 2003).

Aslett, D.: *Office Clutter Cure* (Avon, MA: Adams Media Corp, 2003).

Barney, J.B. and W.S. Hesterly: *Strategic Management and Competitive Advantage: Concepts* (Upper Saddle River, NJ: Prentice Hall, 2010).

Beam, B.T. and J.J. McFadden: *Employee Benefits*, 7th ed. (Chicago, IL: Dearborn Financial Publishing, Inc., 2004).

Beckett, J. and H.O. Koenig: *Public Administration and Law* (Armonk, NY: M.E. Sharpe, 2005).

Bennett, J.: *Evaluation Methods in Research* (New York: Continuum, 2003).

Berry, L.M.: *Employee Selection* (Florence, KY: Wadsworth, 2002).

Bigham, R. and C. Felbinger: *Evaluation in Practice: A Methodological Approach*, 2nd ed. (Cottonwood, CA: QC Press, 2002).

Bird, S. and J. Zauhar: *Recreation and the Law*, 2nd ed. (Milburn, NJ: Carswell CAN, 1997).

Block, S.B., Hirt, G.A. and B.R. Danielson *Foundation of Financial Management* (New York: McGraw-Hill Higher Education Group, 2009).

Bloomfield, B.P., R. Coombs and D. Knights (eds.): *Information Technology and Organization: Strategies, Networks, and Integration* (New York: Oxford University Press, 2000).

Bogsnes, B.: *Implementing Beyond Budgeting: Unlocking the Performance Potential* (Hoboken, NJ: John Wiley, 2011).

Bohlander, G.W. and S.A. Snell: *Managing Human Resources*, 13th ed. (Mason, OH: South-Western, 2003).

Booty, F.: *Facilities Management Handbook* (Oxford, UK: Elsevier Science and Technology Books, 2009).

Breen, A. and D. Rigby: *The New Waterfront: A Worldwide Urban Success Story* (New York: McGraw-Hill Book Co., 1996).

Brewer, P.C., R. Garrison and E. Noreen: *Introduction to Managerial Accounting* (New York: McGraw-Hill Higher Education, 2009).

Burnes, B.: *Managing Change: A Strategic Approach to Organizational Dynamics*, 4th ed. (Tappan, NJ: Prentice Hall PTR, 2004).

Burton, R.M. and B. Obel: *Strategic Organizational Design: The Dynamics of Fit*, 3rd ed. (Higham, MA: Kluwer Academic Publishers, 2003).

Busse, R.C.: *Employee's Rights: Your Practical Handbook to Workplace Law* (Naperville, IL: Sourcebooks Inc., 2004).

Calloway, J., C. Feltz, and K. Young: *Never by Chance: Aligning People Strategy through Intentional Leadership* (Hoboken, NJ: John Wiley, 2010).

Cayer, N.J.: *Public Personnel Administration in the United States*, 4th ed. (Florence, KY: Wadsworth, 2003).

Certo, S.C. *Supervision: Concepts and Skill-Building* (New York: McGraw-Hill Higher Education, 2010).

Cihon, P.J. and J.O. Castagnera: *Employment and Labor Law*, 5th ed. (Mason, OH: South-Western, 2005).

Colquitt, J., LePine, J.A. and M.J. Wesson: *Organizational Behavior: Improving Performance and Commitment in the Workplace* (New York: McGraw-Hill Higher Education, 2010).

Colton, D. and R.W. Covert: *Designing and Constructing Instruments for Social Research and Evaluation* (San Francisco, CA: Jossey Bass, 2007).

Conison, J.: *Employee Benefits in a Nutshell*, 3rd ed. (Eagan, MN: West Publishing Co., College and School Division, 2003).

Cortada, J.W.: *How Societies Embrace Information Technology: Lessons for Business and Government* (Piscataway, NJ: IEEE Computer Society Press, 2010).

Courtney, R.: *Strategic Management for Voluntary Nonprofit Organizations* (New York: Routledge, 2002).

Cutt, J. and V. Murray: *Accountability and Effectiveness Evaluation in Nonprofit Organizations* (Florence, KY: Routledge, 2000).

Dahl, B. and D.J. Molnar: *Anatomy of a Park*, 3rd ed. (Long Grove, IL: Waveland Press, 2005).

David, F.R.: *Strategic Management: Concepts*, 10th ed. (Tappan, NJ: Prentice Hall PTR, 2004).

De Bruijn, H.: *Managing Performance in the Public Sector* (New York: Routledge, 2002).

De Nisi, A.S. and R.W. Griffin: *Human Resource Management*, 2nd ed. (Boston, MA: Houghton Mifflin Co., 2005).

Diedrich, R.J.: *Building Type Basics for Recreational Facilities* (New York: John Wiley, 2005).

Dilenschneidfer, R.L.: *The AMA Handbook of Public Relations* (New York: Amacom, 2010).

Dillinger, W.C.: *Decentralization and Its Implications for Urban Service Delivery* (Washington, DC: World Bank Publications, 1994).

Dolman, E.C.: *Pure Strategy* (Portland, OR: Frank Cass Publications, 2005).

Douglas, R.W.: *Forest Recreation*, 5th ed. (Long Grove, IL: Waveland Press, 2005).

Dunn, J.: *Public-relations Techniques That Work* (Chicago, IL: Thorogood GBR, 2001).

Elliott, C. and F. Quinn: *Tort Law*, 4th ed. (Tappan, NJ: Pearson Education, 2003).

Ewert, R.M. and A. Wagenhofer: *Managerial Accounting* (New York: Springer, 2009).

Eyeston, P.: *Public Policy Formation* (Greenwich, CT: JAI Press, 1984).

Falkenberg, H.: *Pool Design* (New York: teNeues Publishing Co., 2004).

Feinglass, A.: *Public Relations for Non-profits: A Comprehensive Guide and Resource* (New York: John Wiley, 2005).

Filar, J.A. and S. Hourie: *Uncertainty and Environmental Decision Making: A Handbook of Research and Best Practice* (New York: Springer, 2010).

Fontana, V.R.: *Municipal Liability: Law and Practice*, 2nd ed., 2 vols (New York: Aspen Publications, Inc., 2003).

Franklin, B., Hogan, M., Langley, Q., Mosdell, N. and E. Pill: *Key Concepts in Public Relations* (Thousand Oaks, CA: SAGE, 2009).

Fullan, M.: *Leadership and Sustainability: System Thinkers in Action* (Thousand Oaks, CA: Conwin Press, Inc., 2004).

Fulton, R.S.: *Common Sense Management: Quick Wisdom for Managers* (Berkeley, CA: Ten Speed Press, 2009).

Gelb, A.: *Playgrounds* (East Rutherford, NJ: Penguin Group, Inc., 1987).

Gingrich, G.: *Managing IT in Government, Business, and Communities* (Hershey, PA: Idea Group Publishing, 2003).

Glickman, C.D., Gordon, S.P. and J.M. Ross-Gordon: *Supervision and Instructional Leadership: A Developmental Approach*, 6th ed. (Boston, MA: Allyn & Bacon, 2003).

Godbey, G.: *Leisure and Leisure Services in the 21st Century* (State College, PA: Venture,1997).

Goldberg, J.C., Sebok, A.J. and B.C. Zipursky: *Tort Law: Responsibilities and Redress* (New York: Aspen Publishers, Inc., 2004).

Golensky, M.: *Strategic Leadership and Management in Nonprofit Organizations: Theory and Practice* (Chicago, IL: Lyceum Books, 2010).

Goodwin, P. and G. Wright: *Decision Analysis for Management Judgment* (New York: John Wiley, 2009).

Grant, K., R. Hackney, and D. Edger: *Strategic Information Systems Management* (Andover, MA: Cenage Learning, 2010).

Greene, R.J.: *Rewarding Performance: Guiding Principles, Custom Strategies* (New York: Routledge, 2011).

Greer, C.R. and W.R. Plunkett: *Supervision: Diversity and Teams in the Workplace*, 10th ed. (Tappan, NJ: Prentice Hall PTR, 2002).

Griffin, J.: *How to Say it for First Time Managers: Winning Words and Strategies for Earning Your Team's Confidence* (New York: Prentice Hall Press, 2010).

Gruber, J.: *Public Finance and Public Policy* (Gordonsville, VA: Worth Publishers, Inc., 2005).

Guildung, C.: *Financial Management for Hospitality Decision Makers* (St. Louis, MO: Elsevier Science and Technology Books, 2002).

Hackman, M.Z. and E.E. Johnson: *Leadership: A Communication Perspective*, 4th ed. (Prospect Heights, IL: Waveland Press, Inc., 2003).

Hall, I.: *Evaluation and Social Research: Introducing Small-scale Practices* (New York: Palgrave Macmillan, 2004).

Harper, C.A.: *Environment and Society: Human Perspectives on Environmental Issues*, 3rd ed. (Tappan, NJ: Prentice Hall, 2003).

Harrison, J.: *Strategic Management*, 2nd ed. (New York: John Wiley, 2004).

Hartley, J.: *Managing to Improve Public Service* (New York: Cambridge University Press, 2008).

Hendricks, B.E.: *Designing for Play* (Aldershot, UK: Ashgate, 2001).

Heragu, S.S.: *Facilities Design* (Tappan, NJ: Prentice Hall PTR, 2005).

Hicks, M.: *Problem Solving in Business and Management*, 2nd ed. (Independence, KY: Thomson Learning GBR, 2004).

Hilton, R.W.: *Managerial Accounting*, 6th ed. (New York: McGraw-Hill/Irwin, 2005).

Hogan, C.: *Tennis Courts: A Construction Maintenance Manual (Ellicott City, MD: American Sport Builders Association, 2008)*.

Hogg, M.A. and D.V. Knippenberg: *Leadership and Power: Identity Processes in Groups and Organizations* (Thousand Oaks, CA: SAGE, 2004).

Hollingsworth, J.R. and R. Harrneman: *Centralization and Power in Social Service in Delivery Systems* (Higham, MA: Kluwer Academic Publications, 1983).

Huff, A.S., Floyd, W., Sherman, H.D. and S. Terjesen: *Strategic Management: Thought and Action* (New York: John Wiley, 2004).

Hunsaker, P.L. and J. Hunsaker: *Managing People* (New York: DK Publications, 2009).

Hunter, M.G.: *Strategic Information Systems: Concepts, Methodologies, Tools, and Applications* (Hershey, PA: Information Science Reference, 2010).

Hurd, A.R., R.J. Barcelona, and J.T. Mildrum: *Leisure Service Management* (Champaign, IL: Human Kinetics, 2008).

Hussey, D.: *Strategic Management: From Theory to Implementation*, 4th ed. (New York: Elsevier Science and Technology Books, 1998).

Hyman, D.A.: *Public Finance: A Contemporary Application of Theory to Policy with Economic Applications*, 8th ed. (Mason, OH: South-Western, 2004).

Ivancevich, J.M., Konopske, R. and M.T. Matteson: *Organizational Behavior and Management*, 7th ed. (New York: McGraw-Hill, 2005).

Jackson, J.H. and R.L. Mathis: *Human Resource Management*, 13th ed. (Mason, OH: South-Western, 2005).

Janove, J.: *The Star Profile: A Management Tool to Unleash Employee Potential* (Mountain View, CA: David-Black Publications, 2008).

Jensen, C.R. and S.P. Guthrie: *Outdoor Recreation in America* (Champaign, IL: Human Kinetics, Publishers, 2006).

Jerome, P.J.: *Evaluating Employee Performance: A Practical Guide to Assessing Performance*, 2nd ed. (Irvine, CA: Richard Chang Associates, 2004).

Johns, G. and A.M. Saks: *Organizational Behavior: Understanding and Managing Life at Work*, 6th ed. (Tappan, NJ: Prentice-Hall PTR, 2004).

Jones, K.R.: *The Invention of the Park* (Cambridge: Cambridge University Press, 2005).

Judd, D.R. (ed.): *Infrastructure of Play: Building the Tourist City* (Armonk, NY: M.E. Sharpe, 2002).

Judd, D.R. and T. Swanstrom: *City Politics: Private Power and Public Policy*, 4th ed. (New York: Longman, 2003).

Kahn, A.: *Financial Management Theory in the Public Sector* (Westport, CT: Greenwood, 2004).

Kahn, A. and W.B. Hilcheth (eds.): *Budget Theory in the Public Sector* (Westport, CT: Greenwood, 2002).

Katz, P.: *The New Urbanism: Toward an Architecture of Community* (New York: McGraw-Hill Book Co., 1994).

Kaufman, R.A., Brown-Oakley, H., Watkins, R. and D. Leigh: *Strategic Planning for Success: Aligning People, Performance, and Payoffs* (New York: John Wiley, 2003).

Kelly, S.B.: *Community Planning: How to Solve Urban and Environmental Problems* (Blue Ridge Summit, PA: Rowman & Littlefield, 2004).

Kennard, D.: *Staff Support Groups in the Helping Professions: Principles, Practices and Pitfalls* (New York: Routledge, 2009).

Kidwell, R.E. and C.L. Martin: *Managing Organizational Deviance* (Thousand Oaks, CA: SAGE, 2004).

Kotter, J.P.: *Leading Change: Why Transitional Efforts Fail* (Boston, MA: Harvard Business Press, 2010).

Laurini, R.: *Information Systems for Urban Planning: A Hypermedia Cooperative Approach* (Boca Raton, FL: Taylor & Francis, 2001).

Ledermann, A. and A. Trachsel: *Creative Playgrounds and Recreation Centers*, rev. ed. (New York: Frederick A. Praeger, 1968).

Lee, R.D., Johnson, R. and P. Joyce: *Public Budgeting Systems*, 7th ed. (Sudbury, MA: Jones and Bartlett, 2003).

Lefton, R.E. and V. Buzzotto: *Leadership Through People Skills* (New York: McGraw-Hill, 2003).

Leonard, E.C.: *Supervision: Concepts and Practices of Management* (Masan: Ohio South-Western/Cengage Learning, 2010).

Lepak, D. and M. Gowan: *Human Resource Management: Managing Employees for Competitive Advantage* (Upper Saddle River, NJ: Pearson/Prentice-Hall, 2010).

Loomis, M.J.: *Decentralism: Where It Came From – Where Is It Going?* (St. Paul, MN: Black Rose Books, CAN, 2004).

Lucas Jr., H.C.: *Information Technology: Strategic Decision-Making for Managers* (New York: John Wiley, 2004).

Lundberg, J.: "Spatial Interaction Model of Spillovers from Locally Provided Public Services," *Regional Studies* (Vol. 40, No. 6, 2006), pp. 631–44.

Luthans, F.: *Organizational Behavior*, 10th ed. (Blacklick, OH: McGraw-Hill Higher Education, 2004).

Lynch, T.D. and R.W. Smith: *Public Budgeting in America*, 5th ed. (Tappan, NJ: Prentice-Hall PTR, 2003).

Lytras, M.D.: *Information Technology, Information Systems and Knowledge Management* (New York: Springer, 2009).

Maddox, D.C.: *Budgeting for Not-for-profit Organizations* (New York: John Wiley, 1999).

Magee, G.H.: *Facilities Maintenance Management* (Kingston, MA: R.S Means, 1988).

Marcus, A.A.: *Management Strategy: Achieving Sustained Competitive Advantage* (New York: McGraw-Hill/Irwin, 2011).

Martin, L.L.: *Financial Management for Human Service Administrators* (Boston, MA: Allyn & Bacon, 2000).

Martin, L.L. and P.M. Kettner: *Measuring the Performance of Human Service Programs* (Thousand Oaks, CA: SAGE, 2009).

Mayers, R.S.: *Financial Management for Nonprofit Human Service Organizations*, 2nd ed. (Springfield, IL: Troll C. Thomas, 2004).

Mays, V.: *Office and Workspaces* (Gloucester, MA: Rockport, 1999).

McKern, E. (ed.): *Office Professional's Guide* (New York: Oxford University Press, 2005).

McLean, D., Hurd, A.R. and N.B. Rogers: *Recreation and Leisure in Modern Society*, 7th ed. (Sudbury, MA: Jones and Bartlett, 2004).

Mello, J.A.: *Strategic Management of Human Resources* (Mason, OH: Thomson/South-Western, 2011).

Miller, H.T.: *Postmodern Public Policy* (Albany: State University of New York Press, 2002).

Minnaar, F. *Strategic and Performance Management in the Public Sector* (Pretoria: South Africa: Van Schaik, 2010).

Moran, M., M. Rein, and R.E. Goodin: *The Oxford Handbook of Public Policy* (New York: Oxford University Press, 2006).

Morrison, G.: *Nature in the Neighborhood* (Boston, MA: Houghton Mifflin, 2004).

Mosley, D.C., L.C. Megginson, and P.H. Pietri: *Supervisory Management: The Art of Inspiring, Empowering, and Developing People* (Mason, OH: Thomson/South-Western, 2008).

Muir, K.: *Employee Termination Guidebook: Reliable Procedures and Effective Options* (Austin, TX: Turnabout Central, 2004).

Muller, M.: *The Manager's Guide to HR: Hiring, Firing, Performance Evaluation, Documentation, Benefits, and Everything Else You Need to Know* (New York: AMACOM, 2009).

Murphy, M.A.: *Hundred Percenters: Challenge Your Employees to Give it Their All and They'll Give You Even More* (New York: McGraw-Hill Professional, 2009).

National Golf Foundation: *Planning and Building the Golf Course* (Chicago, IL: The Foundation, 1967).

Needles, B.E., Powers, M. and S.V. Crosson: *Financial and Managerial Accounting*, 7th ed. (Boston, MA: Houghton Mifflin College Division, 2004).

Nohr, K.M.: *Managing Risk in Sport and Recreation: The Essential Guide for Loss Prevention* (Champaign, IL: Human Kinetics, 2009).

Norris-Tirral, D. and J.A. Clay: *Strategic Collaboration in Public and Nonprofit Administration: A Practice Based Approach to Solving Shared Problems* (Boca Raton, FL: CRC Press, 2010).

Page, S.J. and C.M. Hall: *The Geography of Tourism and Recreation Environment, Place, and Space* (New York: Routledge, 2006).

Park, Y.H. (ed.): *Computer Technology and Applications* (Fairfield, NJ: American Society of Mechanical Engineers, 2004).

Partington, P. and C. Stainton: *Managing Staff Development* (New York: Open University Press GBR, 2002).

Pearce, J.A. and R.B. Robinson: *Strategic Management: Formulation, Implementation, and Control*, 8th ed. (Blacklick, OH: McGraw-Hill Higher Education, 2005).

Pearlson, K. and C.S. Saunders: *Managing and Using Information Systems: A Strategic Approach* (Hoboken, NJ: John Wiley, 2010).

Penn, L.: *Parks and Playgrounds* (Columbus, OH: Frank Shaffer, 1986).

Peterson, J.A., B.B. Hronek, and J.R. Garges: *Risk Management for Park, Recreation, and Leisure Services* (Champaign, IL: Sagamore Publishing, 2008).

Piersol, J. and H.V. Smith: *Turf Maintenance Facility Design and Management: A Guide to Shop Organization, Equipment, and Preventive Maintenance for Golf and sports Facilities* (New York: John Wiley, 2008).

Porat, A. and A. Stein: *Liability under Uncertainty: Evidential Deficiency in the Law of Torts* (New York: Oxford University Press, 2002).

Powell, R. and R. Sheard: *Stadium Architecture for the New Global Culture* (North Clarendon, VT: Tuttle Publishing, 2005).

Ravetz, J., Roberts, P. and C. George: *Environment and the City* (Florence, KY: Routledge, 2005).

Rice, J.L. and M.L. Carpenter: *Strategic Management: A Dynamic Perspective* (Franks Forest, NSW: Pearson, 2010).

Roadschelders, J.C.N.: *Government: A Public Administration Perspective* (Armonk, NY: M.E. Sharpe, 2003).

Rossman, J.R. and B.E. Schlatter: *Recreation Programming: Designing Leisure Experiences*, 3rd ed. (Champaign, IL: Sagamore Publishing, 2000).

Royse, D., B.A. Thyer, and D.K. Padgett: *Program Evaluation: An Introduction* (Belmont, CA: Wadsworth, Cengage Learning, 2010).

Royse, D.D., Badger, K., Staton-Tindall, M. and J.M. Webster: *Needs Assessment* (New York: Oxford University Press, 2009).

Rue, L.W. and L.L. Byars: *Supervision, Key Link to Productivity*, 9th ed. (New York: (McGraw-Hill Higher Education, 2009).

Russell, R.V. and L.M. Jamieson: *Leisure Program Planning* (Champaign, IL: Human Kinetics, 2008).

Sadler, W.: *Playground Equipment* (Chicago, IL: Heinemann Library, 2005).

Saffody, W.: *Records and Information Management: Fundamentals of Professional Practice* (Lenexa, KS: ARMA International, 2003).

Sashkin, M. and M.G. Sashkin: *Leadership That Matters: The Critical Factors for Making a Difference in People's Lives and Organization's Success* (Grand Rapids, MI: Bethany House Publishers, 2002).

Schneid, T.D. and M.S. Schumann: *Legal Liability: In Safety and Loss Prevention* (Sudbury, MA: Jones and Bartlett, 2011).

Schuler, R.S. and E. Jackson: *Managing Human Resources through Strategic Partnerships*, 9th ed. (Mason, OH: South-Western, 2005).

Seabrook, W. and C.W. Miles: *Recreational Land Management* (Florence, KY: Routledge, 1993).

Seib, O.: *Public Relations Ethics* (Florence, KY: Wadsworth, 1994).

Shivers, J.S.: *Leadership and Groups in Recreational Service* (Teaneck, NJ: Fairleigh Dickinson University Press, 2001).

Shivers, J.S.: *Recreational Services for Older Adults* (Teaneck, NJ: Fairleigh Dickinson University Press, 2002).

Shivers, J.S.: Programming Recreational Services (Sudbury, MA: Jones and Bartlett, 2010).

Siegel, G.B.: *Public Employee Compensation and Its Role in Public Sector Strategic Management* (Westport, CT: Greenwood, 1992).

Shivers, J.S. and G.H. Hjelte: *Planning Recreational Places* (Cranbury, NJ: Associated University Presses, 1971).

Sims, R.R. and A. Scott: *Leadership: Succeeding in the Private, Public, and Not-for-profit Sectors* (Armonk, NY: M.E. Sharpe, 2004).

Smith, L. and P. Mounter: *Effective Internal Communications* (Philadelphia, PA: Kogan Page, 2008).

Spalter, A.M.: *Computer in Visual Arts* (Boston, MA: Addison-Wesley Professional, 1998).

Stacey, R.D.: *Strategic Management and Organizational Dynamics: The Challenge of Complexity*, 4th ed. (Tappan, NJ: Prentice Hall PTR, 2003).

Standiford, K. *Facilities Maintenance* (Albany, NY: Delman Cengage Learning, 2007).

Steiss, A.W.: *Strategic Management for Public and Nonprofit Organizations* (New York: Marcel Dekker, 2002).

Sternloff, R.E. and R. Warren: *Parks and Recreation Maintenance Management* (Boston, MA: Holbrook Press, 1977).

Stiles, D. and J. Stiles: *Playhouses You Can Build: Indoor and Backyard Design* (Westport, CT: Firefly Books, 1999).

Swain, J.W. and B.J. Read: *Budgeting for Public Managers* (Armonk, NY: M.E. Sharpe, 2010).

Taylor, M.: *Public Policy in the Community* (New York: Palgrave Macmillan, 2003).

Tesone, D.V.: *Supervision Skills for the Service Industry: How to Do It* (Tappan, NJ: Prentice Hall).

Torrington, D.: *Fundamentals of Human Resource Management: Managing People at Work* (New York: Prentice Hall/Financial Times, 2009).

Tunnicliffe, N.: *Field of Dreams: Planning and Building Britain's Greatest Sporting Arenas* (Portland, OR: Frank Cass Publications, 2002).

Van Horne, J.C.: *Financial Management and Policy*, 12th ed. (Tappan, NJ: Prentice Hall PTR, 2001).

Vaughn, J. and E.E. Otenyo: *Managerial Discretion in Government Decision Making: Beyond the Street Level* (Sudbury, MA: Jones and Bartlett, 2007).

Vaughn-Williams, J.L. and P. Sander: *Recreational Activities for More Successful Programming*, 2 vols. (Bossier City, LA: Professional Printing and Publishing, 2001).

Wagner, J.A. and J.R. Hollenbeck: *Organizational Behavior*, 5th ed. (Mason, OH: South-Western, 2004).

Warren, R., Rea, P. and S. Payne: *Park and Recreation Maintenance Management* (Champaign, IL: Sagamore, LLC, 2007).

Wei, D. (ed.): *Computer and Information Technology* (Piscataway, NJ: IEEE Computer Society Press, 2004).

Weinbach, R.W.: *Evaluating Social Work Services and Programs* (Boston, MA: Allyn & Bacon, 2004).

Wilcox, D.L. and G.T. Cameron: *Public Relations: Strategies and Tactics*, 8th ed. (Boston, MA: Allyn & Bacon, 2005).

Williams, B.: *Natural World: Biggest and Best* (Chicago, IL: Kelly, Miles Publishing, 2004).

Williams, W.R.: *Recreation Places* (New York: Reinhold, 1958).

Wilson, D.: *Strategic Decision Making* (New York: John Wiley, 2009).

Wilson, J. and N. Corlett: *Evaluation of Human Work*, 3rd ed. (Boca Raton, FL: CRC Press LLC, 2005).

Witting, C.: *Liability for Negligent Misstatements* (New York: Oxford University Press, 2004).

Zimmermann, J.M. and L. Allen: "Public Recreation Administration," *Administration and Society* (Vol. 41, No. 4 2009), pp. 470–502.

Index